OCT 20

D1220824

Propelled

Propelled

*How Boredom, Frustration, and Anticipation
Lead Us to the Good Life*

Andreas Elpidorou

OXFORD
UNIVERSITY PRESS

OXFORD
UNIVERSITY PRESS

Oxford University Press is a department of the University of Oxford. It furthers
the University's objective of excellence in research, scholarship, and education
by publishing worldwide. Oxford is a registered trade mark of Oxford University
Press in the UK and certain other countries.

Published in the United States of America by Oxford University Press
198 Madison Avenue, New York, NY 10016, United States of America.

© Andreas Elpidorou 2020

All rights reserved. No part of this publication may be reproduced, stored in
a retrieval system, or transmitted, in any form or by any means, without the
prior permission in writing of Oxford University Press, or as expressly permitted
by law, by license, or under terms agreed with the appropriate reproduction
rights organization. Inquiries concerning reproduction outside the scope of the
above should be sent to the Rights Department, Oxford University Press, at the
address above.

You must not circulate this work in any other form
and you must impose this same condition on any acquirer.

Library of Congress Cataloging-in-Publication Data
Names: Elpidorou, Andreas, author.
Title: Propelled : how boredom, frustration, and anticipation lead us to
the good life / Andreas Elpidorou.
Description: New York, NY : Oxford University Press, [2020] |
Includes bibliographical references and index.
Identifiers: LCCN 2019053132 (print) | LCCN 2019053133 (ebook) |
ISBN 9780190912963 (hardback) | ISBN 9780190912987 (epub) |
ISBN 9780197524343
Subjects: LCSH: Boredom. | Desire. | Quality of life. | Frustration. |
Expectation (Philosophy). | Emotions.
Classification: LCC BF575.B67 E45 2020 (print) | LCC BF575.B67 (ebook) |
DDC 158.1—dc23
LC record available at https://lccn.loc.gov/2019053132
LC ebook record available at https://lccn.loc.gov/2019053133

1 3 5 7 9 8 6 4 2

Printed by Sheridan Books, Inc., United States of America

*To
Lauren,
Rafa,
and
Penelope*

"There is
no more in life
than in motion,
only because
in motion is
all that is
in life."[1]

Contents

Preface

What would you say if someone were to make you the following offer?

There's a machine that was designed by the world's pre-eminent neuroscientists and engineers. The machine is too complex to describe it in detail, but, trust me, it's been tested and it really works. It reads your every thought and wish; it senses all of your feelings and experiences, even the ones that are too fleeting for you to notice. It carefully alters your brain's electrochemical activity, and in doing so, it can produce in you any experience imaginable. These are real experiences—vivid, forceful, and indistinguishable from the ones that you're having right now. If you were connected to this machine, you would never know it. You would think that you're living your life. Everything would be the same, but with one important difference. The machine is programmed to create in you only those experiences that you find pleasurable. It gives you the perfect life, one in which you would have everything that you ever wanted.

Would you connect yourself to the machine?
Would you want to spend your life in the machine?[2]

I offer this hypothetical choice to my philosophy students every semester. I also offer it to friends, acquaintances, and sometimes even to strangers. Almost everybody rejects my offer. Rejection isn't easy to take, so I try to sweeten the deal. I come back with a better pitch. If my interlocutor is religious, I might claim that the machine is heaven on earth. If erudite, I call it the "Infinite Jest machine." To aesthetes, I emphasize the machine's impeccable design. I bring attention to the inevitable pain and suffering that's contained in our lives and how the machine would erase it. I want people to feel good about the machine, bad about their lives. But, try as I may, the result remains the same. I can't sell it.

Why is that exactly? What could be wrong with always having our desires fulfilled? Imagine: no dull or boring encounters, no frustrating moments, no need to anticipate or wait for future rewards and pleasures. In such a paradise, we're surrounded by instant gratification. Bliss, satisfaction, and enjoyment define us. Our every wish is our reality.

What could be wrong with such a life?
Indeed, what could be better?

In this book, I offer answers to these questions. I argue that the good life not only benefits from, but requires the presence of negative experiences. Science and philosophy concur: negative experiences are extremely valuable, often in ways that many of us have not previously considered. Believe it or not, ubiquitous satisfaction and instant fulfillment of our desires don't promote our well-being; they *hinder* it.

1

"The secret to happiness may be unhappiness"

We think of the good life often, and how could we not? We have to. We continually find ourselves faced with decisions and choices that need to be made. Some are trivial and some are not, but how we decide in either case depends, at least to a large extent, on our view of the good life. Simply put, we wish to do whatever brings about or maintains the good life.

But how do we determine what a good life is? How do we know what kind of life is worth pursuing? Here's a thought: To come up with our conception of the good life we simply imagine a life that's saturated with pleasurable and valuable experiences and bereft of disruptive, meaningless, and aversive experiences. As intuitive as it may appear, this exercise of mentally drafting the good life can lead us astray. In trying to fit as much excitement, pleasure, and gratification as possible into our imagined life, we can lose track of an important fact, namely, that life is motion. Life doesn't just have its ups and downs; it *is* those ups and downs. Life is the desires that we manage to fulfill and those that we don't. It's the things that we gain and the things that we lose. It's the satisfaction we feel when we thrive and the disappointment we experience when we fail.

Life requires failures and pains just as much as it demands successes and pleasures. It does so because life is indisputably a personal thing. No one shares my life. No one shares yours. Whatever else a good life is, it has to be a life that is our own. There is, however, no other way to own a life but to be the subject of its vicissitudes.

To own a life is to author it, and to author it is to try out things for ourselves. It is to strive to uncover and shape our preferences. It is to invest psychological and physical resources in the pursuit of plans. It is to commit to certain objectives and to give up others. Living a life isn't just achieving goals, reaching milestones, or amassing rewards. It is also discovering what goals, milestones, and rewards are worth having in the first place. Make no mistake, such a process of discovery includes effort, struggle, and even sacrifice.

Propelled. Andreas Elpidorou, Oxford University Press (2020). © Andreas Elpidorou.
DOI: 10.1093/oso/9780190912963.001.0001

Discovery involves trial and error. It requires encounters with the unknown and demands that we, at least sometimes, step out of our comfort zone.

To choose a life of instant and perpetual gratification is to forgo a most integral part of life, namely, the part that relates to the discovery of personal values and to the formation of one's own commitments. To choose constant pleasure over change and motion is to give up choice and ownership; it is to surrender life as we know it. What makes life worth living is none other than what often makes it difficult.

Our well-being consists of more than the sum of our positive experiences. We want pleasant experiences, but not only that. We crave for meaning in our lives. We want our lives to be engaging.[1] We demand autonomy over our lives—we want our decisions to be our own and not someone else's. We want independence, but not complete isolation. We seek the respect, approval, and love of others. We chase a sense of accomplishment—we want to feel that we've conquered what's important for us to conquer. We desire many things in life and we have every right to do so.

There's much discussion about the benefits of positive states but little mention of how negative states also have the capacity to enhance our lives and even to help us to flourish. This is unfortunate. To restrict our attention to positive states and feelings (e.g., pleasure, joy, interest, hope, trust) would be to miss out on the full potential that lies within our rich psychological worlds.

• • •

Positive feelings are good, but they aren't the be-all and end-all of life. They aren't even all that there is to happiness. When researchers set out to understand the factors that give rise to happiness, they found that even very happy people aren't always that happy. Although their average mood ranged from mildly happy to very happy, they occasionally reported negative moods and feelings.[2] Not even the happiest among us are altogether immune to bad experiences. Indeed, how could they be? They're human after all. Yet what distinguishes the happiest among us is that they're able to deal with the presence of negative experiences. Such experiences neither thwart nor derail their lives. What makes them happy isn't the absence of negative feelings. It's instead the ability to respond to and learn from those negative feelings.

Focus for a moment on the black letters that you're now reading. What makes them visible isn't the presence of light but its absence. You see them because they absorb light. Indeed, the more light they absorb, the better you see them. Or consider a case of illusory contours as is illustrated in Figure 1.1. What makes the triangle's illusory presence possible is an absence: The

Figure 1.1 A version of Kanizsa's Triangle. Kanizsa figures give rise to illusory contours when incomplete Pac-Men (or Pac-Persons) are appropriately placed.

contours of the triangle are seen only because the circles are incomplete. Complete the circles (Figure 1.2) and the contours disappear. Absences can be revealing; too much presence need not be.

The feeling of our clothes touching our body or that of glasses resting on our ears and nose goes largely unnoticed throughout the day. Our clothes and our glasses, however, are there, constantly making contact with us. Restaurants can be initially overwhelming with their scents and sounds, but after a while both recede into the background. I remember when I moved to a house on a very busy street in Cambridge, Massachusetts, it was loud, especially at night. The heavy traffic kept me up. After a week though, I adjusted. It was as if my brain made the traffic disappear.

In some cases, this is exactly what happens. The phenomenon is known as *sensory adaptation* and has a well-understood neurological explanation. The details are hairy and largely unnecessary but in broad strokes the story goes something like this. All tissues and organs in our body consist of cells. The same goes for our nervous system. The cells that comprise our nervous system are of two types, neurons and glia cells. Glia cells are important, but we can ignore them here. It is neurons that are thought to perform the functions distinctive of the brain. Their job is to detect input, both from the outside world and from our own bodies; to analyze such input; and to respond to it appropriately,

Figure 1.2 Completing or filling out the Pac-Men (or Pac-Persons) takes away the presence of illusory contours.

often by means of coordinating action. Part of what makes neurons suitable for such complicated functions is their morphology—unlike other cells in our body that are self-contained, neurons extend and branch out.

If we focus only on those neurons that are responsible for responding to stimuli, we find that they receive information from the environment and convert it into a signal that our nervous system can understand. How does this translation ("transduction") occur? The quick answer is this: with the help of tiny protein molecules that permit charged particles (ions) either to enter or to exit the neuron cell. This influx and outflux of ions generates an electrical signal that travels along the length of the neuronal cell, which, with the help of other proteins and neurotransmitters, is passed on to other neurons. The world talks to our neurons, charges move around our nervous system, our neurons talk to each other, and then we do all the things—imaginable and unimaginable—that we do.

What's worth noting is that our nervous system thrives on contrast. To put it another way, prolonged or repeated stimulation often suppresses the activity of neurons. When neurons receive too much signal or the same signal over and over again, they have less to say. Sometimes they even turn silent. There are exceptions to this rule, to be sure, but adaptation (the process by which constant or repeated stimulation reduces or even ends the flow of ions) is a common feature of receptors in all senses. And it's not only sensory neurons that adapt. Most neurons, even the ones deep within our brain, adapt to stimulation and become less sensitive to prolonged or repeated stimulus.[3]

At the level of the organism, sensory adaptation gives rise to an important phenomenon: the organism becomes insensitive to constancy, familiarity, and redundancy. Adaptation allows one to ignore or devalue repeated or constant stimuli. Sated animals display no interest when they're given food that they've had before, but are motivated to pursue food if they perceive it as highly palatable.[4] Furthermore, human brains are extremely good at predicting the outcome of familiar stimuli. So good, in fact, that the brain itself cancels out their perception. When everything is the same and is just as expected, we don't need to expend resources attending to or perceiving it. We can save those resources for when things change. Action potential—the firing of neurons—is suppressed for the common and the familiar and our brain goes into energy-saving mode.

What does sensory adaptation have to do with happiness? A lot. Too much of a good thing ceases to be good. Or more precisely, it ceases to be perceived *as* good. The brain gets used to the good. It adapts to it. It devalues it. It ignores it. So, to retain their pleasurable qualities, familiar pleasures need to be punctuated by changes or absences. Neurobiologist Indira M. Raman cites this neurological fact as an explanation of why it's so hard to achieve continuous satisfaction. "Because the brain grades on a curve, endlessly comparing the present with what came just before, the secret to happiness may be unhappiness. Not unmitigated unhappiness, but the transient chill that lets us feel warmth, the sensation of hunger that makes satiety so welcome, the period of near-despair that catapults us into the astonishing experience of triumph."[5] Short-lived negative experiences are shocks to our sensory system. They recalibrate us so that we can continue to enjoy the things that we enjoy. Happiness isn't a stable condition, a plateau that once reached can be our permanent home. Happiness is change. It's the movement from the less pleasurable and less meaningful to that which is more. Without unhappiness or discontent, without short dosages of negativity, the good won't be good. It will be just plain okay.

• • •

Runners are all too familiar with the effects of wind on their performance. Running against the wind, facing, that is, a headwind, is no fun. We must exert more energy to maintain the same pace. The wind becomes the center of our attention, sometimes the object of our wrath. We wish that it would die down or change direction. And then it does. Instead of a headwind, we now find a tailwind. It feels good to get the benefit of the wind. We can pick up the pace. We can relax and let our minds wander. We can finally enjoy the run. Such benefits, however, are short-lived. We quickly adapt to the advantage that the tailwind gives us. The extra push no longer seems significant. It's as if we're running with no wind at all. Just like that, the benefit of the tailwind vanishes.

We perceive difficulties differently than the way we perceive benefits. Whereas difficulties command our attention and have to be overcome, benefits can be enjoyed and thus largely ignored. Psychologists Shai Davidai and Thomas Gilovich have shown how an emphasis on difficulties and obstacles can affect a wide range of attitudes: it makes us think that our political party, our favorite sports team, and even ourselves have been disadvantaged and treated unfairly even when they haven't.[6] Although Davidai and Gilovich's research focuses primarily on the disproportional attention that difficulties command, the fact that we're quick to forget our benefits is equally important. Think back to the last time that you felt really happy. Maybe it was when you finally received a long-awaited promotion, when you bought your dream house, or when you won a prestigious prize. Such extraordinary occasions are accompanied with great joy. Our reactions to them are emotional and often intense. Still, without fail, they fade over time. What was once seen as the apex of our professional trajectory is now just another ordinary achievement. Once possessed, the dream house is no dream but a tangible part of one's reality. And the prize, although still prestigious, no longer makes us feel like we're on top of the world. We've adapted. This time, however, the adaptation isn't the immediate or obvious product of our nervous system. Our neurons are firing with the same vigor and at the same rate as they did before. Yet our world doesn't offer us the same delight as before.

Psychologists Timothy D. Wilson and Daniel T. Gilbert set out to investigate why such emotional adaptation occurs.[7] Through a series of experiments, they found that people's strong emotional reactions to situations tend to dissipate when those situations are turned into well-understood phenomena. The promotion, the new house, and the prize cease to be exceptional events. After a while, they're seen as just another part of our life narrative, the natural consequences of our hard work. Once assigned a place in our lives, they no longer affect us emotionally (either positively or negatively). Human beings are natural-born meaning-makers but such a knack for finding meaning comes with a prize. It takes away the extraordinary. To find meaning in a situation is to understand it. But by understanding it, we render it commonplace. "The more easily one can explain and understand an event," Wilson and Gilbert note, "the more quickly one will adapt to it."[8]

Emotional adaptation through finding meaning may dull our positive feelings but it also protects us from negative experiences. People who recover most quickly from traumatic experiences, such as the death of loved ones, are those who are capable of finding meaning in the event. In line with Wilson and Gilbert's suggestion, the discovery of meaning facilitates recovery from traumatic experiences by allowing one to adapt to such events and to the feelings that they produce in us.

In a 1992 study published in *The New England Journal of Medicine*, researchers reported on the psychological effects of predictive testing for Huntington's disease. Individuals who had a parent with Huntington's disease were given a genetic test to determine if they had inherited the gene that would cause this fatal disorder. Some participants learned that there was a high likelihood that they had inherited the gene. Others learned that there was a low likelihood that they inherited the gene. And there were others for whom the test was inconclusive or who preferred not to be tested. Predictably enough, the participants who received good news showed an initial increase in their psychological well-being and those who received bad news were initially very upset. Yet despite this initial effect, the news, good or bad, had no lasting effects. After 12 months, both groups had returned to their baseline levels of well-being. In fact, people who received the bad news were just as happy after 12 months as those who received the good news. The group that was most affected by the test was the one that included individuals in a state of uncertainty. After 12 months, that group's well-being was significantly lower than that of the two other groups. Without conclusive knowledge, they were incapable of furnishing their lives with meaning. As the researchers note, "knowing the result of the predictive test, even if it indicates an increased risk, reduces uncertainty and provides an opportunity for appropriate planning. Therefore, as our findings suggest, people who receive informative results, regardless of the content, may derive psychological benefits not experienced by those who remain uncertain."[9] Negative emotions don't doom our prospects for achieving the good life. Sometimes, through their ability to inform us about our selves and our situations, they might even be the necessary antecedents both to recovery and to our improvement.

• • •

Xavier's world is emotionally monochromatic. He feels either joy or anxiety, never both, never something else. Anika's existence is more variegated. She experiences eight distinct emotions, four positive ones (joy, love, awe, content) and four negative (sadness, anger, frustration, boredom). Throughout their lives Xavier and Anika experience the same number of positive and negative emotions. As it happens, both Xavier and Anika's emotional experiences have the same intensity. Xavier's joy feels as good as Anika's love and Anika's boredom feels as bad as Xavier's anxiety. It would seem that both are happy (or unhappy) to the same extent. But are they living the same type of life? Xavier and Anika are hypothetical beings, the one-dimensional creations of a poor imagination. But their imaginary existence serves a purpose. It compels us to take seriously the following question: If we had to choose between one of those two lives, which one should it be?

Recently, scientists have started thinking about the role that the variety and breadth of our emotional experiences (what's called "emodiversity") play in our lives. In a study led by Anthony Ong, Professor of Human Development at Cornell University and Professor of Gerontology in Medicine at Weill Cornell Medical College, the relationship between emodiversity and inflammation was investigated.[10] Previous studies have indicated that inflammation is a key risk factor for morbidity and mortality—the presence of inflammation, in other words, was found to be positively correlated with both poor health and early death. The purpose of Ong's study was to examine whether there're any meaningful correlations between emodiversity and inflammation. At the end of every day for 30 days, participants in the study were asked to report the extent to which they experienced a variety of negative and positive emotions. Emodiversity was then calculated on the basis of the variety and frequency of the participants' emotional experiences. As a measure, emodiversity is designed to keep track of the relative breadth and abundance of different emotions. Hence, low emodiversity means that one's emotional experiences are largely homogeneous and revolve around a few emotions, whereas high emodiversity is an indication that one experiences a relatively diverse range of emotions. What Ong and colleagues reported in their study is that although mean levels of emotions showed no association with inflammatory activity, *positive* emodiversity (i.e., the extent to which one experiences a variety of positive emotions) was associated with lower inflammation. Importantly, the association between positive emodiversity and lower inflammation was independent of one's age, gender, anti-inflammatory medication, and even previous medical conditions.

When it comes to inflammation, Ong and colleagues found no benefits attached to *negative* emodiversity. However, two other large-scale studies (involving in total more than 37,000 subjects), conducted by psychologist Jordi Quoidbach and colleagues, found support that emodiversity, in both its positive and negative variety, is a predictor of mental and physical health.[11] Overall emodiversity was associated with decreased depression, whereas negative emodiversity was negatively related to visits to the doctor, days spent at the hospital, and medication costs. The nature of these studies didn't permit the researchers to draw any conclusions about the causal interaction between emodiversity and health. In other words, it's unclear whether emodiversity causes better health or whether better health causes one to experience the world in a more fine-grained emotional manner. All the same, Quoidbach and colleagues do provide reasons to think that emodiversity is a cause or (at least) a contributing factor to better health.

For one, the authors contend that experiencing many different emotional states carries an adaptive value. Richness in emotional experience will be associated with richness in information about one's existence and relatedly with a better ability to respond appropriately to emotionally charged situations. Additionally, the authors argue that emodiversity could protect us against adaptation and ultimately against harm. "[T]he experience of prolonged sadness," they write, "might lead to depression but the joint experience of sadness and anger—although unpleasant—might prevent individuals from completely withdrawing from their environment."[12]

The research on emodiversity is exciting, but new. Before we can draw any final conclusions, we need to wait for it to mature—studies confirming the above results need to be performed and published. Still, what such initial findings suggest is that the presence of negative emotions isn't a sign that we aren't faring well. On the contrary, a mix of positive and negative emotions might be the key to happiness and the good life.

• • •

In the pages that follow, I will defend a similar claim. I won't argue that *all* negative emotional experiences are good for us. Nor will I advocate that we ought to seek out such experiences. My aim is more circumscribed. I wish to make a case for the essential role that three states of dissatisfaction play in our lives. Outrageous as it may at first seem, I will show that boredom, frustration, and anticipation are *good* for us. To live a good life we need boredom and frustration. We also need to anticipate, wait, and long for future events.

Boredom, frustration, and anticipation aren't unpleasant accidents of our lives. They're neither superfluous nor necessarily burdensome psychological states that we should want to eliminate. Instead, they're the elements of a good life. Boredom, frustration, and anticipation are indications that we find ourselves stuck in unpleasant and unfulfilling situations. But they're also the incentives we need to get out of such traps. Boredom, frustration, and anticipation aren't obstacles to our goals. They're our guides. They keep us motivated. They propel us into lives that are truly our own.

2

"I hear you clearly, yet your voice sounds far away—distant and unreal"

"Come here please" the stranger said. No one else was there but S.M. The stranger was sitting, alone on a park bench. It was dark out. In the church across the street, the local choir was finishing up their evening practice. Their voices sonically framed the night. The stranger motioned for S.M. to come over, and she did, perhaps out of curiosity or kindness. What could she have been thinking? *What does he want from me? Is he lost? Does he want money? Does he need someone to talk to? Maybe I can help.* He suddenly stood up, interrupting her thoughts. His fingers crumpled her shirt. He pulled her close. Too close. The cold metal blade of his knife was felt pressing uncomfortably against her throat. "I'm going to cut you, bitch."[1]

Dangerous and life-threatening situations elicit certain reactions. We often flee from danger or fight it. When neither option is available, we freeze. S.M. did none of these. She stood there, composed and still. She didn't tremble from fear. She wasn't paralyzed. She certainly didn't beg for her life to be spared. She instead looked at him calmly and said: "Go ahead and cut me."

Such poise, such confidence packed into five words.

He let her go.

After he released his grip and put away his knife, she didn't run. Slowly, she walked away from him as if nothing had happened. And as if nothing had happened, she walked by the same spot the next day.

Peculiar though it may sound, for S.M. nothing really had happened, or, more precisely, nothing happened that would have left a lasting emotional impression on her. S.M. has a rare genetic condition known as Urbach-Wiethe disease. This disorder is characterized by the hardening of skin, mucous membranes, and internal organs including the brain due to the deposit of waxy infiltrates. In the case of S.M., the deposit of infiltrates resulted in the complete destruction of her amygdalae, a brain structure that's crucial for emotional experiences. As a consequence of her condition, S.M. almost entirely lacks the capacity to experience fear. Horror films, haunted houses,

Propelled. Andreas Elpidorou, Oxford University Press (2020). © Andreas Elpidorou.
DOI: 10.1093/oso/9780190912963.001.0001

tarantulas and snakes, and even life-threatening traumatic events fail to scare her. S.M. doesn't avoid threatening situations. In fact, overwhelmed by curiosity, she is drawn to them.[2]

S.M.'s adult life is mostly fearless.* Yet she wasn't always like that. Fear had been a part of her emotional repertoire as a child. The dark used to scare her, and she still recalls how she felt when at the age of ten a large Doberman Pinscher cornered her and started growling. "I can remember my gut tightening up," she says. "I was afraid to move. I was crying. . . . That's the only time I really felt scared. Like gut-wrenching scared."[3] Even though she rarely experiences fear, she knows what fear is. S.M. understands very well what should scare her. She realizes that certain stimuli ought to be felt as threatening and fearful because they signify potential danger.

What S.M. lacks isn't knowledge of what's dangerous and what isn't. Rather, she lacks an immediate emotional reaction to most threatening and dangerous stimuli. S.M.'s world isn't already presented to her as threatening or dangerous. She has to cognitively and laboriously infer and add those labels and categories for herself. For most of us, our affective and emotional experiences deliver the world as difficult or accommodating, boring or interesting, alienating or welcoming.† As neuroscientist Antonio Damasio explains, "the beauty of emotions is that they're ready-mades. What an emotion is—same way that an instinct or drive—is that you don't need to think about it in order to do it. It's a natural, ready-made way of leading you to the correct behavior."[4]

S.M.'s world is drastically different from ours. Whereas in our world, fear can be found hidden behind every fold, her world is almost entirely devoid of fear. It's a sunnier and more carefree world, and because of that, it's also a much more dangerous world. S.M.'s case offers a vivid and concrete illustration of

---

* Researchers were finally able to induce fear in S.M. by asking her to breathe in nonlethal carbon dioxide–loaded air. Immediately after inhalation, S.M. began to gasp for air and to show visible signs of panic. When asked what kind of emotions she felt, she said, "Panic mostly, cause I didn't know what the hell was going on." When she was asked whether this experience was bad, she said, "Yeah, this was the most, number one, worst." The report is given in Feinstein et al. (2013), supplementary information.

† Affects are feelings, that is, experiences that are felt or sensed by us, that accompany and characterize our thoughts, actions, or situations. Feeling tired or energetic, satisfied or dissatisfied, interested or disinterested, safe or threatened, at home or ill at ease are examples of affects. And so are feeling cranky, moody, just okay, over the moon, so happy that you could cry, and so sad that your heart hurts. All emotions involve affects, insofar as they are felt, but not all affects are emotions. For one, emotions, but not affects, are always about something—ourselves, others, or the world—and involve some kind of appraisal or evaluation. For another, emotions are subject to standards of correctness depending on whether they fit the facts or not. Consider: although it makes sense to ask whether it's correct for me to be angry, even after I told you I'm angry, it doesn't make much sense to ask whether it's correct for me to feel hunger after I sincerely told you that I'm hungry. Despite their differences, affects share with emotions the following two features. They're both characterized by their valence (i.e., the extent to which they are pleasurable/attractive/agreeable or not) and by their level of arousal (i.e., the extent to which our bodies are prepared for action when such affects or emotions occur).

what a life without fear would be like. In doing so, it highlights not only the value of fear, but also of emotions in general.

• • •

What are emotions?

Simply put, emotions are ways of living—of behaving, thinking, and perceiving. When in the grip of our emotions, we encounter a world permeated and structured by our concerns and bodily feelings: our surroundings and ourselves are characterized by the very emotions we have and embody. Awe ushers in a world that's far greater and more powerful than we are. Sadness renders our world gloomy, passive, and unappealing. Happiness can transform our world into an agreeable one, full of opportunities. And then there's rage, an emotion capable of dramatically narrowing our world. While enraged, parts of our world simply disappear as they sink into insignificance, whereas others are elevated and become our primary focus. When we say, "rage blinds," we mean it literally. As our emotions wax and wane, they bring about changes in how we perceive and live in our world.

Emotions don't merely reveal the world to us in specific ways; with our help (our biology, our concepts, our culture), they also construct it for us. Take fear, for example. Fear creates a world of harms, threats, and dangers. It does so not by finding something that's already and independently of us fearful—such a thing doesn't exist. Rather, in a state of fear, the world appears fearful, unwelcoming, and distant. On account of my fear of heights, glass elevators, hot air balloons, and roller coaster rides stand out of my reach. The world contains them, but my fearful existence hides them insofar as it renders them inaccessible. In your world however—or the world of someone who's not afraid of heights—such items can be a source of enjoyment. They attract you, but repel me.

The world of emotions isn't an "inner" world, as some believe. During our emotional states, we aren't operating our bodies like we drive a car in the rain; we don't see the world behind a foggy window, nor do we act rashly, irrationally, or improperly, as if emotions have made us lose our traction with the world. Emotions are as felt as they are lived. They constitute, for the most part, appropriate and rational ways of living. And they're lived "out there," not in our minds but in our world of social and practical concerns.

It's hard to overstate the power that emotions have over our perception of the world. An online study conducted shortly after the terrorist attacks of 9/11 found that fearful respondents made higher risk estimates concerning both subsequent terrorist attacks and other unrelated events.[5] Individuals who've experienced rejection and social exclusion perceive individuals who can fulfill their need for affiliation as being spatially closer to them.[6] Sad people placed at the bottom of a hill overestimate the incline of a hill, and people who are fearful of heights overestimate heights.[7] Fearful subjects reported a decrease in their tactile sensitivity,[8] whereas participants who were instructed to think of a time when they performed an unethical action perceived their world as darker than those who were instructed to recall the performance of an ethical act.[9]

During an emotional episode, our world is clearly transformed: emotions construct it according to their nature. While emotions change our world, they also change us. Emotions influence our thoughts, desires, and expectations. Even our overall orientation and standing in life isn't immune to the forces of our emotions. Consider someone who is feeling pangs of guilt. That individual can't stop thinking about what they've done. They reflect upon the nature of their past actions. They might deem themselves to be a bad person. They feel bad and might decide to act on these feelings: to apologize, to make amends, or to become a better person—all because of guilt.

Or return to fear. During fear, we run, hide, or freeze. We lose our calm. We worry. Yet regardless of how we experience fear, it forces us to see something about ourselves. It speaks to us. It reveals to us the various ways in which we're susceptible and vulnerable. No wonder the experience of fear is so unpleasant. Who wants to be reminded of our limitations?

Other emotions can bring about more beneficial changes and realizations. Positive emotions such as joy, hope, interest, or awe can expand the repertoire of actions that we find desirable.[10] In one study, individuals who watched a short film that elicited amusement were able to come up with more examples of things they'd like to do compared to individuals who watched a short film that elicited anxiety and fear.[11] Furthermore, positive emotions help us process critical feedback better. When happy, we better retain and use negative information about something that matters to us.[12] Lastly, by changing ourselves, such emotions also change our relationships. Positive emotions can give rise to a feeling of closeness with others,[13] and happy people are significantly more trusting than sad or angry people.[14]

Our lives are dynamic. We constantly change and adjust our behavior to meet the demands of our surrounding world. Emotions are there to help us. By changing the world for us, they shine light on what matters to us and obscure what doesn't. In doing so, they inform us of what's out there and how it relates to us. Such differential lighting brings into focus a world that is hierarchically structured, based on our individual values and concerns. Paternal love renders my children special. Fear makes a slithering snake the focal point of my experience. Lust overshadows everything but our sexual objects and desires.

Emotions thus reveal what matters to us and what doesn't. Yet we shouldn't lose track of the fact that those revelations are never just a passive pointing or a showing. Emotions don't merely tell or show; they do. Immediately and without any forethought, they push us in certain directions. By changing our world and ourselves, emotions prompt us to take action. Parental love doesn't just show to me that my children are special. It brings me closer to them; it makes me want to protect them; it makes me happy when they're happy, sad when they're sad. There's more to emotions than feelings or sensations. Think again of fear. Think of what it does to us. It causes us to freeze, to change direction, to drive slowly, to tell lies, and even to perform regretful acts.

We need our emotions. Emotions are necessary not only to experience the world, but also to live it. A life can be successful or unsuccessful, enjoyable or unpleasant, safe or reckless, even moral or immoral, depending on the emotions that govern it. Thus, what emotions rule and characterize our lives ought to be of utmost importance to us. We should be mindful of their presence and attentive to their absence. Emotions are lessons and tricks that we've acquired, either through nature or culture. We can't afford to give them up or to ignore them.

• • •

Our capacity to experience emotions is essential to who we are. We're beings whose actions, desires, thoughts, and preferences are influenced by our emotions. Our emotions and the emotions of others constantly color the entities and projects in our lives, other people, and our own selves.

But emotions aren't mere colorations of our existence. They aren't add-ons or accessories of our human existence. We're humans precisely insofar as we're emotional beings. Imagine, if you can, what our world and lives would be like if they were devoid of emotions. Imagine not a world without *this* or *that* emotion, but a world without any emotions at all. Such a world—almost unimaginable, completely drenched in pallid neutrality—is far from human.

Depersonalization/derealization disorder isn't well known to most people; however, it's a common psychiatric condition. It affects millions of people worldwide—indeed, it's estimated that one in fifty people suffers from it.[15] It can appear by itself or alongside other psychiatric disorders. The exact cause of the disorder remains elusive. It's clear, however, that it's linked to an imbalance of neurotransmitters—the chemicals responsible for the transmission of signals between neurons.[16] There's a strong association between the disorder and childhood trauma and past emotional abuse.[17] The mean age of onset is around adolescence, and the most common triggers of the disorder are severe stress and drug use.[18]

Its symptoms are highly distressing, often debilitating. People with depersonalization/derealization disorder feel estranged either from their entire being or from aspects of their selves, such as their emotions, feelings, thoughts, actions, or even body parts. They can also experience detachment from their world, including their surroundings, other objects, and individuals. Without any attachments but with a constant and profound feeling of unreality, individuals with depersonalization/derealization disorder fear they've gone mad. They often feel as if they've ceased to be alive. Consider, for example, how a woman—let's call her "D"—diagnosed with depersonalization/derealization disorder describes her condition:

> I feel as though I'm not alive—as though my body is an empty lifeless shell. I deem to be standing apart from the rest of the world, as though I'm not really here. Is there something wrong with my ears? I hear you clearly, yet your voice sounds far away—distant and unreal. Whatever has deadened my feelings has deadened my hearing too. It's the same with my eyes. I see but I don't feel. I taste but it means nothing to me. . . . I seem to be walking about in a world I recognize but don't feel. . . . It all makes me feel so lonely and cut off. It's the terrible isolation from the rest of the world that frightens me.[19]

Many of us have experienced a feeling of unreality and detachment from ourselves or from the world, at least once. In fact, it's estimated that about half of all adults have undergone such an episode.[20] Often it's a consequence of a traumatic experience, of extreme stress, or even of finding oneself in an unfamiliar environment. It may be that feeling detached from oneself or from one's world serves a protective function: it distances oneself from traumatic events. Most of us reap the benefits of this defensive mechanism without incurring any costs. That's to say, for most of us, such an experience is transient. Detachment occurs when we need it most and disappears as soon as we're safe. For people affected by depersonalization/derealization disorder, however, the story is radically different. Their experience of unreality and estrangement is either continuous or persistently recurring.

Depersonalization/derealization disorder is best understood through the eyes and testimonies of those who live with it. Their words make it obvious that such a condition is often characterized by an emotional numbing.

Psychiatrist Daphne Simeon and coauthor Jeffrey Abugel, in their book *Feeling Unreal: Depersonalization Disorder and the Loss of the Self*, report the following statement made by an individual suffering from depersonalization/derealization: "I have no moods. . . . I wanted to cry when my mother died but didn't. Not because I didn't love her, I just could not evoke how it should feel; I know she's no longer in the world, but neither am I."[21] In turn, familiarity in the lives of such individuals disappears and attraction subsides. D, the woman previously quoted, reports: "My husband and I have always been happy together, but now he sits here and might be a complete stranger."[22] And objects that used to cause a response fail to do so anymore. The emotional connection to them is lost. They no longer matter. "I really love[d] music," D says, "but now I can't bear it because it doesn't stir me."[23] There's thinking but not feeling and no emotional connection to one's past or future. Perhaps the only emotion that persistently lingers is fear or anxiety.[24] Cheryl, another individual interviewed by Simeon and Abugel, has this to say: "I know that there's something wrong with me, and all it does is fill me with fear, especially fear of being taken away screaming in a straight jacket."[25]

Depersonalization/derealization disorder offers insight into an emotionally muted existence. But so does alexithymia, a construct introduced by psychiatrist Peter Emanuel Sifneos in the early 1970s in an attempt to understand the cognitive and affective behavior of patients with psychosomatic illness.[26] The term "alexithymia," which comes from the Greek "a" for lack, "lexis" for word, and "thymos" for emotion, describes a marked difficulty in experiencing, identifying, and communicating one's emotions as well as paucity of fantasy and the presence of a utilitarian, action-oriented mode of thinking.[27]

Alexithymia isn't classified as a mental disorder by the latest version of the *Diagnostic and Statistical Manual of Mental Disorders*. Nor is it an all-or-nothing matter. Instead, it's a psychological construct resembling a personality trait—similar, for example, to intelligence—that's normally distributed in the general population.[28] About 10% of the population scores high in alexithymia measures and the presence of high alexithymia poses a major risk factor for many medical and psychiatric problems (e.g., chronic pain or anxiety and depressive disorders).[29]

High-alexithymic individuals are at loss for words when it comes to their emotional experiences.[30] They often register them as physical or somatic problems instead of emotional reactions.[31] Anger might be mistaken for being hot; the symptoms of fear can be confused with the effects of caffeine.[32] High-alexithymic individuals have difficulties describing their subjective feelings to others, and so others can't help them. They can't readily imagine others' emotional experiences, and so they can't empathize with and help others.[33]

Such individuals are disconnected both from their emotional selves and from others.[‡]

"Do you know what depression is like?" the doctor asks.

"Yes, I think so, I've certainly looked after a number of people who have been depressed," the patient, a divorced physiotherapist in her late forties, responds.

"Have you felt it yourself?"

"I don't think so."

"Never, ever?"

"No, I don't really think I have."

"What about sadness?"

"No, I don't think so."

"What sort of emotions do you usually experience?"

"I find that hard to say." [34]

Psychiatrist and psychologists Paul Frewen found in his studies that alexithymia is common with individuals with posttraumatic stress disorder.[35] When interviewing a participant in one of his studies about her reactions to trauma reminders, she reported the following: "I don't know *what* I feel, it's like my head and body aren't connected."[36] When she was later asked about her emotions she stated, "I'm living in a tunnel, a fog, no matter what happens it's the same reaction—numbness, nothing. Having a bubble bath and being burned or raped is the same feeling. *My brain doesn't feel.*"[37]

Compared to either individuals with depersonalization/derealization disorder or to high-alexithymic individuals, we live in a world that's saturated with emotions. Our emotions often feel heavy or overwhelming. Bring to mind the power of shame, love, jealousy, or rage. Consider how such emotions affect and sway us. No doubt, emotions can be difficult to deal with. They can change our minds and hearts. They can compel us to engage in action. They even have the potential to derail our lives. At times, we might wish that emotions would go away. Fortunately, they don't. The capacity to have them is, for most of us, a permanent feature of our existence. As testimonies from

[‡] Given our characterization of alexithymia, one would expect the presence of alexithymia to be related to the presence of a dissociative condition such as depersonalization/derealization. Well, that's exactly what a 2011 study found (Majohr et al., 2011). Although the two conditions or constructs are distinct, Swiss psychiatrist Karl-Ludwig Majohr and colleagues observed a strong relationship between difficulty in identifying feelings and depersonalization/derealization in patients with panic disorder. The study by Majohr and colleagues is not the only study that found a relationship between alexithymia and dissociation. Another group of psychiatrists (led by Hans Jörgen Grabe) has offered supporting evidence for a link between alexithymia and depersonalization/derealization (Grabe et al., 2000).

people with depersonalization/derealization disorder and alexithymia make clear, an emotionally shallow life is a life that's unrecognizable, both numb and lifeless. Living in such a state is almost unbearable. The weight of emotions doesn't compare to the weight of their absence.

• • •

Emotions breathe life into our existence: they make our lives meaningful; they reveal and construct our world; they inform us of what matters to us and they propel us to act in certain ways. Emotions, it seems, are almost magical.

Jean-Paul Sartre, the French philosopher, playwright, novelist, literary critic, and political activist, insisted on precisely that point. In his book *Sketch for a Theory of the Emotions*, he argued that emotions *are* magical. They can transform our world, and in doing so, they present to us a world in which certain difficulties disappear. Emotions are ways to overcome life's obstacles.

Sartre illustrates his point with an example. Sadness often arises, he notes, when the conditions that are necessary to achieve certain desirable ends are missing or have been taken from us. I lost my job, yet my need for income persists; I lost a friend but I need companionship. To achieve these ends, I now need to look for, and to secure, new means. The onset of sadness temporarily solves all those difficulties. Or so Sartre holds. Sadness does this by "suppressing the obligation to look for these new ways, by transforming the present structure of the world, replacing it with a totally undifferentiated structure."[38] Sadness changes how we experience the world. If what we wanted to achieve is no longer attractive to us, then there's no need for finding new ways of achieving it. In other words, as long as we wallow in sadness, we're relieved from certain obligations and expectations. Of course, one need not entirely agree with Sartre to appreciate the value of his account. Emotions can still be magical—powerful, moving, transformative, and informative—even if they don't always solve our problems.

In the following chapters, I will follow Sartre in spirit but not in letter. My aim is to reveal the magical character of emotions. I won't be concerned with every emotion or state, of course. Nor will I discuss emotions in the abstract. I've already presented the general view of emotions that will inform the ensuing discussion. Now it's time to move forward. It's time to get specific.

My argument focuses on three common psychological states: boredom, frustration, and anticipation. Although boredom and frustration are readily considered to be emotions, anticipation typically isn't. Such a view of anticipation won't matter for the purposes of the book. What matters for our purposes is the fact that anticipation is all too often an emotionally laden experience that, like boredom and frustration, signifies either a type of dissatisfaction with our present situation or the existence of some unfulfilled desire. The account of emotions presented in this chapter can thus be easily extended to apply to anticipation. Indeed, as it will become obvious later on in the book, the similarities between anticipation, boredom, and frustration are striking.

All three—taken either individually or together—have much to teach us. By discussing their respective characters and how they relate to our experience of time, to motion, and to the good life, I will present their importance in our everyday lives. Boredom, frustration, and anticipation are markers of how we're faring in life. They illuminate our desires and expectations and inform us about our failures and struggles. Most important, they're our indispensable guides in our quest to live the good life. States of discontent might be unpleasant, but they're powerful, moving, and instructive. Positivity is great. Negativity can be tremendously useful.

3

"What do you think it's like being dead?"

Nothing seems to stick.

With the blink of an eye, the whole world is forgotten. Within the span of a few seconds, faces, objects, and indeed, entire scenes are renewed. The same face, the same object, the same scene, yet all of them constantly present themselves to him as new. It's as if he has never seen them before.

Clive Wearing can't read. Nor can he sustain a conversation. Watching television is an impossible task and so are countless other mundane activities. Once, his wife found him holding a chocolate in the palm of one of his hands. Like a practicing magician, he repeatedly covered and uncovered it with his other hand. Throughout this act, he held the chocolate, feeling its light mass pressing down on his skin. Yet every movement of the hand, every act of covering and uncovering, amazed him.

"Look! . . . It's new!"

"It's the same chocolate," his wife assured him.

"No . . . Look! It's changed. It wasn't like that before. Look! It's different again! How do they do it?"[1]

Clive's consciousness resets every few seconds. Five, ten, fifteen, twenty, twenty-five, thirty—his memory is wiped clean. Five, ten, fifteen, twenty, twenty-five, thirty—it's gone again. Oblivious to what came before, he's reborn, confused and scared.

It's very likely that at least once you've woken up in the middle of the night feeling disoriented—unable to recognize where you are, incapable of remembering how you got there. For a few seconds, you're lost. No thoughts, no memories come to mind. Nothing helps you to find your bearing. At the same time, a terrifying feeling of nothingness and complete helplessness arises. But the feeling is ephemeral. Within a matter of seconds, you're able to recall your whereabouts. Terror disappears, but it leaves behind a small taste of Clive's unbearable emptiness.

Encephalitis reduced Clive to a mere temporal slice of himself. He's lost the capacity to form new memories and remembers very little of his life before the contraction of the virus. Utter darkness and oblivion lie behind him and

Propelled. Andreas Elpidorou, Oxford University Press (2020). © Andreas Elpidorou.
DOI: 10.1093/oso/9780190912963.001.0001

beyond him. Clive is constantly coming into consciousness. Every instance for him is the first awakening.

The constant feeling that he's just woken up, that he has for the very first time become conscious, prompts him to inquire about his state. But it's all to no avail. Clive can't come to grips with his condition. He can't understand what has happened to him. He can't understand what's constantly happening to him.

"How long have I been ill?"

"Nine weeks," his wife answers.

"Nine weeks . . . ? I haven't heard anything, seen anything, touched anything, smelled anything. It's like being dead. What's it like being dead? Answer: nobody knows. How long's it been?"

"Nine weeks," his wife repeats.

"Nine weeks . . . ? I haven't heard anything seen anything, touched anything, smelled anything. What do you think it's like being dead?"[2]

Clive is stuck in an ever-repeating now. It's a dark and narrow place. It's entirely disconnected from the past and the future. It irrevocably disappears almost as soon as it appears.

· · ·

We speak of a sense of time, but such talk isn't entirely without an air of paradox. Our sense of time is unlike that of vision, smell, or touch. We have neither time organs nor time receptors. In fact, we couldn't possess either. Time isn't comparable to light or pressure. It isn't a physical quantity. As psychologist J. J. Gibson argued in a 1975 article, events are perceivable but time is not.[3] We don't perceive time as such. What then do we perceive when we say that we experience time? What we perceive isn't time, pure and simple, but its flow. Through the perception of events outside of us and of sensations in us, we take notice of time's passing.

It's hard to conceive what it would be like to perceive time directly—time on its own, unadulterated by change or succession. American writer Kurt Vonnegut tries. In his *Slaughterhouse-Five*, Tralfamadorians—the alien race that abducts Billy Pilgrim, exposes him to their understanding of time, and displays him naked in a zoo—are said to perceive time as we see objects spread out in space. "I am a Tralfamadorian seeing all time as you might see a stretch of the Rocky Mountains."[4]

Such a description of the perception of time stretches the concept of time beyond its yield point. We can't perceive future things. Perception is a causal process. We perceive in virtue of what causally affects us. But since causes can't postdate their effects, future things are causally and perceptually inaccessible to us. Does that mean that we perceive the past? In a sense, we do. Given the finite speed of light (and sound) and the finite speed by which neuronal activation occurs in our brain, every perception is a perception of a thing past. The book or computer that you see is as it were nanoseconds ago. The light of the moon in which the night bathes is a second old. And our perception of the sun is the perception of the sun as it looked approximately 8 minutes ago. The further we look into space, the further back in time we glance. But even that kind of looking back doesn't approximate the Tralfamadorian concept of seeing the past. What we perceive when we perceive far away objects isn't the past but past things *as* present.

Tralfamadorian time is time objectified, doubly objectified to be precise. It's objectified once when it's asserted that time exists independently of us: "All moments, past, present, and future, always have existed, always will exist."[5] It's objectified again when it's rendered an object—a mountain range that can be glanced all at once. To some, this double doctrine would be seen as a straightforward denial of the existence of time. At least this is what the Christian philosopher and theologian Augustine would have thought. "If nothing passed away," he notes in *Confessions*, his philosophical autobiography, "there would not be past time; and if nothing were coming, there would not be future time; and if nothing were, there would not be present time."[6] For Augustine, time isn't something fixed and permanent. Indeed, the past and future don't really exist. All that exists is the present and even that it must, to be present and not eternity, disappear as soon as it appears. Time is the product of the mind. The past is our current memory of things past, the future is our current expectation of things to come, and the present is our current attention to things present to us.

Whereas Tralfamadorians render time inhuman by denying its subjectivity, Augustine renders it solely human by denying its objectivity. The Augustinian take may be extreme, but it's not as extreme as the Tralfamadorian. We could live with Augustinian time but not with its Tralfamadorian counterpart. Billy Pilgrim comes to accept much of the Tralfamadorian doctrine. "It is just an illusion we have here on Earth," he declares, "that one moment follows another one, like beads on a string, and that once a moment is gone it is gone forever."[7] But even Billy, who has come unstuck in time during World War II and as a result travels back and forth in time, is incapable of perceiving time in its Tralfamadorian guise. Thought, speech, comprehension, feelings, emotions—in short, all that makes us human—require that time must be experienced by us as passing.

All the same, realizing the necessity of a subjective dimension of time—that time's passage ineludibly impresses us—doesn't force us to deny its independent reality. Tralfamadorian time is objectified not once but twice. We could reject the second sense of objectification while still accepting the first. And indeed, from our human perspective, both the objectivity and subjectivity of time are unassailable facts. Time is out there—precise and unforgiving, measured by lunar orbits, pendulum swings, or energy transitions of the caesium-133 atom; defined by strikes, births, wars, and deaths; and also and always in us, subjective and fluent, long or short, vulnerable to the vagaries of our inner world.

Our time is a compromise between the Tralfamadorian and the Augustinian, even-handed, it seems, and, above all, anthropic.

• • •

He picks up the phone, and through clenched teeth, shouts repeatedly, "J'en ai marre!" (I've had enough).[8] More than two months ago, he smiled for TV cameras and news reporters, embraced his mother, kissed his new bride, and descended through a 100-foot vertical shaft to the floor of Midnight Cave, near Del Rio, Texas. He would remain in this changeless environment for a total of 205 days, the majority of them alone, disconnected from the sun, calendars, and clocks; all in the name of science—perhaps vanity too. This wasn't the first time that Michel Siffre set out to live "beyond time"—in 1962, when he was just 23 years old, he spent two months in total isolation underground in the French Alps. And it wouldn't be the last time either—almost 3,000 feet underground in a cave in south France, he rang in the new millennium, three and half days late but with champagne and foie gras. So, when he angrily announced that he had enough of the Midnight Cave, he really didn't. He would stay for another 100 or so days. The voice across the line perhaps knew this. It sounded reassuring. "All is well. Everything is going fine," Siffre was told right before he slammed the phone.[9]

Everything wasn't going fine. Everyday Siffre would wake up, phone the surface team and ask them to turn on the lights inside the cave, record his blood pressure and pulse, perform tasks to test memory and mental acuity, ride a stationary bicycle for three miles, practice target with a pellet rifle, and shave and save his whiskers. He would also sweep the cave "energetically," as he wrote later, while trying not to breathe—the dust was mixed with excrements of an erstwhile bat colony and inhaling it could prove fatal.[10] Above all, he would measure. He measured his weight, food intake, and the cave's barometric pressure. He noted his periods of wakefulness and counted his days by cycles, from one waking hour to the next. He measured his temperature with a rectal probe and his cardiac rhythms with electrodes on his chest. Even sleep didn't bring a respite from this incessant measuring: "After carefully cleaning the skin surface, I must apply miniature Beckman electrodes to my head and face; these will record the patterns of deep sleep, light sleep, and dream time."[11]

His daily routine quickly became tedious. He felt like a prisoner in a cave where "the darkness is absolute, the silence total."[12] His memory became fragile: "I recall nothing from yesterday. Even events of this morning are lost."[13] His circadian rhythm went nuts. For most of his stay, his circadian cycle would extend beyond 24 hours. But it would jump. His 44th cycle, for example, would last 51 hours and 44 minutes. When he read in a magazine that bat urine and saliva could transmit rabies through the air, he panicked. On a different occasion, he disconnected himself from all instruments and wires but then felt guilty that his research team may be missing out on important data and so he reattached himself to his machines. He even contemplated suicide—the thought, however, of burdening his parents with all of the debt that he had accumulated proved harder to bear than the cave's desolation.

Chiefly, he felt lonely—"This long loneliness is beyond all bearing"—and longed for companionship, of any kind.[14] When he discovered that a mouse was in his presence, he got excited. "My heart leaps. Another living creature exists in Midnight Cave! If I trap this rodent, I will have a companion."[15] He spent days studying the habits and movements of the mouse. He set up a trap and named him Mus. On the 166th day he tried to capture Mus but failed. On the 170th, he tried again. He used jam as bait. He waited for Mus to approach and then, at the right moment, he slammed down a casserole plate to capture him. "My heart pounds with excitement. For the first time since entering the cave, I feel a surge of joy."[16] His joy, however, was short-lived. The edge of the plate caught the mouse's head. Siffre stared at him. He heard his squeaks of distress. He watched him die. "Desolation overwhelms me."[17]

• • •

> We say time passes. Fine, let it pass for all I care. But in order to measure it . . . no, wait! In order for it to be measurable, it would have to flow *evenly*, but where is it written that it does that?
> —**Thomas Mann,** *The Magic Mountain,* 1924[18]

Unlike Siffre's cave, our *super*terranean worlds come already adumbrated with the marks of time. In our everyday lives, we glide from one event to another: from last winter to the birth of your child in the fall, from yesterday's four o'clock appointment to tomorrow's soccer practice, and from that to the upcoming promotion. Time passes. It passes whether we want it to or not. Yet, our experience of the passage of time can be shaped, altered, or bent.

Our experience of time's passing isn't abstract. It's both felt and lived. We embody time in our activities: time may feel stretched or contracted depending on what we do. "The way in which we experience the day-to-day flow of time depends on what it holds," French philosopher, feminist, social theorist, political activist, and novelist Simone de Beauvoir once remarked.[19] Ask lovers and they will readily attest that a tryst is almost always an event that passes too fast. An intellectually stimulating conversation or a captivating book also makes time disappear. Time slips away from us, and we can't reclaim it. On the contrary, monotony, mandatory work, and repetitiveness have the opposite effect. Time still passes, and if measured, it passes at the same rate of 1 second per second. Yet it appears otherwise. In monotonous, tedious, and repetitive activities, time seems to linger stubbornly and to leave behind a trail. Instruments of time may say one thing, but feelings, sensations, and thoughts indicate another.

Our experience of the passage of time is affected by how we're able to relate to our current situations and projects. Situations that grab our attention—be it because they're engrossing, enjoyable, challenging, distracting, or changing— appear to happen in less time. They direct our attention away from the passage of time, and in doing so, we're led to underestimate the passage of time. A common explanation of this phenomenon appeals to the idea that cognitive tasks compete for resources. When the world captures our attention, it's harder for us to pay attention to the passage of time. Because of that, time slips by.

On the contrary, repetitive, monotonous, and uninteresting situations appear to last longer. Consider what it's like to repeat the same task over and over again, to wait for a plane that never seems to arrive, or to anticipate the end of a tedious shift. Such situations transform our perception of the passage of time. They lack appeal and don't grab us. As a result, our attention drifts away from them. Instead, we think of the passage of time. We think of what lies beyond the now. And we become stuck in a seemingly longer and more unsatisfactory present. "Time travels in diverse paces with diverse persons," wrote William Shakespeare in *As You Like It*.[20] Time travels in diverse paces with diverse situations, we should add.

Unsatisfactory projects, tedious or monotonous activities, and situations to which we can't relate highlight that there's something missing from our current situation. They're unpleasant, and, via transforming our experience of the passage of time, they make us acutely aware of the fact that the now doesn't fulfill us. They tell us that what we're doing right now isn't what we want to be doing. Through them, we can see ourselves as dissatisfied and as standing still, removed from our goals and desires.

Subjects who contemplate suicide experience in an intense way such a transformation of time. Compared to various control groups, suicidal subjects overestimate the duration of time. Suicidal individuals resemble in this respect extremely bored individuals: "The present seems endless," psychologist Roy F. Baumeister wrote in his influential study of suicide, "and whenever one checks the clock, one is surprised at how little time has actually elapsed."[21] In addition, suicidal subjects find it difficult to think about their future. They don't experience their lives as meaningful, and this perceived meaninglessness contributes to the appearance of a protracted present. As psychologists Jean M. Twenge, Kathleen R. Catanese, and Roy F. Baumeister note, "[w]ithout meaning, time seems to drag, and the person remains stuck in a relatively empty present moment, cut off from past and future."[22]

Years after his experiment in Midnight Cave, Siffre talked to an interviewer about his experience of the passage of time. Disconnected from the world, surrounded by night, and living in a changeless environment, he admitted feeling trapped in a seemingly unending present. "The only things that change are when you wake up and when you go to bed. Besides that, it's entirely black. It's like one long day."[23]

• • •

The way we experience the passage of time is indicative of the way we relate to the world.[24] To be stuck in the present often means that we ourselves are stuck in the world. We're confronted with situations that don't resonate with us; they don't match our goals, needs, and desires.

An unsatisfactory present is a now that is either antithetical to or incongruous with our projects and concerns. It traps us without entrancing us. Unsatisfactory or uninteresting situations often lead to the dilation of time and consequently to a feeling of being stuck, yet not every slowing down of time is due to the presence of an unsatisfactory or uninteresting situation. Our sense of the passage of time can also be affected by our emotional experiences.

Consider, for example, how a twenty-four-year-old man experienced the passage of time while he was in a car accident. "I remember, like in slow motion, the sound of glass shattering. As the car started spinning I came up out of my seat and looked at the ceiling of the Volkswagen. I remember being very interested in the roof like I hadn't seen it before. The whole thing must have happened super quick but seemed to take a tremendous amount of time."[25] Due to their effects on our emotional and psychological states, life-threatening situations like this one have the seeming ability to slow down the passage of time. Individuals who have come face to face with life-threatening danger report that time becomes "strung out"; it seems "drawn out" and "expanded"; it feels "endless," like an "eternity."[26]

Other emotional states carry similar effects.[27] The presence of spiders to arachnophobic individuals leads to the overestimation of time.[28] Angry expressions appear to last longer than neutral expressions.[29] An emotionally arousing negative stimulus (a picture of a baby with an eye tumor) is perceived to linger longer than both a neutral stimulus (a picture of a rolling pin) and an emotionally arousing positive stimulus (a picture of a naked couple), even if all stimuli are shown for the same amount of time.[30] Fearful skydivers overestimate the duration of their fall, whereas skydivers who were excited about their fall underestimate its duration.[31] Depression has also been associated with a distorted sense of the passage of time. For individuals battling depression, time appears to pass more slowly.[32] The same appears to hold true for cancer patients in a state of anxiety.[33] Marcel Proust wrote in *In the Shadow of Young Girls in Flower*: "The time which we have at our disposal every day is elastic; the passions that we feel expand it, those that we inspire contract it; and habit fills up what remains."[34] Science agrees.

Our perception of the passage of time is a measure of how the world affects us. But as we've just seen, time isn't just an indication of how rich, interesting, distracting, or appealing our current situation is; time is also an indication of how we emotionally find ourselves when we're engaged with various situations. "Our feeling of time," William James, the father of American psychology, wrote, "harmonizes with different mental moods."[35] Emotions can transform the manner in which we find ourselves in the world and thereby can change our relationship to the present moment. Think of the different ways that fear, anger, rage, sadness, happiness, or boredom open up parts of the world to us and close off others. Objects and situations suddenly become our focus: they're threatening or enraging, difficult or easy, unappealing or simply lacking in possibilities. At the same time, other objects and situations disappear. In rage, anger, and fear, for example, what doesn't matter to us, what's irrelevant to us, recedes into the background. The object of rage, anger, or fear is all that there is for us. In this way, emotions can trap us. Emotions don't merely change our perception of the passage of time or the focus of our attention. They also modify the ways in which we experience our world. They render salient features of our situations. They act as powerful centers of gravity—pulling us toward certain aspects of our situations and away from others.

Emotions are ways through which we experience the world. We walk and move with them; we think, imagine, and perceive through emotions. Not all emotions will confine us within the present, but some will—those that transform our condition into one that's somehow foreign to us, incongruous to our goals, or contrary to our values. Despair and sadness, for example, can make it harder for us to think ahead. During those states, we tend to remain face to face with the present, and yet we can't be fulfilled or satisfied by it. In despair and sadness, we remain, it seems, stuck.

• • •

Sometimes the passage of time appears to have contradictory properties. A minute, hour, or year may seem both quick and unbearably slow.

On December 8, 1995, Jean-Dominique Bauby, then the editor-in-chief of the French *Elle,* suffered a massive stroke while driving his son to the theater. He lapsed into a coma and awoke 20 days later only to find himself locked within his own body—mouth, arms, and legs were paralyzed, but his consciousness remained intact. Imprisoned by an unyielding body, Bauby was able to communicate only by blinking his left eye. Despite that, he managed to produce a touching memoir—a description of his time in a hospital in Berck, France.[36] The book, composed and edited entirely in his head, was dictated, one letter at a time, using a system that allowed Bauby to choose letters depending on how he blinked his eye. "It is a simple enough system," he wrote.[37] "You read off the alphabet . . . until, with a blink of my eye, I stop you at the letter to be noted. The maneuver is repeated for the letters that follow, so that fairly soon you have a whole word, and then fragments of more or less intelligible sentences."[38] Every sentence is spread out in time, punctuated by pauses and blinks. It's in those long, delayed, filled with struggle sentences that Bauby tells us of the paradoxical nature of time—how time can be both long and short. "Sunday. The bell gravely tolls the hours. The small Health Department calendar on the wall, whittled away day by day, announces that it is already August. Mysterious paradox: time, motionless here, gallops out there. In my contracted world, the hours drag on but the months flash by."[39]

Viktor Frankl, the renowned Austrian neurologist and psychiatrist, documents a similar experience. In his profound and widely influential *Man's Search for Meaning,* Frankl provides a description of his grim existence as an inmate in Auschwitz from 1943 to 1945, followed by a system of existential theory that's based on his insight that our main drive in life isn't pleasure or power, but meaning. Frankl wrote his book on scraps of paper that he sequestered while in a concentration camp. On one of the pieces of paper, Frankl wrote the following. "In camp, a small time unit, a day, for example, filled with hourly tortures and fatigue, appeared endless. A larger time unit, perhaps a week, seemed to pass very quickly. My comrades agreed when I said that in camp a day lasted longer than a week. How paradoxical was our time experience!"[40]

How is it that the same length of time can appear to one both short and long? While paralyzed or in a concentration camp, time seems motionless and endless in the present but fast in retrospect. Such diverging, and seemingly contradictory, judgments are rendered perfectly consistent with one another once we appreciate the fact that each judgment is the product of a *different* way of estimating time. We can measure or estimate the duration of an interval *prospectively*: in this case, we're measuring the duration of the interval while this interval is still unfolding. But we can also estimate duration *retrospectively*: after a temporally extended event has concluded, we offer an estimate of its duration.

Memory is the driving mechanism of retrospective timing tasks.[41] To judge the duration of an event that's now past, we have to rely on our memory of that event to determine its duration. Naturally, our estimation of the duration will depend on the type of information that we've stored about the event. That's why unremarkable and mundane events seem short in retrospect. When we try to recall how we filled our time, we come up empty-handed. We did, it seems, nothing much, at least nothing memorable. Because such events seem empty, they appear to us in retrospect as having taken no time at all.

It's thought that the manner in which we prospectively estimate the duration of an event differs markedly from how we estimate its duration retrospectively.[42] Whereas in a retrospective estimation task we rely primarily on memory, prospective timing happens simultaneously with the event and as such, it's assumed that's governed by a different type of cognitive mechanism—one that's susceptible to the influences of physiological arousal (the extent to which our bodies are ready for action), emotions, and attention. Often, prospective timing is explained via the postulation of an "internal clock" that we somehow unconsciously operate. The clock consists of a pacemaker that emits pulses at a steady pace, a switch that when closed begins the accumulation of pulses, and a counting mechanism that's responsible for collecting and counting the accumulated pulses. This idea was first proposed by Michel Treisman in 1963 and later developed by John Gibbon, Russell Church, and Warren Meck. This internal clock model (sometimes called the pacemaker-accumulator model or the information-processing model) does a good job explaining a number of empirical findings. Why does time appear to move faster when we're engaged in a stimulating conversation? Answer: It's because we don't pay attention to the passage of time, and thus some of the accumulating pulses are missed. Why do emotions affect our perception of the passage of time? Answer: It's because our emotions have an effect on the pacemaker—they either speed up the rate of emission of pulses or slow it down.

Having in mind these two different ways of estimating durations—prospectively versus retrospectively—we can account for the seemingly paradoxical nature of Bauby and Frankl's observations. For example, empty and unremarkable activities appear in the moment to last longer because our attention to the passage of time leads us to accumulate more pulses than we would have accumulated had we been distracted. But in retrospect such activities appear short because they're not memorable.* Conversely, a busy and engaging present appears in the moment to pass quickly because we don't pay attention to the passage of time. However, in retrospect such an interval appears long— we remember all the things that we've done. William James summarizes this idea nicely. "In general, time filled with varied and interesting experiences, objects which rivet attention, vivid feelings, etc., seems short in passing, but long as we look back. On the other hand, a tract of time empty of experiences seems long in passing, but in retrospect short."[43]

Despite its popularity and ability to account for a number of findings, the internal clock model lacks any kind of physiological or neurological specificity. What it gives us is a story of how things *might* be unfolding. Many scientists are dissatisfied with this model. They're unhappy with the model's lack of detail of how the various mechanisms are implemented by the brain and are suspicious of the assumption that there exists a master clock. Whatever the fate of the internal clock model ends up being, it's undeniable that we do notice the passage of time differently in different contexts. We estimate durations of events, and our estimations are affected by our cognitive and emotional engagement with the world. Any psychological theory of the perception of the passage of time needs to come to terms with these observations.

• • •

Our behavior in the world is always shaped by our memories, expectations, desires, beliefs, and goals. What we experience is a product of both our past and our future. Imagine how a car mechanic encounters a car, how a chef experiences a kitchen, and how a hacker conceives of a computer. For the car mechanic, the car is an all-too-familiar object, one that calls to be repaired. For the chef, a kitchen is a space of limitless possibilities and opportunities, a venue for creativity. For the hacker, a computer is a tool, a weapon, or even

---

* Complication! Such an explanation of retrospective time estimation seems to run into a problem: it predicts that in retrospect the duration of boring experiences would be typically underestimated—in other words, if boring experiences are unremarkable and fail to grab our attention, then retrospectively it would seem that time flew by when we were bored. However, we know that this isn't the case, for, even in memory, boring experiences appear to be lengthy. So, what accounts for the protracted character of remembered boring experiences? The answer is (once again) memory. Although we don't remember the details of our boring situation (after all, it was boring and we weren't paying particular attention to it), we still remember that time was passing slowly. Our memory of our boring experience is thus shaped by our memory of how time dragged on. As a result, we tend to overestimate the duration of a boring situation even in a retrospective estimation.

a solution to a problem. For most of us, however, cars and computers are just tools, convenient or necessary ones to perform everyday tasks. And kitchens, well kitchens are places in which we prepare and eat food.

Our past furnishes us with a set of skills and knowledge that we bring to bear on any moment. As such, our past isn't a thing of the past. It's constantly informing and transforming our present. It also provides us with a sense of who we've been and who we are. Our future gives our present a focus and a direction. It picks out what's important to us and what matters to us; it helps us to narrow our choices. It's only by keeping in mind who we want to become that we can decide how to act in the now. The future thus informs our present. It stands as our guide. It's that which helps us to realize our dreams and desires.

Recall Clive Wearing. His all-encompassing amnesia has reduced him to a point-like existence. Without a past, he has no self, no sense of familiarity, and no identity. Without a future, his actions are meaningless and purposeless. Whatever he does, it doesn't matter. No action has any consequences for him, for no action can be remembered.

We are not like Clive, yet we can be subject to a similar but much less severe form of psychological entrapment. It happens to us when our future and past cease to be applicable or relevant to our present situation. That is, it happens when a situation either fails to promote our goals and interests or when it fails to relate in a meaningful way to who we are and who we have been. Imagine doing a job that you hate, listening to a lecture on a topic about which you don't care, or having to attend a party with people who you don't respect. Such situations aren't physically inescapable, yet they entrap us. They're unappealing to us. They're meaningless and incongruous with our beliefs and identities. In these situations, there are things to do, yet we don't understand the point of those things. While in them, we experience a form of psychological entrapment: we remain stationary in the present moment, disconnected from our true self and unable to move toward our potential.

Our perception of the passage of time, I wish to suggest, is a metric of our well-being. Specifically, feeling stuck in the present or experiencing a slow or lingering passage of time is an indication that we've found ourselves in situations that aren't fulfilling to us, which fail to promote our interests, and which ultimately don't contribute to—perhaps, they even hinder—our well-being.

We mentioned already that depressed or bored individuals, both of whom are dissatisfied with their situation, report a slower passage of time. But subjects who've experienced social rejection report the same. In a fascinating study, psychologists Jean M. Twenge, Kathleen R. Catanese, and Roy F. Baumeister examined the cognitive and emotional effects of social exclusion.[44] Subjects were randomly assigned into one of two conditions: rejection or acceptance. For the rejection condition, participants were falsely told that no one from a group of peers wanted to work with them and so they had to complete the experiment alone. For the acceptance condition, participants were told (falsely again) that because everyone wanted to work with them, it would be best if they worked alone. What the researchers found was that the participants in the rejected group significantly overestimated the temporal length of intervals compared to the accepted group. "Overestimating the duration of intervals," the researchers note, "occurs when time is passing very slowly, such as when one is severely bored or life is generally empty."[45] Thus, a slower passage of time can be thought of as a sign of an unsatisfactory condition. Equally important was the finding that rejected individuals found it difficult to think of the future and that they were more likely to focus on the present. Once rejected, such individuals saw themselves as being isolated from their future goals and plans. Such temporal isolation, in turn, affected their perception of the present. Specifically, a narrow focus on the present, robbed the present of its meaning, for it disconnected it from the past and future. As the researchers write, "[t]he meaningful construction of human life links different episodes across time, and the present often draws meaning from the future (e.g., when people explain their current activities in terms of goals or other anticipated future outcomes)."[46] They add: "Much of the meaning of present events is eliminated when the future is blocked out of awareness."[47] Each dimension of our time—past, present, and future—is interrelated with the other two. It owes its meaning to the relationship that it bears to them.

Perhaps the most impressive support for the claim that our subjective experience of the passage of time is an important indicator of how we're faring comes from studies that explicitly considered the relationship between well-being and the perception of the passage of time. In a study published in 2006 in the journal *Palliative and Supportive Care,* the authors investigated how patients with hematological malignancies (i.e., cancers that affect blood and lymph system) experience the passage of time. The authors reported a negative correlation between well-being and the perception of a slow passage of time. "Patients who prospectively estimated the time span as being longer showed a higher anxiety level, lower quality of life, and less spiritual well-being."[48] The authors explain their findings by suggesting that cancer patients who are anxious are less satisfied with their lives and thus perceive them as lacking in meaning. Without meaningful activities or distractions to surround them, such patients are forced to think of the passage of time. But attention to the passage of time leads them to a feeling that time passes slowly. The researchers conclude by emphasizing the diagnostic value of asking individuals of their experience of the passage of time. "The results of our study indicate that the experience of the passage of time should be investigated and taken seriously in psycho-oncological interventions."[49] In other words, the rate by which time appears to move is informative of one's existence. "The feeling that time passes slowly," the researchers write, "could indicate psychological distress resulting from an inability to focus on meaningful thoughts and to engage in purposeful actions."[50]

A different study, conducted by Steve K. Baum, Russell L. Boxley, and Marcia Sokolowski, reported similar findings. Intrigued by the claim, often repeated in the literature on time, that time speeds up with age, the researchers set out to examine whether one's age affects the perception of the passage of time.[51] What the researchers discovered wasn't that time speeds up with age but rather that it speeds up with *better* psychological well-being. Data from 296 institutionalized and community-dwelling elderly participants (aged 62–94) showed that faster time perceptions were associated with less clinical depression, an enhanced sense of purpose and control, and an image of oneself as younger than one's chronological age. On the contrary, participants who perceived time as moving slowly exhibited more depression, less purposed activity, and a self-concept of themselves as older than their chronological age.

The aforementioned findings are both revealing and important. They suggest rather strongly that the manner in which we relate to time is an indication of how we're faring in life. Being stuck in an unsatisfactory, unyielding, and seemingly unending present is a sign that our well-being is under threat.

• • •

The notion of temporal entrapment discussed in this chapter can be readily discerned in the three psychological states that are the focus of this book. In boredom, we find ourselves engaged in unfulfilling and uninteresting situations, and we desire to replace them with something else. Consider a typical example of situational boredom. While waiting for our flight that is delayed, we might remain bored despite the fact that opportunities for engagement present themselves: there are magazines to read, emails to reply to, and phone calls to make. Such opportunities, however, offer no relief. They aren't what we want to be doing. What will promote our interests and goals is to get to our destination, but the flight delay holds us in limbo. We're stuck in an unsatisfactory present, one in which our unfulfilled desire to board the plane is made all the more apparent to us.

In frustration, we're engrossed by the now but only insofar as we wish to overcome it. We seek to reach a future point in time during which the difficulty that we're currently facing no longer exists. An artist's frustration with her work signifies not only dissatisfaction with how her work is going, but also a desire to create an end product that meets her expectations. To state the obvious, frustration isn't apathy. We might be dissatisfied with our situation, but we aren't detached from it. In frustration, we remain engaged with our current situation. We try to overcome our frustration, but as long as frustration lasts, we can't succeed. In frustration, we stand face to face with an unsatisfactory situation. Thus, in contrast to boredom, we don't (at least immediately) wish to jettison the situation that fails to satisfy us. If boredom is a call to give up on our present situation and to do something else, frustration is a call to stick with and ultimately overcome our frustrating situation.

Finally, in anticipation, we long for what's to come and not for what we have. Indeed, the now may even stand as an obstacle to our goals. Bring to mind what it feels like to anticipate meeting a lover. The anticipation of this future event transforms our present. The *now* before meeting your lover becomes the *before* of meeting your lover. The now is important only because it will lead to the anticipated future. As a result, the now is drained of its flexibility and openness. It remains bound to the future, for not everything is allowable in this now. You won't do something that would interfere with meeting your lover. In anticipation, we may thus find ourselves stuck in the present. When we do, the present is nothing but time that has to be endured or, perhaps more tellingly, spent so that we can finally reach the anticipated future.

If being stuck in the present is a way of failing to do what matters to us, and if it results in an inability to connect with who we really are, then it's of utmost importance to understand the nature of such an entrapment. We need to understand it because we need to know how to get unstuck, how to set ourselves free, how to promote and flourish in our lives.

• • •

Boredom, frustration, and anticipation are three ways in which we find ourselves stuck. They're certainly not the only states that can give rise to such a condition, yet they're ones that demand our attention. This is the case not merely because they're common occurrences in our everyday lives, nor even because their presence signals our entrapment. Rather, they're important because within them, they already contain the potential to liberate us.

In their own ways, these three states tell us that there's something that we aren't yet accomplishing. They're reminders that what matters to us still lies ahead of us. But they do more than that. They can also act as motivating mechanisms that push us to pursue what's important to us. These three states set us on a trajectory to seek what's truly our own.

But how, exactly?

4

"Confined in an invisible bubble that prevents contact with the world"

The inscription reads: "In order to play the theme 840 times in succession, it would be advisable to prepare oneself beforehand, and in the deepest silence, by serious immobilities." Erik Satie's *Vexations* (1893) consists of a bass "theme" of nineteen notes (the last two notes are tied together) followed by two harmonizations.[1] It's eccentric, skewed, and unnerving. But, somehow, it's also pleasant. The sheet of musical notation doesn't exceed half a page, yet the inscription that lies at the top of the page carries the potential to open it up and to confer on it unforeseeable and superlative qualities (Figure 4.1).

The precise meaning and force of the inscription remains, even to this day, elusive. However, if understood as a directive to perform the piece eight hundred forty times in succession, the inscription doesn't only greatly alter the length of the piece, it also changes the way it emotionally affects us. What at first might be pleasant or interesting, might cease to be so after one hears it continuously for hours: incessant repetition tires the soul, numbs the senses, and according to pianist Peter Evans, who attempted a solo performance of the piece and had to stop abruptly after 16 hours, "wear[s] the mind away."[2] Never perhaps has a single sentence had such a profound effect on a musical piece.

American composer John Cage was the first to stage a complete live performance of *Vexations*.[3] On September 9, 1963, a relay of twelve pianists took twenty-minute turns and executed the piece in its entirety. The performance lasted over eighteen hours. The audience waxed and waned. The *New York Times* critic fell asleep at four AM. Yet one man, an off-Broadway actor named Karl Schenzer, remained present for the entire performance. He must have liked it. But how could he have?

To state the obvious, *Vexations* is repetitive and seemingly unending. But is it also boring? One might legitimately wonder. "Only at first," wrote Dick Higgins, a composer, poet, and member of the art collective Fluxus, in his essay "Boredom and Danger."[4] "After a while the euphoria . . . begins to intensify. By the time the piece is over, the silence is absolutely numbing, so much

Propelled. Andreas Elpidorou, Oxford University Press (2020). © Andreas Elpidorou.
DOI: 10.1093/oso/9780190912963.001.0001

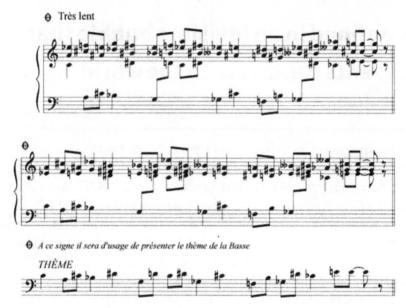

Figure 4.1 The score of *Vexations*.
© Sonia y Natalia / Wikimedia Commons / CC-BY-SA-3.0.

of an environment has the piece become."[5] For Higgins, boredom occupies an important, perhaps essential, place in art. Boredom, Higgins notes, "is a necessary station on the way to other experiences."[6]

Boredom emphasizes what it disrupts or takes away. It forces us to see things anew.

•••

It was a hazy afternoon, but the building could be seen clearly in all its grandeur.

The date was July 25, 1964. Andy Warhol, accompanied by poet and photographer Gerard Malanga, filmmaker and critic Jonas Mekas, filmmaker John Palmer, and member of the camera crew Marie Desert, entered the TimeLife Building at the corner of 50th Street and the Avenue of the Americas in New York City. They were carrying bags and boxes filled with camera equipment. They ascended to the forty-first floor, the headquarters of the Rockefeller Foundation, where they met up with Henry Romney, the vice president of the foundation, who escorted them into an office. Outside the window, the Empire State Building stood tall, resilient, and clear of any obstructions. With meticulous care, a camera was placed on a tripod, turned on, and left running for a total of six and a half hours.[7]

This is how Andy Warhol's *Empire* was shot. A silent, black and white film with one protagonist: the immovable Empire State Building (Figure 4.2). The movie was shot at twenty-four frames per second but was projected at sixteen. The result? A touch of unreality and a total running time of eight hours and five minutes. *Eight hours and five minutes.* Eight hours and five minutes of passivity. "Nothing was to happen in the film," art critic and philosopher Arthur Danto notes in his book *Andy Warhol*, "other than what happened to it."[8]

The film begins with a brilliantly white image. Slowly the outline of a cityscape emerges. The Empire State Building becomes visible, front and center. Two smaller buildings can be discerned to its left. One of them is the Metropolitan Life Tower, which, throughout the film, acts as a clock: the light on its top flashes once every fifteen minutes and the correct number of times every hour.

Figure 4.2 Andy Warhol, *Empire* (1964), 16 mm film, black and white, silent, 8 hours 5 minutes at 16 frames per second.

© 2018 The Andy Warhol Museum, Pittsburgh, PA, a museum of Carnegie Institute. All rights reserved.

As the sun sets, the scene begins to darken. The light at the top of the Empire State Building glows, and, suddenly, the floodlights are turned on, illuminating the top thirty floors. Natural light eventually fades to blackness, and for the remainder of the film, the Empire State Building stands still. Occasionally, this stillness is interrupted. Bubbles, marks, speckles, and flashes of white flare—all of them artifacts resulting from either the production or the development of the film—appear. Still, the same image persists. Minute after minute the Empire State Building stands there, visible and motionless, until the floodlights are turned off. After that, the film takes place almost in darkness. One watches a nearly black screen. The film ends.

The lack of action and movement is resounding. Once a viewer asked when the film was going to start, even though unbeknownst to him the film had started several minutes earlier.[9] On a different occasion, viewers found *Empire* so abhorrently empty and lacking in any discernable features or progression that they threatened to destroy the theater. Jonas Mekas recalls in the *Village Voice*:

> Ten minutes after the film started, a crowd of 30 or 40 people stormed out of the theater into the lobby, surrounded the box office, Bob Brown and myself, and threatened to beat us up and destroy the theater unless their money was returned. "This is not entertainment! This movie doesn't move!" shouted the mob.[10]

Early critical discussions of *Empire* also focused on its apparent concern with demonstrating that one can fill over eight hours of cinematic time with, if not quite nothing, then just one thing that does nothing at all. The film is about "a big nothing," *Village Voice* art critic Gregory Battcock wrote in an essay.[11] For some, this lack of action leads to the conclusion that Warhol's early films are about duration or the passage of time.[12] Even Warhol himself admits as much.[13] Nothing really happens in them, but time still relentlessly and uninterruptedly passes. For others, such as philosopher Arthur Danto, *Empire* is a "philosophical masterpiece."[14] A film in which nothing moves is a film that has managed to capture the very essence of film.

The lack of action and the presence of monotonous repetitiveness inevitably bring up the issue of boredom. Passivity and lack of stimulation invite it. The viewer is left to her own devices. Can one find interest in *Empire* or not? Is it boring? "If I were the camera, I would faint with boredom staring that long at one thing" wrote art dealer and writer John Bernard Myers in an essay on *Empire* that appeared in *The New American Cinema: A Critical Anthology*.[15]

• • •

Contrast our reaction to pain with that to boredom. The experience of the former is disruptive. It prompts concerns and often morbid thoughts. We don't want to be in pain. We dread it. And we go to great lengths to avoid and alleviate it: we take painkillers, exercise regularly, meditate, and even choose to undergo surgery. But when bored, rarely do we drop what we're doing to seek help or treatment. We don't even protest much. We acknowledge its presence often silently and with acquiescence. There's no hidden side to boredom. What feels like boredom is boredom, and boredom, we believe, isn't that terrible even if it is unwelcome and displeasing.

We often like to distinguish between appearances and reality. What appears to be gold, for example, isn't necessarily gold. The outward appearance of a specimen doesn't guarantee that it's a specimen of gold. What makes gold *gold* isn't its appearance but its atomic constitution. That's why fool's gold isn't gold. The same goes for biological species. A Bengal tiger is a tiger not because it merely looks like a tiger but because it's a member of the species *P. tigris* and bears the right phylogenetic relationship to other related species. Cleverly disguised automata—self-operated machines—that look like tigers aren't tigers. They're just tiger-looking automata.

When it comes to boredom, the reality–appearance distinction seems to vanish. The experience of boredom signifies boredom and not something else. We don't confuse boredom with something else. At least most of us don't. Jane Austen's Emma Woodhouse is a notable exception: "This sensation of listlessness, weariness, stupidity, this disinclination to sit down and employ myself, this feeling of every thing's being dull and insipid about the house!—I must be in love."[16]

But we aren't like Emma Woodhouse. We know very well what boredom is. We're familiar with it and recognize it when it comes. To be clear, our familiarity with boredom doesn't guarantee that we always know *why* we're bored; often boredom seems to have no cause. Boredom can even silently sneak up on us. It can engulf us without noticing it. Sometimes we realize we've been bored only in retrospect. The party was boring, but it didn't strike us as such while we were there. It was only later—while thinking about the conversations we had, the music we listened to, and the food we ate—that we realized we were bored.

What we mean when we say that we're familiar with boredom is that we know how it feels. The experience of boredom is unpleasant. In it, we find shades of frustration, displeasure, sadness, anxiety, and even anger. We feel empty and constrained by our surroundings and by what's afforded to us. In boredom, it's hard to concentrate on the situation at hand. We find ourselves disengaged from the world and others. Our mind wanders. We become restless and irritable. We grow mentally tired. We become aware of the passing of time—time seems to have slowed down. As such, we linger even longer in this disagreeable present situation becoming increasingly aware of its unpleasant and unsatisfying nature. In boredom, we're trapped in our current situation. Boredom is there but we don't want it to be. We feel stuck. We seek relief. We desire a world richer in stimulation and interest. We wish to do something, often *anything* other than what we're currently doing. We wish to become active and to move out of this unappealing and tiresome situation.

Boredom has an uncanny capacity to find us. It finds us at home or at work, in open spaces or behind closed doors, alone or in the company of others, on computers or exercise bikes, while standing up or lying in bed. It finds travelers in airports and on planes, patients in doctors' offices, drivers behind the wheel, students in classrooms, and inmates in prison. A 2003 survey found that 91% of North American youth experience boredom.[17] Another survey from the same year reported that 51% of teenagers are bored easily.[18] More recently, a 2015 study conducted by Pew Research reported that the second most common reason that smartphone owners use their phone is to avoid boredom. (The first reason was to coordinate meeting someone.) Given how prevalent the use of smartphones is, boredom must be everywhere. It's even in the bedroom—23% of French men and 31% of French women reported being bored while making love.[19]

There's more. A NASA-published report on the effects of reduced sensory stimulation mentions boredom as one of the main effects and problems of space travel and exploration.[20] "Funny thing happened on the way to the moon: not much," wrote Gene Cernan, an Apollo 17 astronaut.[21] And he regretted that he didn't bring crossword puzzles for the trip. Incredibly, boredom finds us even when we're out of this world. "[E]ven though it's space flight and all of that, you still get bored," said astronaut Norman Thagard about his experience aboard Mir in an interview.[22] Yet another astronaut who preferred to remain anonymous commented that the trip to the International Space Station, which took almost three days, all the while being cramped in a miniscule space capsule, was extremely boring.[23] Not even the most exciting, awe-inspiring of all activities lie outside of boredom's reach.

Boredom appears to be ubiquitous, but despite its prevalence and omnipresence, we aren't particularly worried by it. I suspect that such a nonchalant attitude stems from the fact that most often boredom is a fleeting state that can be easily pacified. That is, boredom finds us easily, but it also leaves us quickly. Most of us aren't continuously bored. We're bored in one moment, but not in the next. Partly because of its transient and tolerable nature, boredom is thought to be a trivial, inconsequential, or banal state. More often than not, we're able to fight it, to mask it, or to make it, temporarily at least, go away. Without much thought, we look for an alternative situation or engagement: a book, a movie, a friend, a phone call, a text message, a magazine, a mobile app, a walk, an inner thought, or a fantasy—anything that will keep our interest.

What's ephemeral, it seems, can't be taken seriously. Instead, like a gadfly, boredom is a pestering but passing emotion. It doesn't befit our busy, achievement-orientated lifestyles, and we would rather live without it. Still, life is bearable, perhaps enjoyable, even if it contains low to medium doses of boredom.

• • •

Boredom isn't merely a fleeting psychological state. It's also situational and remarkably personal.

Boredom is often the product of our circumstances. It arises because of how the world is. Waiting in a doctor's office for an appointment that's running late yields, almost invariably, boredom. So does waiting for a bus or a plane that never seems to arrive. In our everyday lives, we're forced to endure countless situations. When those situations don't fulfill us, when they fail to capture our interests, when they hold us in limbo and postpone our goals, they can give rise to boredom and make us aware of an unsatisfactory present. Finding ourselves in such situations, boredom finds us. Boredom is *out* there: in monotonous, repetitive, mandatory, lackluster, banal, or trite situations. Change those situations and you change the experience of boredom. Some changes diminish boredom, others increase it, and others bring about its complete dissolution.

But boredom is as much out there as it is in us. We shouldn't always blame the world for our boredom; sometimes it's our fault that we're bored. Our beliefs, desires, intentions, and goals can also be responsible for when and how boredom arises. They affect the ways in which we engage (or fail to do so) with our situations and in doing so, they can give rise to boredom. How many times have we found something to be boring simply because we didn't know enough about it? Think of a new music album, an art exhibition, or a lecture that we couldn't appreciate. And how often does lack of care result in boredom? Think of our apolitical friend. No political debate or conversation will ever grab their attention or entertain them.

Thus, we don't only find boredom in our world; we also carry it with us. We move it from place to place. We can take it almost everywhere. Boredom is *that* portable. Think of the bored tourist who finds every sight, museum, or ancient ground boring. Think of English writer Samuel Johnson's reminder: "Triflers may find or make any Thing a Trifle."[24]

In this manner, boredom becomes personal. It's personal insofar as its presence and character depend on our psychological make-up—our beliefs, desires, dispositions, and intentions. It's personal insofar as *my* boredom isn't *your* boredom. Nor is it anyone else's. It isn't Warhol's, who was fond of saying "I like boring things."[25] It isn't John Cage's, who in his book *Silence* famously wrote: "In Zen they say: If something is boring after two minutes, try it for four. If still boring, try it eight, sixteen, thirty-two, and so on. Eventually one discovers that it's not boring at all but very interesting."[26]

And clearly, my boredom isn't that of Kenneth Goldsmith's, the self-proclaimed "most boring writer that has ever lived."[27] Goldsmith spent an entire day dictating his every bodily movement into a tape recorder and then transcribed it hour by hour in his book *Fidget*. On a different occasion, he recorded and then transcribed every word he spoke for an entire week. And if that weren't enough, he once retyped a day's copy of the *New York Times*, page by page, column by column, line by line. The resulting transcription is a book that spans close to nine hundred pages. One can read it, but few would want to. One can retype it, but even fewer would want to engage in such a mindless, repetitive, and, no doubt, boring activity.

Boredom is personal not only in the sense that our thresholds for boredom differ. It's also, and more important, personal in the sense that the object of boredom differs from person to person. Some are bored with sex, drugs, money, and social status—everyone in Bret Easton Ellis' *Less than Zero* is bored with all four. Others become bored with religion and God. And yet others lose interest in their own friends and even their children. "It would amuse me for a few seconds, maybe, hearing her, but it would bore me soon enough," the protagonist of François Mauriac's marvelous *Thérèse Desqueyroux* thinks when she remembers that she hasn't seen her child for a while.[28] Imagine for a minute the things that bore you and make a list of them. Your list will not be identical to mine. Undoubtedly, there will be agreement between the two. Dare I say that we both find monotony boring? But there will be disagreement too. Our interests, after all, differ. It's to be expected then that our boredoms will differ as well. I am fascinated by biographies of obscure mathematicians, by reruns of old soccer matches, and by trying to figure out whether one can hear silence or not. Are you? Probably not.

If it changes from person to person, from time to time, and from place to place, is there something meaningful to be said about boredom? If almost everything can potentially bore us, then what could boredom mean or signify? Is boredom simply a matter of personal taste? Is boredom trivial or inconsequential?

• • •

There isn't, however, only one kind of boredom.

In an essay commenting on the developmental value of boredom, British psychotherapist Adam Phillips makes precisely this point: "Clearly, we should speak not of boredom, but of the boredoms."[29] There's the simple, everyday, mundane, or trivial type of boredom, and then there's a boredom that's far more serious. Depending on its object, frequency, and duration, boredom can change.

One can find almost anything boring, but when certain objects or situations that are almost universally considered important become boring, boredom takes on an ominous character. A failure to find interest in things that matter can signify a moral failure or a character flaw. Consider becoming bored with life, with your marriage, with your children, with your civic duties, or with social affairs. We typically think that one *ought* not to be bored with such important matters. And "ought" here carries moral force: it's wrong to experience such boredom.

The moral dimension of boredom has been noted for centuries. Early Christian Fathers were concerned with a type of spiritual boredom that was endemic to monastic life and which besieged monks. It instilled laziness in them. It distracted them. It made the monastic life appear lengthy, harsh, and undesirable. Ultimately, it resulted in a loss of a sense of commitment or dedication to the goals and aims of the ascetic life.[30]

The term used for this type of spiritual boredom is "acedia." It's made up of the negative prefix "a" and "kedos," the latter means to care about. The term carries distinctively negative connotations. Acedia, as a form of lack of concern or care, isn't merely a psychological state or a fleeting experience. Its presence is indicative of a deep flaw or shortcoming. Such a shortcoming can't, of course, lie with God. One can't find fault in that being who is most perfect. The problem lies instead with the individual experiencing this type of boredom. It's the individual who lacks the necessary emotional and intellectual resources. It's he who can't allow himself to be taken by God. It's he who has fallen.

The fallen state of those who suffer from acedia is depicted in the darkest and most sinister fashion by Dante in his *Inferno*. Dante and Virgil discover the slothful in the fifth circle of hell. The slothful lie hidden underneath the slimy surface of the river Styx. They have words to say: "Sluggish we were in the sweet air made happy by the sun, and the smoke of sloth was smoldering in our hearts; now we lie sluggish here in this black muck!"[31] They have words to say, but they can't properly voice them. Speech and voice need air. They have none. The slothful can only gurgle their words, for they remain completely immersed in black mire.

When boredom becomes spiritual, when the object of boredom is the monastic life, prayer, or even God herself, boredom changes. It ceases to be a trivial state. It's no longer inconsequential. Boredom becomes a sin. Its presence signifies a character failure. It demands a solution, a fix—or, in Dante's account, it warrants extreme and perhaps eternal punishment.

We shouldn't, however, be misled to think that the problematic nature of boredom is specific to spiritual boredom. A monk's boredom with God seems to be both unacceptable and worrisome. Yet the same goes for a politician's boredom with the public good, a judge's boredom with fair judicial procedures, a doctor's boredom with beneficence, a father's boredom with his children's well-being, or a soldier's boredom with their patriotic duties. Under the appropriate circumstances, anything can appear boring. But when certain objects of boredom move from the sphere of potentiality to that of actuality, boredom is immediately transformed. It becomes a darker and more ominous psychological state. It becomes forbidden. This dark boredom says more about us than about its objects. It reveals our own shortcomings and flaws.

• • •

The passage from trivial to serious can take yet another path. Boredom can become a problematic state not only when the object of boredom is something culturally or morally important or even sacrosanct, but also when one is frequently bored in a wide array of situations. Psychologists have been studying the propensity to experience boredom for years. They call it "boredom proneness."

In the summer of 1997, Mansur Zaskar swallowed over seventy aspirin and antinausea tablets.[32] His suicide attempt however failed. His overdose caused him to hallucinate and to fall into convulsions. He was discovered by an apartment-mate and was rushed to the intensive care unit. Zaskar survived and was referred to a psychiatric clinic. This wasn't the first time that Zaskar tried to end his life. In conversations, he expresses that he has no desire to live. He dwells in suicidal thoughts and is constantly dysphoric. "Everything seems trite and insubstantial," he says.[33] And his life is difficult: "Everything for me is an effort. I feel heavy, slothful, as if merely existing is a burden, and even small talk requires too much effort."[34] Zaskar is deeply and profoundly bored, not with this or that situation, but with *every possible situation*.

> I feel I lack a sense of purpose, and completeness. Most of all I feel extremely bored. Bored of everything—work, friends, hobbies, relationships, music, reading, movies, bored all the time. I do things [merely] to occupy my time, to distract my- self from trying to discover the meaning of my existence, and I would gladly cease to do anything if the opportunity arose. No matter what the activity is it leaves me feeling unfulfilled. . . . What possible difference does it ultimately make whatever I do? What difference does anything make?[35]

Zaskar is an instance, extreme perhaps, of a boredom-prone individual.

Boredom proneness isn't a disposition that can remain hidden or nonactualized. Rather, boredom proneness affects one in visible and signif- icant ways. Boredom proneness is different than the simple and everyday boredom that most of us experience and which can be dispelled by a change of situation or mind. The boredom-prone individual often and easily finds her- self to be bored, even in situations that others typically find interesting and stimulating. She regularly becomes incapable of maintaining sustained atten- tion and interest in her activities. She lacks excitement for, or can find no pur- pose in, what she is doing. She easily becomes frustrated, restless, or weary by situations that are either challenging or lacking in variety.

To be sure, there is a relationship between the common and short-lived ex- perience of boredom that most of us experience and boredom proneness—in some sense, the boredom-prone individual still experiences the same experi- ence that we experience when we are bored. But there's also a great difference. Our world isn't boring, only this or that situation is boring, and only some- times. For the boredom-prone individual, however, existence itself becomes boring. Because of that, it would be misleading to call boredom proneness a psychological "state." It isn't a state, at least not one of our familiar psycholog- ical or mental states. One doesn't go in and out of boredom proneness in the way that one goes in and out of a headache. Boredom proneness isn't just what we feel when we find ourselves in a boring situation. Boredom proneness is an existential condition; it's a way of life. It's a person's total comportment to the world—affective, cognitive, volitional, and behavioral—when the world appears to be almost always boring.

The frequent experience of boredom transforms the way that the boredom- prone individual inhabits the world and lives her life. The world doesn't sat- isfy her. She isn't captured by the world. Instead, she stands at a distance from the world and others. She seeks diversions and excitement. She moves from project to project, from activity to activity seeking relief from boredom. But relief is nowhere. Interest is nowhere. The boredom-prone individual seems barred from the possibility of finding interest. She can't become captivated, mesmerized, or seduced by her world. "I feel I am in this world but not of this world, confined in an invisible bubble that prevents contact with the world," Zaskar reports.[36]

A 2015 *Time* magazine headline reads: "Terrorists' Most Powerful Recruiting Tool: Boredom." If boredom is a recruiting tool, it can't be the boredom that we occasionally experience at the dentist's office. It must instead be boredom proneness—the frequent, almost omnipresent, experience of boredom that is coupled with an inability to find meaning and interest.

In one of his lecture courses, the twentieth-century German philosopher Martin Heidegger, discussed at length a form of boredom that bears remarkable resemblance to boredom proneness.[37] According to Heidegger, when we find ourselves in its inescapable embrace, a type of total withdrawal from the world takes place. This boredom is so pervasive and powerful that it strips away all of our identifying characteristics, history, and projects. What overtakes us is nothing less than absolute indifference. In this extreme boredom, we can relate to nothing, not even to ourselves.

Boredom-prone individuals are there, but the world exists as if they weren't. They've become specters of themselves, and their everyday existence can be summarized without a trace of excitement and without a hint of personal connection. They describe themselves as "phonies."[38] They think of themselves as "observers of [a] passing scene, watching it all happen as though from some distant vantage point."[39]

The world of boredom proneness is almost devoid of interest and excitement; it is characterized by a scarcity of fulfilling situations and lacks entities and activities to which one can meaningfully relate. "The plains of ennui," Baudelaire wrote in *The Flowers of Evil*, are "vacant and profound."[40] Boredom of this extreme form is profoundly vacant.

• • •

"Boredom is the root of all evil."[41]

In the span of fifteen pages, Søren Kierkegaard, the nineteenth-century Danish philosopher, makes such a sweeping pronouncement, not once, not twice, but four times. Kierkegaard doesn't assume authorship of this claim. Rather, he makes it through the pseudonymous voice of A, the main author of the first part of his *Either/Or*. A is an aesthete whose sole purpose in life is the incessant pursuit of sensual and artistic pleasures. His existence is utterly egotistic, characterized both by a complete immersion in pleasures and by a flight away from boredom. The aesthete calls boredom "corrupting,"[42] "demonic,"[43] and "infinitely repulsive."[44] He offers suggestions—often elaborate and preposterous—for how to deal with boredom and how to transform the boring into the interesting. He insists that all people are boring. He claims that boredom is as old as the world itself. And he echoes French mathematician and philosopher Blaise Pascal when declaring that boredom is a human condition.

Kierkegaard's pronouncement that boredom is the root of all evil should be understood within the context of his discussion of the life of the egotistic and hedonistic aesthete. For someone who requires that all things are interesting, boredom *is* evil. It isn't evil in the moral sense. Still, it's evil in the aesthetic sense. Boredom is tantamount to triteness, banality, and the uninteresting. Boredom is the lack of excitement. Boredom is unimaginativeness.

Outside the context of A's aesthetic life, it might seem like a stretch to call boredom the root of all evil. Yet, somehow, such a broad and unconditional assertion manages to capture many of the lessons that we've learned in the last thirty years from the scientific study of boredom proneness.

Take depression, anxiety, anger, and aggression. Boredom proneness is positively correlated with all of them.[45] And the same holds for loneliness, apathy, and hopelessness.[46] Boredom is pervasive in psychiatric and neurological populations and has been reported to be a complicating factor in the rehabilitation of mental disorders and in recovery from traumatic brain injury. Within the environment of the hospital, psychiatric patients often experience boredom and the decrease of meaningful relationships. A 2003 study conducted by psychologist and professor of mental health at the University of Haifa David Roe and legal scholar and lecturer of social work at Ben Gurion University Ya'ir Ronen and published in the *International Journal of Law and Psychiatry* reported that 87% of inpatients at four hospital facilities in the Yale University Department of Psychiatry experienced a profound passivity. The same study included testimonies by psychiatric patients. "It's not good being on this chronic ward," a patient reported.[47] "I stagnate."[48] Another patient describes how boring his life in the hospital is: "All you did was just sitting around and there was nothing for you to do. There was no program. There was no program to keep you busy and occupied and stuff."[49]

Patients who have suffered traumatic brain injuries (including concussions) also experience boredom often.[50] Indeed, one distinctive way in which their preinjury life differs from their postinjury existence is the presence of boredom. The injury has diminished their ability to be stimulated and has turned their lives into ones that are filled with, and ruled by, boredom.

Within an educational context, boredom proneness has been linked to poor grades, early dropout rates, and school dissatisfaction.[51] Within the workplace, boredom proneness has been associated with lower job satisfaction and job involvement, increased accident rates, and increased job stress.[52] In the case of delivery truck drivers, it was found that the experience of boredom is related to property damage.[53]

In everyday life, boredom proneness is related to poor performance on tasks that require sustained attention.[54] It's also related to a propensity to make mistakes in completing common tasks, such as misplacing one's keys or putting milk in the pantry instead of the fridge.[55] Boredom proneness leads to poor interpersonal and social relationships. Boredom-prone individuals have difficulty in social situations and in forming and maintaining relationships.[56] Boredom proneness is also associated with a lower life satisfaction.[57] Indeed, boredom-prone individuals have a harder time finding meaning in life than those who aren't prone to boredom.[58] They also report disordered agency—they don't know what they want to do in life—and diminished self-determination.[59] What's more, boredom-prone individuals experience impulse control deficits.[60] Looking for something to excite them, they're more likely to engage in risk-taking behavior (e.g., reckless driving) and are more prone to binge eating, excessive smoking, drug and alcohol abuse, and gambling.[61]

And if all of this was not enough, there's even evidence suggesting that too much boredom can be an indication of early death. In the 1980s, British epidemiologists Annie Britton and Martin J. Shipley surveyed more than 7,500 civil servants about their experience of boredom.[62] When they followed up in 2009, they found that those who initially reported to experience a great deal of boredom were more likely to have died than those who reported no boredom at all. The authors were careful to make it clear that boredom wasn't the direct cause of death. Still, boredom is an indication of poorer health prospects.

Boredom proneness is a serious matter. There can be no question about it. Boredom in this extreme form is capable not only of greatly altering our behavior, but also of derailing our lives. It can take away the possibility of finding rest, peace, and happiness. It can severely harm us.

• • •

There's no inconsistency, paradox, or contradiction in insisting that boredom can be both trivial and serious. As a tolerable and easily allayed psychological state, boredom is, for the most part, trivial and inconsequential. However, boredom can undergo a transformation. Depending on its object, boredom can signify a character flaw or weakness. Depending on its frequency, boredom can cease to be a fleeting state and become a way of life. Either way, boredom can change from trivial to serious, from inconsequential to harmful.

But boredom isn't necessarily a toxic condition. There can be value in boredom. And I will show how this can be the case in the next chapter. So far, we've only seen the negative side of boredom. We've seen what boredom takes away from us and what absence it leaves. It's now time to see what boredom can do for us. There's another side to boredom that waits to be discovered. A bright side of boredom exists.

5

"Like water after days in the desert"

Your life was a hypothesis. Those who die old are made of the past. Thinking of them, one thinks of what they have done. Thinking of you, one thinks of what you could have become. You were, and you will remain, made up of possibilities.

Your suicide was the most important thing you ever said, but you'll never be able to enjoy the fruits of this labor.[1]

On October 15, 2007, Edouard Levé committed suicide. He hung himself. Just ten days before this final act, he submitted a book manuscript to his editor. The passage with which this chapter begins is taken from that work. It's titled *Suicide*.

Suicide is a fictional work written in the second person. It offers an incomplete, nonchronological, and tessellated portrait of a friend of the narrator who killed himself twenty years ago. It reads like a letter to the deceased.

For the most part, its language is simple, controlled, precise, and to the point. Playfulness is sometimes allowed to emerge. But when it does, it's fugacious: the bleakness and gravity of the subject manner quickly consume it.

Some novels are attractive because in them we find a home—an emotionally comforting landscape, a place to relieve our minds of heavy thoughts. *Suicide*'s allure lies elsewhere. What attracts us to it is its ability to push us out of a state of equipoise. Whatever else it is, *Suicide* is disquieting. It can make our minds race. It populates them with thoughts about the value of life. Nothing seems to put our life more forcefully in perspective than the unbearable projection of its absence. As the narrator tells the deceased, "[y]our suicide makes the lives of those who outlive you more intense. Should they be threatened by boredom, or should the absurdity of their lives leap out at them from the curve of some cruel mirror, let them remember you, and the pain of existence will seem preferable to the disquiet of no longer being."[2]

Propelled. Andreas Elpidorou, Oxford University Press (2020). © Andreas Elpidorou.
DOI: 10.1093/oso/9780190912963.001.0001

Given Levé's own death, it's hard not to read *Suicide* as a work about him. Levé knew this. Indeed, he must have wanted it to be this way. Why else would he have committed suicide right after he had completed a work titled *Suicide*? Sometimes the storyteller is part of the story. Levé's act of taking his own life is as textual as it is real.

Suicide, however, isn't simply a work about Levé. To understand it as such is to uncharitably and unnecessarily confine it. It's to reduce it to something that it isn't. *Suicide* is essentially ambiguous. When the narrator says, "[y]ou died because you searched for happiness at the risk of finding the void," the denotation of "you" seems clear enough.[3] "You" picks out a singular individual, Levé himself. Yet, at other times, one forgets of Levé. The second-personal declarative narration has a soporific effect. The repetitive use of "you" is hypnotic. And as one glides from sentence to sentence, one loses track of the referent of "you." We're accustomed in seeing ourselves in everything. So, we come to see ourselves even in *Suicide*. Slowly and unavoidably, *Suicide* becomes a work about everyone.

Levé discusses boredom in *Suicide*. The narrator accuses the deceased of impatience. "Your impatience deprived you of the art of succeeding by being bored."[4] The accusation sounds off-key, if not straightforwardly oxymoronic. How does one succeed by being bored? The narrator offers an explanation. "You believed that only action and thought, which seemed absent here, carry life. You underestimated the value of passivity, which is not the art of pleasing but of placing oneself. Being in the right place at the right time requires accepting long moments of boredom, passed in gray spaces."[5]

There's value in the experience of boredom, the narrator informs us. We have to give time to boredom. We have to sustain it and withstand it. Only then, perhaps, we will achieve satisfaction.

• • •

Afterwards there's bliss.

The idea that there's value to withstanding boredom isn't a new one. Nor is it unique with Levé. The philosopher Friedrich Nietzsche claimed that boredom is—at least sometimes—a component of creative work. Boredom is the emotional storm before the creative calm: "that disagreeable 'lull' of the soul that precedes a happy voyage and cheerful winds."[6] One has to ask or even long for boredom. One has to wait for it. And then, one has to endure it. Its effects are beneficial. One seeks boredom, it seems, as sailors seek wind in their sails: to be moved forward.

Nietzsche isn't alone in extoling the creative powers of boredom. In a brief diary entry, Susan Sontag suggested that the most interesting art of her time was boring: "Jasper Johns is boring. Beckett is boring, Robbe-Grillet is boring. Etc. Etc. . . . Maybe art has to be boring, now."[7]

British philosopher, writer, political activist, and Nobel laureate Bertrand Russell and the psychoanalyst Adam Phillips both spoke of the importance of being able to endure boredom. And they both underscored the value of teaching children how to be bored, how to live through it. For Russell, a certain degree of tedium is unavoidable in one's life. So, we better learn how to deal with it. The capacity to weather boredom is thus "essential to a happy life."[8] Relatedly, Phillips maintained that "boredom is integral to the process of taking one's time."[9] To endure boredom is to take time to find what interests one. As such, learning how to endure boredom is learning how to experience a paradoxical and unpleasant form of waiting: in boredom, we're waiting and longing for something of which we know not.

Perhaps the most provocative claim about the value of enduring boredom comes from David Foster Wallace. In his posthumously published novel, *The Pale King*, he asserts "if you are immune to boredom, there is literally nothing you cannot accomplish."[10] For Wallace, boredom appears to be an experience that can lead, somehow, to greatness. It contains the potential of utter bliss, even transcendence. But one can reap the benefits of boredom, only if one can withstand it. He writes:

> Bliss lies on the side of crushing boredom. Pay close attention to the most tedious thing you can find (tax returns, televised golf) and, in waves, a boredom like you've never known will wash over you and just about kill you. Ride these out, and it's like stepping from black and white into color. Like water after days in the desert. Constant bliss in every atom.[11]

Wallace's words might sound like an encomium. But do we really pay boredom a compliment when we claim that withstanding boredom can lead to something good?

Consider the following. For most of us, states of "normalcy"—for example, being healthy or not being in pain—don't usually have associated feelings; there're no distinctive sensations that accompany and mark them. That's true, except when such states of "normalcy" arrive after their prolonged absence. Being not in pain after an intense and long experience of pain feels good. Reclaiming your health after a debilitating illness also feels good. But neither fact shows that enduring the experience of pain or illness has any value. What has value is that which we lost and which returns once pain and illness disappear. Similarly, proclamations of the value of the capacity to endure boredom aren't necessarily claims about boredom's value. The experience of boredom may very well lead to something valuable or important. But if boredom doesn't play a role in taking us there, then boredom isn't what is valuable; what has value is only that which follows it.

Hence, in our attempt to find value in boredom, we mustn't look only to what follows boredom (bliss, creativity, happiness) but also to boredom itself. If boredom is a doorway to a good and happy life, it isn't because goodness and happiness happen to lie at the end of boredom. It must be because there's something *in* boredom that leads us to those desired ends.

• • •

> "You be good," Alex said. "I love you."
> "I love you too," she responded.
> "You'll be in tomorrow?" he asked.
> "Yes, I will be in tomorrow."[12]

Alex didn't make it through the night. At the time of his death, Alex was something of a celebrity. He made appearances on television shows and was featured on many scientific articles and books. There's a film dedicated to him and both the *Times* and *The Economist* published obituaries about him. While alive, Alex could identify more than fifty different objects and could distinguish and label seven colors and five shapes. If you were to show him a mixture of blue and red blocks and ask him how many blue blocks were there, he would get it right, as long as the number was below eight. He could add small sets up to six and was able to infer the equivalence between Arabic numerals, vocal English number labels, and sets of objects. He could report on whether two objects had the same or different color and shape, and he could tell you which object was smaller or bigger. If nothing was the same or different, or if the objects were of equal size, he would respond with "None." He used "I want X" and "Wanna go Y" correctly and intentionally. Alex did all that and many more with a brain the size of a walnut. Alex was a parrot, the most studied parrot in the history of avian psychology.[13]

Dr. Irene Pepperberg, the animal psychologist who bought Alex from a Chicago pet shop and spent thirty years training and studying him, likened Alex's abilities to those of chimpanzees and dolphins. Although other parrots shared some of his abilities, Alex was unique. He showcased impressive behavioral complexity. He appeared capable not only of having emotional responses to situations but also of being motivated by those responses to act in ways that were hard to predict on the basis of either his training or his biology.

One example of such unexpected behavior comes from a study investigating Alex's numerical competence. Dr. Pepperberg and colleagues wanted to determine whether Alex was able to represent quantities and apply them to sets of items. It was previously shown that Alex could label triangles and squares as "3-corner" and "4-corner," respectively, and that if he were to be asked "How many blue blocks?" he could correctly respond verbally with the number of blue blocks (e.g., "six"). Still, the investigators weren't convinced that such findings demonstrated that Alex understood what numbers represent. To test that, they decided to run an additional test. They presented Alex with a tray containing either one type of object in three different colors (e.g., a collection of red, blue, and green keys) or three different types of objects of the same color (e.g., a collection of blue blocks, keys, and rods). Without training, Alex was asked "What color is X?" or "What object is X?," where "X" stood for a numerical quantity.

Alex did so well that Dr. Pepperberg and colleagues claimed that Alex exhibited numerical comprehension comparable to that of chimpanzees and very young children. His success rate was greater than 80%. And yet, this particular finding wasn't what impressed them the most.

After Alex responded to the first eight questions correctly, he changed his behavior. He became noncompliant. "He would, for example, stare at the ceiling, reply with a color or object label not on the tray, fixate on that label, and repeat it endlessly; this behavior was interspersed with requests to return to his cage or with requests for water or various foods."[14] This noncompliance period lasted for about two weeks, at the end of which Alex returned to testing. But soon after his return, a curious thing happened. Alex was presented with a set of two, three, and six objects and was asked "What color three?" He replied not with a color but with another number. He said "Five." The experimenter insisted—"What color three?" Alex insisted too. He responded again with "Five." The experimenter tried once again, but to no avail. Then, the experimenter said "OK, Alex, tell me, what color five?" Alex immediately responded "None." This was big.[15]

Alex was previously trained to respond "None" if no category (color, shape, or material) was same or different when he was asked about the similarity or difference between two objects. But Alex was never taught to use "None" to represent the absence of quantity. To judge the absence of quantity is to engage in abstract reasoning; it's to think of something (in some sense of "thinking") that isn't there. And, in fact, quantifying absence in this manner wasn't obvious to earlier human cultures. What's more, Alex set up the question himself! It's as if Alex wanted to show to the experimenters that he was smarter than what the experiment would and could show. The task at hand was too easy for him.

What could have prompted Alex's behavior? What could have been the impetus for making him modify the task in a way that would make it more challenging? Given that his action occurred after a period of noncompliance, it's plausible to think, and the researchers thought precisely this, that it was the consequence of lack of interest. Alex, in other words, was bored by the study. And it was his boredom that propelled him to an unexpected, novel, and cognitively impressive act.

•••

There are crimes of passion, of rage, and of love. And then, there are crimes of boredom. If found guilty of the charges that he's facing, German nurse Niels Hoegel would become the worst serial killer in post–World War II Germany. In 2015, Hoegel was sentenced to life in prison after he was found guilty of two counts of murder and two attempted murders. During his trial, however, a shocking confession was heard: he admitted to killing more, many more. After extensive investigations and toxicological analyses, Hoegel has been charged with ninety-seven additional murders. Hoegel injected patients with drugs that caused them heart failure or circulatory collapse so that he could try to revive them. He was searching for a thrill to escape his boring routine and an opportunity to impress his colleagues and supervisors. "It is very curious," Danish philosopher Søren Kierkegaard once noted, "that boredom, which itself has such a calm and sedate nature, can have such a capacity to initiate motion."[16] Kierkegaard's observation has proven to be remarkably prescient.

In a much-discussed series of studies, University of Virginia psychology professor Timothy D. Wilson and colleagues touched upon boredom's power to initiate motion indirectly when they set out to investigate whether or not distraction-free and deliberative thinking is enjoyable. In six of their studies, they gathered a total of 409 college students and instructed them to entertain themselves only with their thoughts for six to fifteen minutes in a "sparsely-furnished room in a psychology building."[17] Once the thinking period was over, participants were asked to rate their levels of enjoyment, entertainment, and boredom. On average, participants found thinking somewhat enjoyable, somewhat entertaining, and somewhat boring. Participants didn't love their thinking period. But they didn't hate it either.

Still, Wilson and colleagues concluded that "just thinking" is something that most people don't enjoy. Even though first-person reports don't establish their conclusion, the results of an additional study (study 10) are more supportive of their outlook on thinking. For this study, they again asked participants to entertain themselves alone with their thoughts. However, in this variation of the experiment, participants were allowed, if they were so inclined, to self-administer a mildly unpleasant electric shock, one to which they were exposed prior to the thinking period. Focusing only on participants who before the thinking period stated that they would pay not to receive the shock again, they found that twelve out of eighteen men and six out of twenty-four women chose to shock themselves at least once. Wilson and colleagues concluded: "What is striking is that simply being alone with their own thoughts for 15 min was apparently so aversive that it drove many participants to self-administer an electric shock."[18]

Although widely publicized, the conclusion of Wilson and colleagues' shock study has been contested. Whatever one makes of Wilson and colleagues' findings, it's instructive to consider what the subjects themselves said about the shocks. Four subjects cited boredom as the reason for shocking themselves. One had this to say: "I chose to willingly shock myself because I was so bored during the thinking period that I chose to experience the mild unpleasant shock over the oppressive boredom."[19] Perhaps what the Wilson and colleagues shock study demonstrated isn't the aversive character of thinking but the motivational power of boredom.

But would one really shock oneself just to escape boredom? Two recent studies suggest so. In the first one, psychologist Remco C. Havermans and his colleagues at the University of Maastricht tested whether the induction of boredom was capable of motivating participants to seek a change in stimulation.[20] They found that individuals in a monotonous, boring condition ate more chocolate (M&Ms) and shocked themselves both more often and with higher intensity than individuals in a neutral condition. Havermans and colleagues concluded that boredom is such an aversive experience that some individuals would choose to subject themselves to negative stimuli to make it go away.

Is there something unique about boredom that motivates one to seek ways (even unpleasant ones) to escape from it, or is this a feature that boredom shares with other negative emotions? In a 2016 study, psychologist Chantal Nederkoorn and colleagues (one of whom was Havermans) set out to answer this question.[21] Sixty-nine participants were randomly divided into three conditions: a boredom condition, a sadness condition, and a neutral condition. In each condition, participants viewed a sixty-minute segment of a film that was supposed to induce, respectively, boredom, sadness, and no specific mood. While watching the film, participants had the option to self-administer electric shocks. What the researchers observed was that compared to the neutral and sadness condition, the onset of boredom gave rise to an increase in the total number of self-administered electric shocks. Their study not only confirmed Havermans and colleagues' previous findings, but also showed that the reason why individuals chose to self-administer shocks isn't to avoid emotional experiences in general but rather to escape boredom specifically.

What do such findings show? At first sight, they seem to demonstrate boredom's toxic nature. After all, they're consistent with previous studies that reported a relationship between chronic boredom (boredom proneness) and a tendency to engage in risk-taking activities.[22] But such a grim picture of boredom is both partial and inaccurate. Boredom is neither essentially nor irredeemably problematic. It's a powerful affective state that can at the same time disengage us from uninteresting or meaningless situations and also move us away from them but not necessarily toward negative, self-destructive actions, as the studies would have us believe. Boredom informs us of the fact that what we're currently doing isn't what we want to be doing and propels us to do something else. What that something else is, however, is never spelled out by boredom. Boredom carries us only part of the way. For the rest, we're on our own.[23]

• • •

Alice was beginning to get very tired of sitting by her sister on the bank, and of having nothing to do . . .

So she was considering in her own mind (as well as she could, for the hot day made her feel very sleepy and stupid), whether the pleasure of making a daisy-chain would be worth the trouble of getting up and picking the daisies, when suddenly a White Rabbit with pink eyes ran close by her.

There was nothing so *very* remarkable in that; nor did Alice think it so *very* much out of the way to hear the Rabbit say to itself "Oh dear! Oh dear! I shall be too late!" . . . but when the Rabbit actually *took a watch out of its waistcoat-pocket*, and looked at it, and then hurried on, Alice started to her feet, for it flashed across her mind that she had never before seen a rabbit with either a waistcoat-pocket, or a watch to take out of it, and burning with curiosity, she ran across the field after it, and fortunately was just in time to see it pop down a large rabbit-hole under the hedge.[24]

Stories of rabbits with waistcoats and pocket watches are the products of fiction. Real rabbits don't jump out of nowhere, they aren't in a hurry, and they don't care for time. But mechanical rabbits, ones created for the sole purpose of a scientific study, do. In an elaborate and ambitious experiment, a group of over twenty scientists, engineers, and computer scientists, led by Dr. Matthias Rauterberg of Eindhoven University of Technology in the Netherlands, set out to recreate important narrative arcs from Lewis Carroll's *Alice's Adventures in Wonderland*.[25] They built an installation that involves both virtual and augmented reality elements called "ALICE" and that takes up two stories and an area of 144 square meters (1,550 square feet). It's fitted with computers, cameras, projectors, microphones, speakers, a smoke machine, artificial grass, a 360-degree surround canvas print, a chair-lift running on a monorail, and secret rooms and hiding places. It also includes a rabbit hole.[26] The aim of the experiment was to study participants' reactions when they were placed inside the installation as the narrative arcs from *Alice's Adventures in Wonderland* were unfolding. One of those narratives that they chose to recreate was the very beginning of the story—Alice is tired of doing nothing, the white rabbit appears, and intrigued and "burning with curiosity," Alice follows the rabbit down the rabbit hole. The role of Alice was to be played by the participants. Everything else was provided. But would participants do as Alice did? This is precisely what the researchers wanted to find out.

And so they placed participants in a part of the installation away from the rabbit hole. They asked them to engage in a repetitive and meaningless task to make them feel what Alice felt at the beginning of the story, namely, boredom. They were given a big pile of paper and were instructed to fold sheets of paper one by one and then put them in an empty box. The task was futile, and its futility was emphasized. The participants were informed that the investigators didn't care about the number of folded sheets of paper nor their folding method nor even the time taken to fold the paper. They let the participants fold sheets of paper for ten minutes. After that, a mechanical, pink-eyed, jacket-and-scarf-wearing and watch-carrying rabbit appeared. The rabbit was made out of carbon fiber, was painted white, and was placed on top of a radio-controlled vehicle platform. Through a hidden walkie-talkie that was attached to the rabbit, the rabbit could talk. Once the rabbit emerged, it said, "Oh my dear, my dear, I shall be late," and consequently disappeared in the rabbit hole. The researchers then observed whether the participants would follow the rabbit, explore the environment, and eventually enter the rabbit hole. If a participant didn't follow the rabbit, then the rabbit would make another "run," trying to entice the participant into seeking and finding the rabbit hole. If that didn't work, then there was a third and final run during which the rabbit asked the participant to follow it.

All of the participants entered the rabbit hole. Two, in fact, did so even before the rabbit made its appearance. They were so bored with folding sheets of paper, and perhaps intrigued by the installation, that they started their exploration prematurely. From the subjects who completed the ten-minute folding task, only one didn't follow the rabbit after its first appearance. And even this reluctant subject did enter the rabbit hole at the end. On the basis of their findings, the researchers concluded that the deliberate arousal of boredom proved to be an effective and predictable manner of guiding behavior. They also concluded that the appearance of the rabbit aroused participants' curiosity and led to exploration. To anyone who has been in the grip of boredom before, the findings aren't surprising. Being in a state of boredom is unpleasant, and it's natural to seek escape from it. What's surprising, however, is once again the force of boredom. Boredom can make us stop working on a task; it can get us out of our chair; it can make us follow a mechanical rabbit; it can even make us go down a rabbit hole.

●●●

Not all situations in which boredom arises permit escape. We might experience boredom during work, in a meeting or a classroom, while driving or doing chores. When we can't escape boredom by changing our situation around us, we may try to change ourselves. How? We can turn our attention inward to our inner thoughts, feelings, expectations, and experiences. We can let our minds travel. We can alter the manner in which we perceive our situation. We can modify our expectations or intentions. And we can look for meaning where meaning was previously absent. The change that boredom brings about isn't always physical.

"When I started there," he says with a not too loud but clear voice, "I was still in high school and they had a school-to-work program." Austin is one of the most hardworking, down-to-earth, polite individuals that I've met. He also carries with him a contagious sunny disposition: the glass is always at least three quarters full. "I was in container unload," he tells me and then explains. "So, they bring you these big metal containers. They look like sheds off a plane and they bring them into the building and I take the packages out and put them on a belt." Austin worked and still does, although no longer in container unload, at one of the biggest logistic and transportation centers in the world. He doesn't brag when he tells me that "not a lot of people can put the physical effort into stuff that I do." It sounds sincere. "A lot of it is heavy, a lot of it is awkward and the sheer volume of packages is unreal."

His job had the absurdity of a Kafka story and the sonic variation of a broken record. "It's so monotonous, and easy, and repetitive that two packages in, your mind is bleeding. You are sitting there going 'Oh my god, I got to do this all day long.' . . . It's hard to see what you are accomplishing. You are picking up a box and you are setting it down. That's literally all that you are doing." The job is boring, undeniably so. All the same, Austin did it without being bored.

He couldn't change the nature of his job—he still had to unload those packages. Yet he was able to change his attitude about the job. "That job gets really boring unless you are able to entertain yourself," he tells me. And that's exactly what he did. First, he would turn his job into a game or a competition. "We would have competitions to see who got the most packages down, to see who had the best read rates, you know, with the placement of the stickers right side up, things like that. We'd do little competitions like that, something to keep your mind off of moving that box." Second, although Austin couldn't physically do anything but move boxes and unload containers, his mind was free to wander. "I like to think about things and the job was so easy, it doesn't require any mental involvement. . . . The whole time I was thinking about things, thinking about school, trying to figure out things in my head. I don't know. I guess I'm kind of weird in that kind of sense."

Austin isn't weird in that sense. The psychology literature reports many findings that show that what Austin was doing was, in fact, common. Studies monitoring the behavior of workers who are forced to work in extremely monotonous conditions show that they can find ways to occupy themselves by turning aspects of their work into a game.[27] More generally, individuals who have a reason to persist in a boring task are likely to engage in interest-enhancing strategies that transform the boring task into something more enjoyable. Furthermore, although bored individuals experience their situation as lacking in meaning, the very experience of boredom triggers in them a drive to look for and discover meaning. Put individuals in a boring situation and make salient to them the fact their situation lacks meaning, and they will act appropriately. They may change their expectations or attitudes about a specific task; they may alter the manner in which they evaluate and perceive social groups; they may adopt more extreme political views; and they may form prosocial intentions.[28] In an attempt to establish or re-establish a sense of meaningfulness, boredom changes the manner in which we perceive and relate to the world.

What's more, it has also been noted that there's a close relationship between the experience of boredom and mind wandering (daydreaming).[29] While performing mindless, boring, or repetitive tasks, our mind often drifts away from the task at hand. We think not of what we're currently doing. Instead, we draw up future plans, dwell in past events, and think of personal concerns. Mind wandering is defined as task-unrelated and stimulus-independent thinking. It is task-unrelated insofar as the content of our thinking isn't about the task that we're currently performing. It is stimulus-independent insofar as our thinking isn't affected by the stimuli present in our current environment. Mind wandering isn't unique to boring tasks. It can occur during almost every kind of activity. Studies, in fact, suggest that we spend somewhere between 25% and 50% of our waking lives engaging in thinking that is unrelated to our current situation.[30] We don't think that we want to mind wander and then, we mind wander. Nor do we dictate what we will mind wander about. Mind wandering happens. It unfolds, without our consent and often even without our notice.

Such mental excursions come at a cost. Because of its very nature, mind wandering decouples us from our current task—our attention no longer lies with the task at hand. As such, mind wandering can adversely affect our performance on a variety of tasks that require sustained attention or the use of working memory. Bad reading comprehension, poor performance on monitoring tasks, and failure to monitor one's environment while driving have all been associated with the presence of mind wandering.[31] Furthermore, depending on the content of our thoughts, mind wandering can adversely affect our mood. It has been reported, for example, that mind wandering is both the cause and a consequence of unhappiness. "A Wandering Mind Is an Unhappy Mind," the title of a famous science paper reads.[32]

The effects of mind wandering aren't however monolithically negative.[33] First, many of our mental digressions are both prospective and self-related. During episodes of mind wandering, we think about important future goals; we survey obstacles and devise solutions. Mind wandering is, in a sense, our own spontaneously generated executive assistant. Second, while thinking about future and past events that are of personal significance, we organize, even unbeknownst to us, our life. Mind wandering imposes a narrative and in doing so, it furnishes our life with meaning. Third, mind wandering can offer us a much-needed relief from tedium. Although it's true that sometimes mind wandering may lead to a worse mood, it can also help us to alleviate an unpleasant mood. Mind wandering "focused on the future and self was linked to increases in positive mood, even if the content of thought was negative."[34] Finally, researchers found a positive relationship between mind wandering and the generation of creative and novel thoughts. In a 2012 experiment conducted by neuroscientist Benjamin Baird and colleagues, individuals were instructed to work on a task that was designed to measure creativity. Some of the participants were asked to take a break from the task and then return to it. It was shown that those who took a break by engaging in an undemanding task outperformed those who took no break, those who performed a demanding task during their break, and even those who simply rested.[35] The researchers also found that during the undemanding task, participants reported significantly greater mind wandering. They hypothesized that it's the presence of mind wandering that explains why "taking a break involving an undemanding task improved performance on a classic creativity task . . . far more than did taking a break involving a demanding task, resting, or taking no break."[36]

Insofar as Austin engages in meaning-finding activities, attempts to turn his tasks into games, and mind wanders, he's exhibiting an ideal behavior in the face of boredom. Austin, it seems, gets boredom. He gets it, not because boredom gets him. He gets boredom precisely because he doesn't allow boredom to define his situation. He knows how to use boredom's force. He rides the wave of discontent that boredom brings. And through boredom, he carries himself mentally away.

• • •

Here's a task for you. For each of the following lines, think of a word that relates to the other three words on the same line.

SHOW	LIFE	ROW	_____
BASKET	EIGHT	SNOW	_____
FORCE	LINE	MAIL	_____
DUST	CEREAL	FISH	_____

The answer to the first one is BOAT. So, the first line reads: SHOWBOAT, LIFEBOAT, and ROWBOAT. Can you find the other ones?[37] This task, called the Remote Associates Task or RAT for short, was devised by psychologist Martha Mednick in 1962 and is currently widely used as a test for creativity. The more creative one is, the better one performs in RATs, or so the thought goes.

Could one's performance on such a task depend on one's emotional states? Certainly. Suppose that you have received some terrible news right before you're about to complete the above task—your child, you've been told, was in a bad accident, nothing life-threatening but still serious. You'd be feeling anxious and scared, fretting for what's to happen. Your mind would be racing, and you wouldn't be able to concentrate. Getting the right answer on such a task would be of little or no significance to you. If anxiety and fear could hinder your performance on the task, could a different emotional state help?

Happiness, it appears, could. If you're happy while performing the task, you will feel secure with your situation and excited to engage in a novel task. You will welcome the task as an opportunity to challenge yourself and perhaps to show to yourself what you can do. To a happy mind, the task will be something that it wants to do and not something that it wishes to avoid.

Our emotions can affect our performance on cognitive tasks. Boredom is an emotion. So, what kind of influence would boredom have on RAT in particular and on tasks measuring creativity in general? There's a quick and by now all-too-familiar way of seeking an answer to this question: Google it! If you type into Google "boredom and creativity," what you will find are pages upon pages of news articles, essays, blog posts, and even videos praising boredom's ability to foster creativity and claiming that their pronouncements are grounded in scientific findings. Unfortunately, the manner in which the relevant findings are, for the most part, being reported and appropriated resembles a broken telephone. Results are distorted, conclusions are magnified, and warnings aren't heeded. A search engine is as good as its searchable database. When reading through quick presentations of boredom in popular media, one ought to tread carefully.

The relationship between boredom and creativity has received little empirical attention. The published studies divide broadly into two types: those that study the effect of task-related boredom on creativity and those that study the effect of task-unrelated boredom on creativity. The distinction between the two is simple but important. Only in the former type of experiments, boredom is a feature of the task at hand. In cases of task-unrelated boredom, what bores individuals isn't the task that is supposed to measure creativity, but something else.

A look at the relevant literature yields at first good news for the optimist: both types of experiments appear to lend support to the claim that boredom fosters creativity. For example, in a 1977 experiment conducted by Daniel Schubert, a professor of psychiatry at Case Western Medical School, it was shown that subjects' performance on a creative imagination task increased as a function of time: the longer the subjects were allowed to work on a problem that had multiple solutions, the more creative their solutions were. Schubert postulated that boredom could be responsible for the observed increase in creativity. "[T]he subjects," he wrote, "became bored with their less creative responses and became more creative in the second half of their responses."[38] This wasn't the first time that a connection between boredom and creativity was hinted in the empirical literature. A few years earlier and while still working on his psychology PhD at Ohio State University, Stephen Morin noticed that working continuously in one session leads to the generation of more original ideas compared to working on the same task but in several shorter sessions.[39] Such a finding is once again suggestive of the role of boredom. Other things being equal, longer working sessions are more boring than shorter ones.

Now, fast-forward forty years and two more experiments have reported boredom's positive effects on creativity. Unlike the experiments in the 1970s, the more recent experiments, both published in 2014, were measuring the effect of task-unrelated boredom on creativity. In the first study, psychologists Sandi Mann and Rebekah Cadman from the University of Central Lancashire in the United Kingdom induced boredom by asking individuals to copy telephone numbers from a phone directory.[40] After the completion of this ostensibly boring task, individuals were given two polystyrene cups and were asked to write down as many different uses for the cups as they could think and subsequently to circle the two that they thought were the most creative ones. Mann and Cadman found that the boring writing task led to an increased number of reported uses compared to a control sample. However, the answers given by the bored individuals were not judged to be any more creative than the ones given by the control subjects.

In light of their somewhat unexpected conclusion, Mann and Cadman repeated the experiment in an amended form. They added an additional boring task (a boring reading task that involved reading the phone book for fifteen minutes) and two extra creativity-related tasks, one of which included RAT problems. This time they found that both boring tasks led not only to an increase in the number of reported uses of the cups but also to an increase in creativity compared to the control condition. Cups were seen as possible musical instruments, as telephones, and even as a Madonna-style bra. The bored subjects also performed better than the nonbored ones in the two additional tasks that aimed to assess creativity.

A different experiment also found a positive relationship between boredom and creativity, at least when boredom was contrasted with other negative affective states. Researchers Karen Gasper and Brianne L. Middlewood at the Department of Psychology at the Pennsylvania State University explored whether so-called approach-oriented emotions promote creativity more than avoidance-orientated ones.[41] An approach orientation is one that motivates individuals to explore their environment and to expand their ways of thinking. On the contrary, an avoidance orientation narrows one's gamut of possible actions and thoughts and allows one to focus on potential threats. Fear is a prototypical avoidance-orientated emotion, whereas happiness is an approach-oriented one. Gasper and Middlewood conceptualized boredom as an approach-oriented emotional state and compared its effects on creativity to those of relaxation (avoidance-oriented), distress (avoidance-oriented), and elation (approach-oriented). After inducing the four states in different individuals, they asked individuals to work on tasks that measured creativity. What they found was that bored individuals outperformed both relaxed and distressed individuals.

• • •

The temptation to carry the findings of the aforementioned studies too far is strong. It should, however, be resisted. The earlier studies by Schubert and Morin didn't include any measures of boredom. Consequently, one can know neither whether the subjects were indeed bored nor whether their boredom increased as a function of time. More important, their findings admit of an alternative interpretation that doesn't implicate boredom: the observed improved performance on creativity tasks could have been due to practice. After all, the subjects had more time and more opportunities to work on the given tasks. If practice makes perfect, then why couldn't it also increase creativity?

Indeed, psychologists Julia S. Haager, Christof Kuhbandner, and Reinhard Pekrun have shown precisely that. In a study published in the *Journal of Creative Behavior*, they found not only that practice positively affects creativity but also that task-related boredom hinders it.[42] The researchers asked participants to perform a "semantic generation task" in which participants were given a list of categories (e.g., animal) and were asked to generate exemplars of those categories (e.g., lion). Such a task is thought to be a measure of creativity insofar as it can measure both fluency and originality of responses (i.e., how many exemplars are provided and how original those are). The task was divided into six parts (two categories were given at each part) and after each part, the researchers measured both creativity (fluency and originality) and boredom. What they found was that an increase in boredom was correlated with an increase in fluency—the more bored the subjects reported to be the more answers they were able to provide. However, when a more detailed statistical analysis was performed, the researchers found that what was in fact responsible for the observed increase in fluency wasn't the increase in boredom but rather the increase in task practice. What's more, when the researchers controlled for practice effects, they found that boredom actually impaired fluency. By performing more and more tasks, participants were getting better at them, even though they were also becoming increasingly more bored. Boredom was hindering their performance but, as it turns out, to a lesser extent than how practice was improving their performance.

It appears that task-related boredom doesn't foster creativity. What about task-unrelated boredom? Does it yield the desired effects on creativity? Although the findings of the studies by Mann and Cadman and Gasper and Middlewood can't be attributed to practice, the results of the studies ought to be carefully evaluated. The study by Mann and Cadman gave rise to contradictory findings. Findings from the two variations of the experiment disagree as to whether the induction of boredom increases both fluency (reported number of uses for the cups) and creativity (how original the reported uses were) compared to a control group. More studies are needed to determine the validity of the reported results. Furthermore, drawing conclusions about the effects of boredom on the additional two creativity-related tasks that were part of the second variation of the experiment is no simple matter. Those tasks were no longer immediately preceded by a boring task but instead by a task that was designed to assess creativity. Hence, it's possible that any observed effect is due not to boredom but to fact that such tasks were preceded by another task of broadly the same nature.

The Gasper and Middlewood study was a comparative study. So, the findings don't show that boredom is the emotional state that's most beneficial in terms of creativity—in fact, a look at the reported data from the Gasper and Middlewood study demonstrates that elation consistently outperforms boredom. Thus, at most, what the study shows is that it's better to be bored than distressed or relaxed right before performing a task that requires associative thinking. Although such a result is important, it's a far cry from the idolized version of boredom found in the media. Contrary to what many have said and written, it's inaccurate to proclaim that boredom is good *because* it fosters creativity. Companies shouldn't start boring their employees to produce more creative results. If the goal is to maximize creativity, then companies should make their employees happy.

So, what can we conclude from all this? First, in line with the findings reported by Haager and colleagues, task-related boredom within an experimental setting fails to promote creativity—in fact, it seems to do something worse: it thwarts it. The conclusion shouldn't be too surprising though. If we're bored with our task, then our task ceases to be meaningful and interesting to us. Consequently, we won't be attentive to it. And we won't care how we're performing on it. If performance on a task depends on our ability to engage with the task in a creative fashion, then the fact that we find the task to be boring will lead us to underperform.

Not all hope is lost though. It's important to bear in mind that individuals who typically participate in psychology experiments aren't *forced* to care about their tasks. So, they have no reason to deter the onset of boredom. Nor do they care enough to find ways to alleviate boredom when it arrives. But what holds true inside the confines of an experimental setting doesn't necessarily hold true in the real world. In fact, as previously mentioned, studies that have observed the behavior of workers who work under monotonous conditions found that those who are forced to perform a boring task will often do so in a more interesting or creative way. Hence, not every occurrence of task-related boredom must lead to poorer performance. If one finds oneself in a boring situation and has to perform a task, then one might as well perform it creatively. Think of Austin. Think of him moving one package after another, sometimes deep in his thoughts and sometimes joking and competing with his colleagues. Depending on our situation, task-related boredom may be beneficial.

But there's another piece of good news. This stems directly from the 2014 studies. If our situation is boring, then boredom could prevent the production of creative ideas that relate to our boring situation. However, boredom may lead to a redirection of attention and energy toward new tasks. If we're bored with our current task, then the push that boredom contains may motivate us to approach an *alternative* task with renewed interest and energy and as such, boredom may lead to an increase in creativity when performing the new task. After all, bored individuals found more uses for polystyrene cups than nonbored ones, and they performed better than distressed or relaxed ones in associative thinking tasks.

• • •

Boredom may help us to find uses for polystyrene cups. It can push us to shock ourselves when we're left alone with nothing to do. It may force us to mind wander when we're driving, reading, or moving boxes. It can motivate us to discover meaning when there is none. It may even force nurses to kill, individuals to eat more M&Ms, and curious participants to enter rabbit holes. But all these outcomes of boredom are too specific; they reveal boredom only partially. If we focus on them, we run the risk of failing to see the full picture. What boredom does to us is something bigger, more general, and more significant. Boredom promotes movement. And movement is protean: it comes in a plenitude of ways. Physical exercise, eating, daydreaming, thrill seeking, caring, and even harming are all forms of movement.

What is boredom most fundamentally? Boredom is an unpleasant state that signals to us the presence of an unsatisfactory situation and which, at the same time, contains a strong desire to do something else. During boredom, we feel both frustrated and listless. We're disengaged from and dissatisfied with what we do. Our situation doesn't hold our attention. It doesn't interest us. Rather, in a state of boredom, we're moved to think of alternative situations and goals, ones that are more interesting and meaningful to us than our current ones. We itch to leave boredom behind. If all goes as planned, we do just that.

Boredom plays a double role in our lives. It informs us of the need to change something about ourselves or about our environment and pushes us to do something else. It demarcates the interesting from the noninteresting. But it also sets us in motion. Boredom is that which helps us become unstuck when we become stuck.

But there's more. Because of its very nature, boredom should be classified as a self-regulatory state. It is, in plain language, an emotion that aims to regulate our behavior. Consider this. Boredom aims to move us. Yet the movement that it promotes isn't pointless. What boredom facilitates is goal-directed motion. We're moved out of an unsatisfactory state and into one that is satisfactory and congruent with our needs and goals. When we're bored we don't simply wish to replace our situation with any other situation. What we strive for is to stop engaging in this boring situation. In addition, we wish to engage in a situation or task that's more satisfactory. By promoting motion, boredom keeps us in line with what we find interesting and meaningful. It safeguards us from long-term pitfalls of dullness or meaninglessness. Support for this view of boredom comes from a variety of studies that detail the character of boredom, its effects, and its causes.[43] Thinking of boredom as a regulatory emotion allows us to see how its experiential, cognitive, volitional, and physiological components work together to facilitate the performance of its function. Such a take on boredom also brings together numerous and diverse findings on the character of boredom and offers a natural and compelling explanation of its effects. A regulatory approach thus provides a synoptic picture of our current knowledge of boredom.[44]

Boredom, it turns out, is a curious state. Given its regulatory function, it appears to have a self-effacing effect. Boredom arises only to make itself disappear. When it succeeds, boredom will push us out of boredom. We find ourselves in boring situations when we find ourselves in uninteresting, unsatisfactory, or meaningless situations. Precisely because those situations are uninteresting, unsatisfactory, or meaningless they don't attract us but repel us. Boredom can be, paradoxically, its own escape. It can set us free.

• • •

"Oh! Ennui! Ennui! What an answer to everything." Thus wrote French novelist and essayist with a penchant for the bizarre, Barbey d'Aurevilly, in his journal on November 25, 1836.[45] But, no, boredom is no psychological pan-acea. Most emotional states have both beneficial and harmful consequences—fear, for example, protects us from threats and dangers, yet it often forecloses opportunities and possibilities for action. Boredom is no exception. Thus, even though boredom can facilitate escape from an unsatisfactory situation and promote the pursuit of goals that appear to us to be more interesting, meaningful, or engaging, there's no guarantee that the goals toward which boredom will move us are good or even beneficial. New habits, opportunities, and careers often start with the thought "I am bored." But so can unhealthy eating habits, binge drinking, drug use, or destruction. "I guess I was just bored," Keith Eugene Mann said explaining why he scorched sixteen acres of wild forests in North Carolina.[46] The philosopher Bertrand Russell famously wrote, "Boredom is a vital problem for the moralist since half of sins of man-kind are caused by it."[47] Russell's claim is, of course, an exaggeration. But its hyperbole is instructive. In its search for meaning, interest, and fulfillment, boredom straddles the line between the good and the bad, the beneficial and the harmful.[48]

To fulfill its potential, boredom needs our guidance. To deal with boredom one not only needs to be able to motivate oneself to change one's situation—when such a change is possible—but one must also know what alternative situations will be interesting or meaningful. Boredom helps us to keep moving when we cease to. Motion is good, but not when it lacks the proper direction. We don't want to be moved from one bad situation to another. We don't want to replace one bout of tedium with another. Nor would most of us like to al-leviate boredom by engaging in dangerous activities. Not every escape will be one that brings us closer to what we wish to accomplish in life, to what we value and care for. And not every escape will necessarily be moral. We value motion, it seems, but only to the extent that it can lead us to a better state.

A "better state" doesn't simply refer to a state that is more interesting than our current one. It also refers to one that serves our interests and is in line with our desires and overall preferences and principles. To guarantee that we use boredom in a way that promotes our interests and contributes to our self-actualization, we have to be weary of potential dangers that lie all too close to boredom.

Boredom offers us direction but only minimally. It tells us "Do something more interesting!" but the "more interesting" is an empty placeholder. It's up to us to determine the content of that placeholder. More important, it's up to us to figure out which of our many available options will positively con-tribute to our well-being. One may escape boredom by engaging in a risky activity such as, reckless driving, binge drinking, or taking selfies on top of tall buildings. Such behavior is exciting or thrilling. It will vitiate our sensation of boredom in one fell swoop. But it could very well harm us or at least fail to promote our well-being. Knowing oneself is thus necessary to use boredom beneficially.

In turn, boredom may arise when it shouldn't. Inevitably, there will be situations that are important to us, but for whatever reason they don't attract us. Think of a difficult lecture that you must attend, a long report that you have to complete for your work, a weekend with your in-laws, or an entire afternoon accompanying your child to an unbearable birthday party (not your child's birthday party, of course). All these situations are important to you. You need to be able to follow the lecture to get a good grade in the class; your job depends upon your performance on the report; having a meaningful relationship with your in-laws is part of your obligations of being a good partner; and spending time with your child is essential to the well-being of your family, even if that requires that you occasionally jump on bouncy castles and sing along to Disney songs. Boredom may arise in those situations, and it's a fitting reaction: these are situations that fail to grab us and they leave us indifferent. All the same, the onset of boredom is, in another sense, inappropriate and hence unwelcome. The experience of boredom in those situations doesn't permit us to be present. It can hamper our understanding of the lecture, hinder the quality of our report, and even make us seem distant, indifferent, or even rude to in-laws, our children, and others. Classes, jobs, family events may be boring, but often they shouldn't be. All this is to say that boredom signifies a lack of interest but not a lack of importance. As a consequence, boredom has to be, at least sometimes, endured. Its call for movement should be resisted or at least reinterpreted as a call to change our perceptions of the task at hand or our expectations.

What do the previous considerations tell us about boredom and its value? A great deal. They underline the fact that boredom by itself will not solve our problems. We can't surrender to boredom. It needs our direction and a kind of know-how that allows us to use it properly. Using boredom to our benefit is a skill, one that requires knowledge of oneself, the ability to know how to read a situation, and the facility to respond appropriately to it. Listening to what boredom tells us when it arises, and being able to use its motivational power to promote movement, can help not only to reduce the duration of our current boring experience but also to increase the chances of later finding ourselves in situations that are congruent with our desires and in line with our interests. Boredom is a powerful emotional state that can at once disengage us from uninteresting or meaningless situations and move us away from them. As such, boredom plays a unique and useful role in our mental economy. There's no emotion like boredom. And thus without boredom, we wouldn't be who we are. In fact, without boredom to help us chase after our goals, we wouldn't even be who we can be.

• • •

To hold that there's value in boredom isn't to insist that our well-being is promoted by the chronic or frequent experience of boredom. Nor do I wish to suggest that we should strive to be bored. Given what we know about the dangers of boredom proneness, it would be both foolish and irresponsible to make such claims. Still, there's value in boredom when it's experienced occasionally by healthy individuals. To see where its value lies, it's instructive to draw a parallel between pain and boredom. Although the sensation of pain is unpleasant, the capacity to feel pain is good for us. Just consider what happens in cases where the capacity to feel pain is missing. Subjects with congenital insensitivity to pain—that is, individuals who have never experienced pain— live hard, hazardous, and often tragically short lives. They suffer innumerable injuries, all of them in the absence of the sensation of pain.[49] Although most of us don't want to be in pain, it would be foolish to wish to live a life without the capacity to feel pain. Despite its unpleasant and distressing character, the sensation of pain is of great value to us. It isn't just a reliable alarm mechanism that notifies us of harm done to oneself. It also motivates us to change our behavior and to take defensive measures to protect ourselves. As such, pain is valuable to us.

Something similar holds for boredom. Boredom protects us from certain situations. It does so by informing us of the presence of situations that aren't in line with our interests and desires and by motivating us to do something else. If we were to lack the capacity to be bored, we wouldn't notice when we're faced with an unsatisfying, nonstimulating, or monotonous situation. Nor would we do something to get out of it. Boredom is valuable to us precisely because it helps us to keep moving, and in doing so, it brings us closer to what's in line with our desires and goals.

If we think of boredom as something that needs to be eradicated, we miss the point. Boredom isn't an enemy but a friend—not our closest friend, but the type of friend who is bearable in small doses and who offers sobering and sound, even if hard to take, advice. In this chapter, we've seen the force that boredom carries. We've seen what boredom can do for us. And we've seen how boredom, with our help and direction, can set us in motion and propel us into situations that are meaningful and interesting to us.

6

"An energizer, but not a guide; an engine, but not a steering gear"

Our desires can be thwarted, our expectations violated, and our goals blocked. It happens often. When it does, we become upset; we burn up inside. Failure strikes us and with words or actions, with plans or thoughts, we strike back. "Rule. In difficult circumstances always act on first impressions," wrote Leo Tolstoy in a diary entry dated March 1, 1851.[1] In frustrating moments, we do just that. Faced with palpable failure and dissatisfaction, we react. Sometimes it's for the better; other times it's not.

• • •

He couldn't take it anymore. He looked at Dr. Pepperberg and made his request loudly and clearly. Alex, the celebrity parrot of the previous chapter, wasn't given what he was expecting. He became frustrated. And moved by his frustration, he did what he couldn't otherwise have done.

Alex had been trained to associate human phonemes. Spread a number of colored plastic or wooden alphabet letters in front of him (e.g., B, CH, I, K, S, SH) and ask him "What sound is red?" or "What color is /i/?" Alex would respond correctly: "/Sh/" for the sound of the red phoneme and "blue" for the color of the phoneme that makes the sound /i/. Dr. Pepperberg was showcasing Alex's phonological skills to a number of CEOs at the MIT Media Lab. She asked Alex questions about the letters and sounds. He obliged and responded correctly. Yet, he was told to wait for his reward—pressed for time, Dr. Pepperberg didn't have the luxury to pause after each correct response. The lack of immediate reward must have taken Alex aback. He was always rewarded immediately after he had performed a task correctly. In his mind a nonreward meant only one thing: he made a mistake. But he knew that this wasn't the case. Alex grew visibly agitated with the waiting and nonreward. He couldn't suppress his desires any longer. So, he spelt out to them exactly what

Propelled. Andreas Elpidorou, Oxford University Press (2020). © Andreas Elpidorou.
DOI: 10.1093/oso/9780190912963.001.0001

he wanted: "Wanna nut . . . N-U-T!", said Alex, emphasizing each individual sound—"Nnn," "uhh," "t."[2]

Alex's response was unexpected. He separated and sounded out the letters composing "Nut," but Alex was never taught to do that before. In a state of discontent, in a state in which his desires were being thwarted and frustrated, he went beyond his training. As Dr. Pepperberg notes, his behavior "was unlikely to have appeared had he not been thwarted (i.e., had his expectations not been violated), had he not been somewhat angered and in search of some way to obtain his desired goal."[3] Alex, it seems, found a way to use his negative emotions to achieve something that was previously out of his reach.

Even if boredom has had some, admittedly few, famous defenders, it's much harder to find authors who have sung the praises of frustration—and for good reasons. No one wishes to be in a state of frustration. Frustration is thoroughly unpleasant. To be frustrated is to be made vividly and painfully aware that what you desire can't be obtained. Frustration is an unpleasant and bothersome reminder that we're currently engaging in a situation that isn't satisfying. It's a reminder that there's something missing from our current situation. Where frustration is, pleasure, tranquility, and satisfaction are not.

To many of us, a frustrating experience appears to be a breakdown—a disruption to an otherwise smoothly flowing existence. There's certainly truth to that view of frustration. Yet such a conception of frustration delivers only half the story. The other half, the part that often remains untold, is that frustration carries adaptive value. Although frustration is aversive and opposes— initially, at least—progress, it's extremely energizing. Numerous experimental findings, theoretical considerations, and personal stories demonstrate how frustration can invigorate our responses to perceived difficulties and provide us with the psychological resources needed to keep pursuing our goals. Frustration isn't a failure, but a temporary setback, fraught with the possibility of success. It isn't a bug, but a feature of human existence.[4]

Frustration is an opportunity to be invigorated by the various obstacles that life inevitably lays in our paths.

• • •

In the early 1950s, in the basement of Newcomb College at Tulane University, the late, Montreal-born psychologist Abram Amsel spent a considerable amount of time observing rats traversing mesh-covered runways searching for food. Out of his observations, one of the most discussed statements about animal behavior and learning was born.[5]

Amsel's apparatus was strikingly simple. It consisted of a starting box, a first runway, a first goal box, a second runway, and then a second goal box, all arranged in that order. The rats that Amsel was keen on observing were familiar to the apparatus. For twenty-eight days, three times a day, the rats, which incidentally had been kept on a low-intake diet, would repeat their routine—they would be placed in the starting box and once the door of the box was raised, they would travel through the first runway and into the first goal box where they'd find a reward pellet; the door of the first goal box would then be raised and on they'd go again, through the second runway and into the second goal box where another pellet would be waiting for them. Amsel and colleagues noted their behavior, including the speed by which they moved through the apparatus.

After their twenty-eight-day "training" period, the rats were in for a surprise. Three times a day, Amsel would again place them in the apparatus, but now the rats would find a reward waiting for them in the first goal box only half of the time. For the other half, the rats, driven by hunger and expecting a reward, would come up empty-handed. The training period conditioned the rats to expect food every time they would enter the first goal box. The actual test was an attempt to upset this expectation. If training was a hungry rat's dream, the test was real life—sometimes frustrating, sometimes fulfilling, but never entirely predictable. It was this violation of their expectations coupled with uncertainty that led Amsel to the observation that provided the basis for his theory of frustration and animal behavior.

What Amsel witnessed was that the rats ran faster in the second runway when their run through the first runway wasn't rewarded. An absence of reward caused the rats to try harder—to run faster through the apparatus in the hopes of receiving the expected reward at the end of the second runway. Amsel interpreted their behavior as the product of frustration. "[F]rustrative nonreward appears to have an invigorative . . . effect," he writes, "on any behavior that it immediately follows it."[6] The energizing effect of unexpected nonreward on behavior is often called "frustration effect" or "Amsel's effect." Amsel's finding has been replicated numerous times, in different labs and is manifested in different behaviors. Frustrated rats run faster through runways, but they also jump over hurdles, omit odors that affect the behavior of other rats, and become more (ultrasonically) vocal.[7] Frustration effects have also been observed in other species: monkeys, dogs, and pigeons, for example, all become frustrated in the face of unexpected nonrewards and react in ways that suggest that they're looking for an escape out of their currently unsatisfactory situation.[8] And we too—or at least, earlier versions of ourselves—behave in a similar fashion. Infants, who become frustrated when a barrier is placed between them and a desirable object, fuss more, are motivated to overcome the blockage, and display facial expressions suggestive of the experience of anger.[9]

The frustration effect is emotional—it's not the product of cognition or strategic planning—and, at least in rats, it's eliminated by bilateral lesions of the *amygdala*, a structure thought to be responsible for nonspecific arousal and fear conditioning.[10] Surprising nonrewards thus affect the animals in emotional ways, and it's precisely on account of such an emotional upheaval that they're energized. Equally important, frustration in the face of surprising nonrewards is a negative, unpleasant experience. Indeed, frustration is what it is because of its disagreeable character. Without the negativity of frustration, an organism would have no reason to seek escape from frustrating situations nor would it be motivated to overcome obstacles to its goals. The discontent inherent in frustration is paradoxically frustration's own redeeming quality.

• • •

"Bennett Foddy makes frustrating video games."[11]

Musician, moral philosopher, and video game programmer Bennett Foddy is known for his simple yet incredibly challenging, at times maddening, games. Consider QWOP. It gets its name from the four keys that the player uses to control an avatar's thighs and calves. The purpose of the game is to make an avatar (a virtual, low-resolution male runner) complete a hundred-meter dash (Figure 6.1). That's it. There are no opponents. The speed doesn't matter, nor does one's time. All that matters is that you're able to make the avatar move forward. It sounds simple, but it's not. Coordinating the individual parts of the body in a way that offers the avatar forward momentum is a skill that requires hours of practice. There's a rhythm to be found somewhere in the depths of the algorithm. Yet our fingers fumble, constantly pressing the wrong keys, bringing the virtual runner to a stop or hurling him clumsily to the ground. I've never made it past the two-meter mark, but some heroes on YouTube have completed, even semigraciously, the run. "If it wasn't such an everyday task that the guy was performing," Foddy says, "you wouldn't think of it as hard. You expect to know how to do it, and you fail horribly. For a certain group of people, that is motivating."[12]

Foddy is right. As evidenced by the popularity of QWOP and other games like it, there's a demand for frustrating video games. Not because gamers enjoy frustration, but because they savor the completion of frustrating tasks. In the context of video games, frustrations are perceived as challenges. They require

Figure 6.1 Screenshot of QWOP.
Reprinted with permission from Bennett Foddy. All rights reserved.

effort and dedication, and their completion affords gamers a type of status. To complete a frustrating game is, after all, to accomplish something difficult, something that many can't do.* Frustrating games can become successful and popular. When they do, it's because of their ability to attract gamers. They invite approach; they cultivate in gamers a strong desire to overcome their frustrations, not by giving up on the game, not by finding a different game, but by striving to win the game.

Foddy has found a niche in frustration. His newest game, Getting Over It with Bennett Foddy, is a massive hit. At the time of writing this paragraph, more than six million people have played the game. It's received thousands of reviews, most of them positive, and there are scores of YouTube videos documenting players' efforts (mostly unsuccessful) to complete the game. In Getting Over It, you play a silent man by the name Diogenes who's stuck in a cauldron (Figure 6.2). Diogenes carries a Yosemite hammer and the purpose of the user is to use Diogenes's hammer to climb mountains composed of everything from rocks and boulders, to coffee cups, pumpkins, chairs, beach balls, slides, ladders, and buckets. The mountains are unforgiving—it's so easy to fall—and thus any mistake threatens to erase significant and hard-won

---

* In one of the Urbandictionary.com entries for QWOP, the game is described as follows: "QWOP is a game Chuck Norris can't even win."

Oof, you lost a lot of progress. That's a deep frustration, a real punch in the gut.

Figure 6.2 Screenshot of Getting Over It with Bennett Foddy.
Reprinted with permission of Bennett Foddy. All rights reserved.

progress. There are no checkpoints—places that once reached you can return to in case of a fall. And although you never die in the game, Diogenes' immortality offers little solace. Every swing and movement of your hammer is accompanied by the fear that you'll fall, lose progress, and be forced to start over again.

It's not impossible to finish the game—many have. But doing so is certainly not easy, not even for Foddy himself. "[I]n the weeks leading up to the . . . release I was trying to play through it to make sure there weren't too many bugs, and I couldn't beat it," he admits. "I kept getting right to the top and falling right down; some terrible falls, and not for lack of practice."[13] The game is hard, but difficulty isn't its point. Its point is frustration. As one website puts it, "*Getting Over It* is an indie game that can best be described as an exploration into frustration and the human condition."[14]

Gamers play this game precisely because it's frustrating. "It's the kind of game that you want to master despite the difficulty," a gamer reviewing the game writes.[15] "This game is frustrating beyond belief," another gamer notes, and then adds, "it'll keep you playing for weeks."[16] The experience of frustration draws one in, it's almost entrancing: "I have thrown furniture and punch [*sic*] the wall so many times . . . and I keep coming back for more. . . . I have to defeat this game, I have to get to the top no matter what it takes."[17] Some have even found beauty and catharsis in frustration. "When I started this game a couple of weeks ago, I thought I could never beat it. . . . But when I climbed to the top, I nearly cried. This is more than just a game, it's art; beautiful art. I couldn't feel more happier, than getting over it. Thank you."[18]

Asked why he created such a frustrating and difficult game, Foddy had this to say: "I think anything that is pleasurable can be engaging, even addictive, and frustration can (counterintuitively) be quite pleasurable. Or at least, it's a type of pleasure. It's not just video games—people seek out frustration in all parts of their lives . . . in their relationships, in their work. It gets an unfairly bad rap. It's strange because we enjoy discordant notes in music, and bitter flavours in cooking."[19] There's something both trivial and profound about reactions to the game. It's trivial to become obsessed with it; it's a game after all. As a gamer writes: "The game is meaningless unless you want to climb random objects with a hammer."[20] Yet it's popularity and addictive nature deliver a profound message about human experience, namely, that difficulty and frustration have their own appeal. They can motivate us and furnish us with an energy that can help us to persist and to conquer our goals. Frustration has a powerful aesthetic. Foddy has found it.

• • •

It isn't always fun, though. On April 21, 2018, in Durban, South Africa, the Kaizer Chiefs were playing against the Free State Stars in the semifinal of the South African soccer cup. The Kaizer Chiefs, the most successful club in the history of the knockout tournament, lost to the Free State Stars 2–0. In a fit of rage, the Kaizer Chiefs supporters stormed the field after the end of the game. Security guards were brutally assaulted; cameras were smashed to pieces; parts of the venue were torched; and players and officials were pelted with objects.[21] At least nineteen people were injured. The Moses Mabhida Stadium, one of the stadiums that South Africa used for the 2010 FIFA World Cup, was severely damaged—authorities estimated that it would take close to a quarter of a million dollars to repair the damages.[22] Talking to the press, the Durban mayor Zandile Gumede made mention of the involvement of emotions in the violence: "No amount of frustration and anger should lead one to cause violence and injure other citizens in the name of sport."[23]

Economists Ignacio Munyo and Martín A. Rossi studied the effects of frustration on crime. Munyo and Rossi were given access to a massive database that included the exact time of all crimes reported in Montevideo, Uruguay, between 2002 and 2010. In addition, they had access to the results of all soccer games played by the two most popular Uruguyan soccer clubs (*Nacional* and *Peñarol*) along with a database that included the odds in the betting market of those games. Whereas the betting odds gave the authors an indication of the expected outcomes of the games, the actual results allowed them to determine for which games the odds were verified. A comparison between the expected outcome (as provided by the betting market) and the actual outcome allowed the authors to determine the presence of frustration. According to the authors, frustration occurred when either soccer club lost when it was expected to win. The authors then looked at the number of crimes committed after an unexpected loss and compared it to the number of crimes after an expected loss. What they found was that more violent crimes followed an unexpected loss than an expected one. "Violent crime (as measured by robberies)," they write, "shows a significant jump after a frustrating loss. The increase in violent crime after frustration is quantitatively important: robberies increase 70% with respect to the control group."[24]

Curiously, the authors found no similar increase in the number of nonviolent crime (as measured by thefts) after a frustrating loss. If frustration carries an effect on crime, it's one that applies only to violent crimes. Furthermore, the authors found a significant relationship between frustration and increase of violent crime only for the first hour from the end of the game. This finding suggests that whatever effects frustration carries are short-term. Their result might be a confirmation of Tolstoy's rule. Frustrated individuals act immediately, on first impressions. But because of that, they can often be led astray, even steered to violence and crime.[†]

The authors aren't the first to report the onset of violence after a frustrating loss. Swedish economist Mikael Priks found that frustration generated by a team's unexpectedly bad performance leads to an increase in unruly behavior.[25] Additionally, in a study conducted by economists David Card and Gordon Dahl, it was reported that upset losses by professional football teams in the United States lead to a significant increase in police reports of at-home male-on-female intimate partner violence.[26]

The link between frustration and aggression has been observed in other domains in life. In addition to studies that suggest a relationship between violence (and thus aggression) in the face of a frustrating loss by one's favorite team, studies also found that children who behave aggressively toward their peers are ones who themselves experience high levels of stress and frustration at home.[27] Furthermore, workers who have been laid off from their jobs (and are presumably frustrated) are nearly six times more likely to act violently compared to those who are still employed.[28] In a more direct test

---

[†] Not always though! Studies conducted by psychologists Timothy D. Wilson and Jonathan Schooler (1991) suggest that people who verbalize pros and cons may end up making worse decisions than those who merely express their preferences without going through a conscious deliberation process. Sometimes not acting on first impressions prevents one from tapping into the wisdom of one's emotional (gut) reactions.

of the relationship between frustration and aggression, psychologist Mary B. Harris of the University of New Mexico monitored the behavior of unsuspecting individuals when another individual (either a male or female graduate student) stepped in front of them while they were waiting in line in stores, banks, ticket windows, and airport passenger check-in counters.[29] Harris found that people near the front of the line behaved more aggressively than people near the end of the line when both of them lost their place in line by the graduate student. But why should there be a difference in one's reactions depending on one's place in line? For Harris, the answer lies in the presence of frustration. Previous studies have shown that the closer an individual is to a desired goal, the greater the experience of frustration would be, if the goal were to be blocked. So, people near the front of the line, Harris suggests, have acted more aggressively precisely because they were more frustrated.

• • •

What can explain such findings? What, in other words, is the connection between frustration and aggression or violence? In 1939, a team of researchers at the Yale University Institute of Human Relations published a short but influential monograph titled *Frustration and Aggression*.[30] On the very first page, they lay out their view with unmistakable clarity: "the occurrence of aggressive behavior always presupposes the existence of frustration and, contrariwise, . . . the existence of frustration always leads to some form of aggression." Their view, now widely known as "the frustration-aggression hypothesis," is marked not only by its clarity, but also by a striking simplicity. There's only one cause of aggression: frustration; there's only one effect of frustration: aggression.[31]

Although theoretically attractive, the simplicity of the frustration-aggression hypothesis proved to be untenable. As the American scholar George Herbert Palmer once wrote, "We all desire through study to win a swift simplicity. But nature abhors simplicity."[32] The absolute, bidirectional link between frustration and aggression posited by the Yale researchers wasn't the link that subsequent investigations discovered. "The eagerness to find a 'law of Nature' has evidently tempted the [Yale] investigators to presume, too hastily, the existence of a necessary connection," a reviewer wrote in the pages of the journal *Nature* in 1944.[33] Indeed, frustration is neither necessary for the emergence of aggression nor does its presence guarantee the emergence of aggression. The connection between frustration and aggression appears to be broken both ways.

To begin with, instrumental forms of aggression can't be easily explained by the frustration-aggression hypothesis. Consider a contract killer carrying out his bid, a player committing a strategic but aggressive foul play in hockey or football to stop the opposing team from gaining an advantage, or a powerful dictator who orders to kill only to instill fear and submission. Such acts of aggression are counterexamples to the hypothesis: they show that aggression needn't always be preceded by the presence of frustration. The Yale researchers seem to have missed the existence of cool-headed, calculative violence, and even aggression.

It's then a mistake to hold that frustration is necessary for aggression. At the same time, it's also wrong to insist that frustration is *sufficient* for aggression. The presence of frustration doesn't invariably lead to aggression. Let me begin by offering a personal example. For me, a source of great frustration is software malfunction. The worst of all takes place when my word processor crashes unexpectedly and precious unsaved text is lost. The experience is frustrating beyond description. Yet such an experience doesn't lead me to aggression. Instead, I fall in despair and engage in scornful self-blame—I overreact, to be certain. But I'm tempted to cry more than I'm tempted to hit my computer.

Anecdotal stories aside, research in the years ensuing the publication of *Frustration and Aggression* has found that not every instance of frustration leads to aggression. Some studies have shown that the effect of frustration on aggression is greatly reduced when frustration is expected.[34] Other studies have reported that whether one responds aggressively to a frustrating situation depends on what one believes about the source of their frustration. Specifically, unjustified frustration—that is, frustration that is believed to have arisen for no good reason—is more likely to lead to hostile aggression than justified frustration.[35] As psychologist Nicholas Pastore wrote in 1950, "the occurrence of the aggressive response [to the emergence of frustration] depends on the subject's understanding of the situation.[36]" If we can rationalize and understand the source of our frustration, then it's less likely that we'll be carried away by our frustration.

Further difficulties for the frustration-aggression hypothesis arise when we turn our attention to investigations into the triggers of aggression. Researchers don't think that there's a single trigger or cause of aggression. Frustration might be one of them but it's not the only one. A different and rather unexpected trigger is ambient temperature. Archival studies of violent crimes show an increase in crime rates on hot days compared to cold days, in hot months compared to cooler months, and in hot years compared to cooler years. [37] Moreover, field studies have found that individuals driving behind a car that failed to drive forward when the light turned green, honked more if the outside temperature was hotter and if their cars didn't have air conditioning.[38] Finally, by analyzing archival data from the 1986–1988 base-ball seasons, researchers found that pitchers struck batters more frequently on hot days than on cooler days.[39] Importantly, this last result held true even after the researchers controlled for a number of game-related factors, such as errors, wild pitches, and walks, all of which might contribute one way or another to the experience of frustration.

If that's not enough, the simplicity of the frustration-aggression hypothesis is problematic in yet another respect: it ignores the important role of self-control—that is, the set of complex psychological processes that allow us to override our impulses and habitual responses. Indeed, aggression, in cases in which one has previously experienced frustration, could be attributed not to the presence of frustration itself but to a depletion of the resources needed for individuals to exert self-control.

Self-control is a conscious and effortful form of regulating one's actions, thoughts, emotions, and desires. Studies have demonstrated that the exercise of self-control requires the expenditure of some sort of energy (most likely glucose) that may become depleted with use.[40] What this means is twofold. First, given that attempts at self-control draw from the same limited pool of resources, individuals who have already exerted self-control are more likely to fail at later attempts at self-control. Second, individuals who have more resources (higher levels of blood glucose) to fuel their attempts at self-control will be more successful at such attempts than those who operate with depleted resources (low levels of blood glucose). Both of these claims are relevant in the case of the purported link between frustration and aggression. Not only has low self-control been linked to criminal and aggressive behavior, but the same connection has also been found in cases of low glucose and poor glucose tolerance.‡ Consider: a study that measured the glucose levels of delinquent individuals right after they were apprehended found that approximately 90% of them exhibited glucose levels below the normal range.[41] Another study reported that individuals with antisocial personality disorder exhibited poorer glucose tolerance than individuals without this disorder.[42] Another noted that diabetics are more impulsive than those who are not diabetic.[43] A different one reported that poor glucose tolerance was found to be common among arsonists.[44] And lastly, researches even used glucose tolerance as a prediction of criminal recidivism: 84% of the time, glucose tolerance was able to predict correctly whether an individual released from prison would commit a violent crime.[45]

---

‡ What does it mean to have poor glucose tolerance? It means that your body, compared to the bodies of those who are glucose tolerant, is less efficient in using and storing glucose.

Given such findings, it isn't a stretch to hold that many cases of aggression are preceded by one's inability for self-control. Thus, whether frustration may or may not lead to aggressive behavior might be a matter of self-control and the resources available to fuel self-control. To be clear, the experience of frustration is effortful, likely one that will be demanding in terms of energy, and a factor in consequent attempts at self-control. But even if that's the case, frustration isn't necessarily the culprit for aggression. Instead, the fault could lie with our inability to control ourselves and not with an emotional state that may be effortful. More self-control (and more resources available for self-control) would then affect how we act in the face of frustration or other experienced emotions and difficulties. A clear demonstration of this claim is provided by a study that examined the effects of glucose intake on aggression and frustration.[46] The researchers divided participants into two groups—one received a glucose shake; the other, a placebo. Both groups were asked to engage in an impossible computer task. Researchers noticed that the task was frustrating: it led some participants to curse out loud or to hit the computer equipment. However, they also reported that such aggressive bursts were much reduced for participants who received the glucose shake. Although both groups were faced with a frustrating task, only one group exhibited aggression. Glucose intake thus reduced aggressive behavior by facilitating self-control. Frustration, thus, doesn't necessarily entail aggression. And even when aggressive behavior follows the experience of frustration, the connection between the two is not direct but instead mediated by a set of complex factors. In sum, the frustration-aggression hypothesis is guilty not only of oversimplifying the relationship between frustration and aggression but also of obfuscating the wonderfully nuanced workings of human psychology.

To be fair, the limitations of the frustration-aggression hypothesis didn't go unnoticed by the authors of the hypothesis. In fact, two years after they introduced the hypothesis in the literature they came to qualify their position. "Frustration," they wrote, "produces instigation to aggression but this is not the only type of instigation that it may produce."[47] This qualification is important. It doubly weakens their initial position and, in doing so, casts frustration in a more flattering light.

First, frustration, according to the revised account, no longer yields aggression. What it gives rise to is *instigation* to aggression. But, as the authors themselves note, instigation to aggression isn't the same thing as the occurrence of aggression. We might be instigated or tempted to act aggressively but for various reasons we might not act in such a fashion. Maybe that is because we're afraid of punishment. Maybe we came to realize that acting aggressively isn't the right, beneficial, or smart thing to do. Or maybe we figured out that the energy that we get from frustration is spent better elsewhere. A computer programmer who finds herself in the grips of frustration because of a buggy piece of code might react by giving up on the code or by breaking her keyboard. But she might also persist despite the initial failure. She could harness the energy of frustration in an attempt to overcome her obstacle.

Second, although frustration can produce instigation to aggression it may also give rise to other types of instigation. Frustration, in other words, isn't necessarily related to aggression: It's not a law of nature that one will move from frustration to aggression.

The frustration-aggression hypothesis has undergone much additional refinement and modification. What's now clear, eighty or so years after the publication of *Frustration and Aggression*, is that although the hypothesis has once served as a useful theoretical starting point, it's no longer an acceptable explanation of human aggression. The link between frustration and aggression is far more complicated than it was once thought. Frustration might not be all fun and games. It isn't, however, just violence and aggression either.

• • •

There within,
she saw that Envy was intent upon
a meal of viper flesh, the meat that fed
her vice. Minerva turned aside her eyes.
But Envy sluggishly rose from the ground
leaving the half-chewed dregs of serpents' flesh
and coming forward with her faltering steps.
And when she saw the splendid goddess dressed
in gleaming armor, Envy moaned: her face
contracted as she sighed. That face is wan,
that body shriveled; and her gaze is not
direct; her teeth are filled with filth and rot;
her breast is green with gall, and poison coats
her tongue. She never smiles except when some
sad sight brings her delight; she is denied
sweet sleep, for she is too preoccupied,
forever vigilant; when men succeed,
she is displeased—success means her defeat.
She gnaws at others and at her own self—
her never-ending, self-inflicted hell.

—Ovid, *Metamorphoses*, Book 2[48]

Not everyone has Ovid's way with words. Yet many see envy in a similar light. Envy is a sickness, it's said, "a mental pain."[49] It is to flesh what rust is to iron, ancient Greek philosopher Antishenes thought. It is that with which Satan in Milton's *Paradise Lost* is fraught. It is that which Chaucer's Parson character in *The Canterbury Tales* finds to be, echoing the Christian tradition, the worst of all sins. It is that which according to *Genesis* makes Cain kill Abel and which forces Joseph's brothers to sell him into slavery.

Envy is a source of misery. "The heartburn of envy is horrible. How oppressive it is to envy! Envy squeezes the throat with a spasm, squeezes the eyes out of their orbits."[50] That's how Ivan Babivech recalls his first experience of envy in Yury Olesha's novel *Envy*. Envy appears to be a sign of ill will. It "aims, at least in terms of one's wishes," German philosopher Immanuel Kant wrote, "at destroying others' good fortune."[51] The envious rejoices when the target of envy fails. "The man who is delighted by others' misfortunes," Aristotle claimed, "is identical with the man who envies others' prosperity."[52] "Envy is an emotion that is essentially both selfish and malevolent," wrote William L. Davidson in 1912, aptly summarizing the nature of envy in the *Encyclopedia of Religion and Ethics*.[53]

Given such a negative conception of envy, it's no surprise that envy is rarely owned. In his final novel, *Billy Budd, Sailor*, Herman Melville, takes note of this feature of envy. "[T]hough many an arraigned mortal has in hopes of mitigated penalty pleaded guilty to horrible actions, did ever anybody seriously confess to envy? Something there is in it universally felt to be more shameful than even felonious crime."[54] Indeed, it's so hard to get individuals to admit of envy that psychologists who study it often find recourse in indirect and creative ways of measuring it.

Why do we experience envy? Its presence doesn't appear to be dictated by a law of human nature. It's not contradictory, in other words, to imagine humans existing without envy. Yet most of us experience it. Most cultures have a word for it. And various literary and religious traditions have made much of it.

To find the reason for envy's existence we need to look to its social function. Envy arises when we compare unfavorably to others. To admit of envy is to admit that we lack something that others possess. But such an admission brings about, inevitably I think, an even more painful realization. Through envy we come to see ourselves as inferior to others. Thus, envy doesn't merely offer a description about our social status, it also makes a value judgment about it: it tells us not only that we're different than others but that we're worse than them. Such unflattering and painful social comparisons motivate us to compete with those who are socially superior to us. Envy, I wish to suggest, exists precisely because it inspires competition. It arises on account of the perception of a gap between ourselves and the more fortunate others; it functions as a mechanism that pushes us to reduce the gap.

The gap that gives rise to envy can be reduced in one of two ways. We can either pull ourselves up to the level of others, or pull others down to our level. This double manifestation of envy's work is eloquently noted by English writer and poet Dorothy Sayers. "Envy," she writes, "is the great leveler: if it cannot level things up, it will level them down. . . . At its best, Envy is a climber and a snob; at its worst it is a destroyer—rather than have anyone happier than itself, it will see us all miserable together."[55] Sayers' description of the work of envy suggests that envy isn't a monolithic experience. There's malicious envy, an emotion characterized by ill will and a desire to destroy, demonized by writers and religious thinkers. But there's also benign envy, an emotional experience capable of motivating individuals to work harder to get what others have.

It's benign envy that the Rotterdam-born philosopher Bernard Mandeville had in mind when in *The Grumbling Hive*, a poem that begins his famous *The Fable of the Bees*, he writes "Envy it self, and Vanity, / Were Ministers of Industry."[56] *The Grumbling Hive* uses the metaphor of a bee colony to describe human society and in it Mandeville suggests that vices such as envy are necessary for the flourishing of commercial societies. "So Vice is beneficial found . . . As necessary to the State, / As Hunger is to make 'em eat."[57] In one of his remarks to the poem, he addresses the value of envy explicitly. "Envy, as it is very common among Painters, so it is of great Use for their Improvement."[58] Clearly the envy that Mandeville speaks of isn't malicious, but benign. If it's the great leveler that Sayers speaks of, it isn't the type that levels things down, but the type that levels things up.

Sayers was right about the double nature of envy. Many languages, Dutch, German, Polish, Russian, Thai, and Turkish, have two words for envy: one for the malicious variety and another for the benign. Although the English language doesn't draw a distinction between these two forms of envy, our expressions of envy often do. When one says "Congratulations on your new job, I envy you," one doesn't necessarily wish ill on their friend. In a study conducted by psychologists Niels van de Ven, Marcel Zeelenberg, and Rik Pieters and published in the journal *Emotion*, they asked participants to write one or two sentences about a situation in which they experienced envy. What they found was that about half of the participants described an experience involving benign envy, whereas the other half described an experience involving malicious envy. In addition, the researchers articulated and provided support for a distinction between benign envy and admiration. From the outside, benign envy looks like admiration, but from the inside, the differences between the two are pronounced. Even though in a state of benign envy we wish no harm to others, we still foster some negative attitudes toward them—we're still bothered by their fortunes. Benign envy is unpleasant; admiration is not. Most important, benign envy is a much more powerful motivator than admiration. To admire someone is to accept one's superiority; to envy (benignly) someone is to want for ourselves what the other has.[59]

Regardless of its type, envy is unpleasant. That's not just because it casts us in an unfavorable social light, but also because it essentially involves a frustrated desire. We're envious of others' possessions precisely because we can't have them. In envy, we wish to have not only what we don't have but also that which is out of our reach. As psychologists Richard H. Smith, David J. Y. Combs, and Stephen M. Thielke write, "[t]he experience of envy would be quite different if it simply involved noticing a desired attribute and then going about obtaining it without delay."[60]

Envy thus presupposes and involves frustration. Both types of envy involve the experience of a painful frustration—the realization that someone else has what we can't (at least immediately) have. And both of them constitute attempts to overcome the frustration, either by taking away something from someone or by doing our best to acquire it. In summarizing their conclusions about the existence of benign envy, psychologists Niels van de Ven, Marcel Zeelenberg, and Rik Pieters highlight the importance of the role of frustration in understanding envy. "We expect that exactly this frustration is what triggers the positive motivation that results from benign envy, as the frustration signals to the person that the coveted object is worth striving for.[61]" Even though they were surprised to find that a high level of frustration is involved in the experience of benign envy, they had no difficulty in understanding why frustration is present in envy. If envy is the great leveler, frustration is the great motivator behind it.

• • •

"My back pain gets so bad I want to cry. It hurts so bad, I feel like taking a knife and cutting it out."[62] The capacity to experience pain is an essential feature of human existence: it signals the presence of injury or illness; it protects us from dangers and further trauma; it motivates us to protect our bodies. All the same, pain's efficiency and beneficial character dissipate once pain becomes persistent and unremitting. We want pain to arise only when trouble arises; we want it to disappear the instant trouble disappears. But pain is transformed when it becomes a chronic condition. It loses its usefulness. It turns into a toxic influence on one's life.

Chronic pain is any pain that endures more than six months, that stems from non-life-threatening causes, that's persistent, and that isn't typically amenable to treatment or methods of pain control.[63] It's estimated that between 10% to 20% of the general population experiences chronic or recurrent chronic pain.[64] Chronic pain is associated with poor physical and emotional health. It takes a toll on individuals' social, professional, and familial relationships.[65] It diminishes one's quality of life. It even harms areas of one's brain![66] The effects of chronic pain on one's life are pervasive. "Sometimes," a woman living with chronic pain confesses, "I feel it has taken over my life."[67] "Sometimes," someone else admits, "I feel like, uh, my whole *being*, my whole *identity* is wrapped up in this pain."[68]

An astounding 97% of pain-clinic patients with chronic back pain or postherpetic neuralgia (nerve pain caused by shingles) report high levels of frustration.[69] In fact, individuals living with chronic pain report experiencing frustration more intensely than four other negative and pain-related emotional experiences—fear, anxiety, anger, and depression.[70] The presence of frustration makes sense. People in chronic pain are frustrated by the fact that they're in constant pain. "I'm upset because I'm in pain every day."[71] They're frustrated because they can't do the things that they wish to do. "My back pain is ruining my life. There are times when I feel consumed by the pain. It has robbed me of my right to a better, more enriched lifestyle."[72] They're frustrated because they can't even complete the simplest of tasks. "It takes ages to get out of bed and into the bathroom. It is like moving mountains. I'm so extremely stiff, and the pain is just unbearable."[73] They're frustrated with the medical profession and its inability to help them. "[Y]ou're in pain but you are being told by your doctors, 'No, no you haven't got pain, it's just a pin you're feeling in your head.'"[74] They're frustrated with the lack of others' understanding. "[E]ven people that have known me for long periods of time, don't understand that. And I, I find that frustrating and can't explain it enough, you know, how, how pain affects my life."[75] They're frustrated with the invisibility of their pain. "I've lost friends because they haven't understood.... They can't see anything physical so they don't believe you've got anything wrong with you."[76] They're frustrated to watch their interpersonal relationships deteriorate and being transformed through the medium of pain. "I know he loves me very, very much.... He just doesn't seem to want to make love a lot lately."[77] They're frustrated with everything, it seems.

Where there's chronic pain, there's frustration. So, how does one respond to the frustration of chronic pain? The answer is what one would expect: different people respond to frustration differently. Some become angry and resentful. "I fell [*sic*] like I'm losing time every day—which I've worked very hard for years to maintain—I resent my body for failing me, especially when I work so hard to be good to it!!"[78] Some experience disappointment and regret. "My kids are growing and I feel like time is running out and I am missing something."[79] Some feel powerless and depressed. "I can't do anything. This body is totally useless. Is this my body? You cannot imagine how useless I feel, how can it be? . . . You cannot imagine how depressed I am."[80] "I am so depressed that I could go to sleep and never wake up."[81] Some have given up hope that the pain is ever going to go away. "I don't think there's a lot, I mean when it's full on and giving me as much as it can there is nothing, there is nothing you can do except to just grin and bear it, and hope like hell there's no one around there listening to you moaning and groaning."[82]

Yet, despite the adversity that heavily impresses them on a constant basis, some have managed, against all odds, to become resilient. The resilience stems not from the absence of pain but paradoxically from the pain itself. "I just get up and get on with it . . . no matter how bad it is."[83] "You know this is actually how hard life can get. You can survive this if you don't put on blinkers and pretend this is not nasty, it hurts, it sucks, but you know, such is life."[84] "I fight pain even when it wears at me and it makes me tired, I won't let it win."[85] "I refuse to let my back pain interfere with my life."[86] What one discovers in descriptions of individuals who face up to frustration and become resilient to chronic pain is both an honest admission of their difficult situation and a determination to make the best of it. In their study of resilience in chronic pain, psychologists John A. Sturgeon and Alex J. Zautra summarize their findings as follows:

> Those individuals that we may consider to be resilient to pain are those who adopt more adaptive coping strategies to pain . . . possess a greater belief that they can effectively control their pain, and thus expend more effort when implementing these strategies. . . . Resilient individuals possess greater emotional knowledge and direct more attention within in order to evaluate their current emotional state.[87]

Resilience to pain thus begins with awareness of one's condition and emotional experiences and with a search of how one can use the pain and frustration to motivate oneself. Thus, to help oneself, one needs both to know oneself and to be able to carry oneself forward, not alone but by using the energy afforded to oneself by the experience of frustration. Such a finding isn't limited to resilient individuals with chronic pain. Resilient adults with mental illness report the same. "I think that I have knowledge so that I can understand myself. I say that this is what is keeping me here—otherwise I would have killed myself ages ago."[88] And in the face of adversity, they seek energy and a way to strike back. This attitude is captured perhaps best in the following comment, given by an individual with spinal cord injury. "I don't see it [the injury] as a 'You're fucked. Give up. Go shoot yourself. Go live in a nursing home.' I see it as a challenge."[89]

• • •

Frustration is a challenge too. And once we come to see it as such, we can realize that it's something that calls for a response. We have to deal with it and to do so in the right way—in a way that benefits us by carrying us forward toward the resolution of problems and the accomplishment of personal goals. Of course, that's easier said than done. Yet if individuals with chronic pain and spinal cord injuries have found ways to bounce back, ways to use their emotional worlds in advantageous manners, then the rest of us should be inspired by them to try to do the same. We're clearly in a better position than them—frustration isn't a constant emotional texture of our lives. But perhaps because we're in a better situation, we might not appreciate the power of frustration. Thankfully, our brains do. We're hardwired not only to detect obstacles to our goals and to take notice of our frustrating experiences, but also to become energized by such experiences and to strive to overcome our obstacles.

Psychologists Naomi I. Eisenberger, Matthew D. Lieberman, and Kipling D. Williams conducted a fascinating study in which they examined whether social exclusion activates the same areas of the brain that are activated during physical pain.[90] The psychologists asked participants to play a virtual ball-tossing game while in a functional magnetic resonance imaging (fMRI) scanner. The participants were led to think that two other participants, also in fMRI scanners, were playing the game with them. In reality, however, each participant was playing with a preset computer software that was programmed to exclude eventually the participant from the ball-tossing game. After a few throws to the participant, the program stopped tossing the ball to the participant. The participant was then left watching the ball being passed from one virtual participant to another. When the researchers observed the brains of the excluded participants they found that, compared to a control group, there was increased activation of the anterior cingulate cortex (ACC) and such activation correlated positively with self-reported distress. Furthermore, they also observed that a different area, the right ventral prefrontal cortex (RVPFC), was also more active during exclusion; however, this area was negatively correlated with self-reported distress. What this means is that social exclusion leads to an increased activation of ACC, but for those individuals who are able to deal with exclusion, another area of the brain is activated, namely, RVPFC.

The significance of these findings is twofold. First, ACC is active during physical pain. ACC is thought to act as a neural "alarm system" that detects when an environmental or bodily response is inappropriate or incongruent with the organism's goals.[91] Pain activates ACC, but it's important to note that ACC is primarily associated with the affective (i.e., emotional) distress associated with physical pain and not with the sensory component of pain.[92] Increased activation of ACC during the experimental condition reveals not only that social exclusion and physical pain activate some of the same areas of the brain, but that they are both distressing. Social exclusion hurts, not in the way that a paper cut or a burn hurts, but in an emotional way. Second, previous studies have suggested that RVPFC is implicated in the regulation of pain distress.[93] For instance, electrical stimulation of the ventral prefrontal cortex in rats diminishes pain behavior when they experience painful stimulation.[94] So, in the case of social exclusion, the activation of RVPFC, which was found to be correlated with decreased self-reported distress, plays a similar role as in physical pain: it helps to regulate the emotional distress experienced following social exclusion.

How do these findings relate to frustration? In a neuroimaging study published in *NeuroReport*, German psychologists Birgit Abler, Henrik Walter, and Susanne Erk frustrated individuals while in an fMRI machine by not rewarding them when they successfully completed a task.[95] What they found when they looked at the areas of the brain activated in the frustrating condition was that ACC and RVPFC showed increased activation compared to the nonfrustrating condition. Just like social exclusion, frustration activates areas involved during physical pain and areas known to be responsible for the regulation of pain. The findings suggest not only that frustration is a distressing experience but also that the very experience of frustration brings about a need to deal with it. Neurologically speaking, frustration prompts us to do something about our frustrating experience. As the researchers write, "the feeling of frustration, more than cool reasoning, might be a trigger for changing behavior."[96]

Additional findings shed more light on what our brain does when we're frustrated. Healthy adults exhibit increased activation of the amygdala when frustrated.[97] This observation is consistent with previous studies that have found that the amygdala plays an important role in detecting events of negative emotional salience such as fearful situations.[98] Moreover, both neuroimaging and electroencephalographic studies of healthy children show that the performance of frustrating tasks brings about the involvement of attentional and cognitive resources and makes it harder for individuals to disengage from the frustrating task.[99] In a different neuroimaging study that involved Braille training, researchers found that individuals who were frustrated during a novel and highly difficult tactile discrimination task showed brain activity in neurological structures thought to be responsible for acute stress and in the primary and secondary somatosensory cortex (the areas of the brain that are engaged during tactile discrimination tasks).[100] These findings once again confirm the aversive (negative) character of the experience of frustration. But they also show that during the performances of a difficult task there is additional neuronal involvement to counteract the effects of frustration. The brain during frustration works harder. "We found," the authors of the study write, "that frustration and stress during performing a well-trained perceptual task do not impair the level of accuracy, but this happens at a cost of increased brain activation."[101]

Lastly, neuroscientist Rongjun Yu and colleagues developed an experimental procedure during which participants were required to successfully complete a series of consecutive trials to obtain a reward. Just like previous experiments on frustration, the experiment was set up so that participants would be, at certain times, blocked from obtaining a reward. However, given the fact that a reward would only be obtained if participants were able to complete the entire series of trials, the researchers were able to measure how the participants would be affected if the blockage happened either near the beginning or near the end of the series of trials. The researchers made a number of important observations. First, they demonstrated that the closer one is to the reward, the more frustrated one becomes when the reward is blocked. Importantly, such an increase of frustration correlated with an increase in participants' self-reported motivation to obtain the reward. As Yu writes, "[p]articipants reported stronger frustration after being blocked from obtaining proximal rather than distal rewards, and the self-reported frustration was significantly correlated with the motivation to obtain the reward and the force applied to buttons after blockage."[102] Such a finding is a confirmation of the existence of Amsel's effect in humans. Frustration invigorates one's response and motivates one to keep trying to overcome the obstacle. Moreover, when Yu and colleagues turned their attention to the neural structures responsible for frustration, they found that frustrative nonreward (the inability to obtain reward following effort) activated the amygdala and periaqueductal gray, both of which are regions that have been implicated in animal models of reactive aggression.[103] "I propose," Yu states in a 2016 essay on the neuroscience of frustration, "that the adaptive value of frustration may reside in its ability to motivate or energize subsequent behaviors, allowing individuals to continue pursuing goal-directed activities despite frustrating nonrewards and obstacles."[104] Or, as he puts it a few lines later: "The evolutionary significance of frustration is to transfer the unfulfilled motivation aroused by proximal reward into subsequent behavioral vigor."[105] The neuroscience of frustration might be in its early stages, yet its message is clear: we aren't hardwired for failing but for bouncing back when we fail.

• • •

"Drive is an energizer, but not a guide; an engine, but not a steering gear," wrote Donald O. Hebb, one of the most important psychologists of the twentieth century.[106] What Hebb said about drive also applies to frustration. Frustration, after all, is, I've been arguing throughout this chapter, a drive—perhaps, one of the most important drives that we possess. Frustration is a psychological mechanism capable of springing us into action and of propelling us toward the completion of personally important goals. It has the potential for good but also for the worst. It can grant us the energy we need to overcome obstacles to important goals. It can help us achieve what we perceive we're missing. Yet it can also promote aggression or fuel malicious envy. When frustration arises, we should take advantage of its energy but also take notice of it. Just like a powerful wave, we can either ride it or be carried away.

7

"Impossible to stop just now. Why, if I could only prove one simple little lemma"

Faced with limitations, exclusions, failures, and affronts—all which are obstacles to our goals—we become irritated, distressed, and dissatisfied: in a word, frustrated. Such an affective transformation modifies our relationship to the world. The world, no longer agreeable to us, has become stubborn to our wishes, inflexible to our pleas. What's given to us just doesn't do it—we want something different. But through disappointment and dissatisfaction, we become energized. Fueled by frustration, we're moved to take action. We seek to reduce or to completely eliminate the obstacles that lay in our way.

Frustration is key. It's a tool that permits us to navigate the world and to negotiate obstacles that bar us from achieving our personal goals.

• • •

Like boredom, frustration is informative. It can tell us about features of our situation and about qualities of our selves. When we're frustrated, it's because we're blocked from achieving something that we desire. The presence of frustration is thus an indication of a mismatch between our desires and expectations, on the one hand, and reality, on the other hand. The world of frustration, in other words, is a world that isn't to our liking.

What's more, frustration reveals to us something about ourselves. We become frustrated when what's being obstructed is a matter of personal significance. Not every thwarted desire, limitation, or affront will give rise to frustration, only those that are important for our personal goals and desires. "You know someone matters to you if they can frustrate you," Adam Phillips writes.[1] Where there is frustration, personal meaning lies. Frustration is a personal matter. It's no wonder we take it seriously.

Propelled. Andreas Elpidorou, Oxford University Press (2020). © Andreas Elpidorou.
DOI: 10.1093/oso/9780190912963.001.0001

Frustration is also vexing. We're bothered with how frustration feels and this badgering feeling of discontent, which is inherent and essential to frustration, allows frustration to play an important role in our everyday existence. We become upset by, sometimes even obsessed with, the unfulfilled desires or perceived blockages that give rise to frustration. We're disturbed by our inability to move on and to carry out our desires. And it's this burning irritation and dissatisfaction that gives us the energy to persist.

Seen in this light, frustration has a clear adaptive value. An organism that can become frustrated is more likely to adapt to a changing and unpredictable environment than one that can't. If an organism were to lack the ability to become frustrated, then such an organism would remain passive in the face of disappointment; it wouldn't persist nor would it attempt to overcome its difficulties; perhaps it would even quickly resign in the face of failure. An organism that's capable of experiencing frustration, however, won't give up—at least, not immediately and not without a fight. Frustration can lead to victories—triumphs, indeed.

• • •

It's not exactly clear when and how it began. But it's clear when and how it ends: May 1995, in the pages of the journal, *Annals of Mathematics*. Despite uncertainty about the beginning, it's customary to start the telling of the story by describing a late 1630s act of writing. It was then that, in the margins of a Latin translation of a Greek text on mathematics, the French mathematician Pierre de Fermat wrote a statement that not only frustrated generations of mathematicians but also forever changed the course of mathematics.

The text that bears Fermat's epoch-making marginal comment was authored by the "father of algebra," the Hellenistic mathematician Diophantus, who is thought to have lived during the third century AD.[2] Very little is known about Diophantus's life. His exact date of birth is a matter of historical controversy; so is the date of his death. A fifth-century AD anthology of puzzles contains a riddle about Diophantus's age; if accurate, Diophantus would have been eighty-four years old at the time of his death. Details about his life might be sparse; Diophantus's legacy, however, is rich. During his time in Alexandria, Diophantus compiled mathematical problems in a text called *Arithmetica*. Originally composed of thirteen books, of which only ten have survived, the text was famous throughout the Middle Ages and studied closely by both Greeks and Arabs—the famous philosopher and mathematician Hypatia wrote commentaries on the first six books of the text.[3] It includes hundreds of mathematical problems with detailed solutions. It constitutes a tremendous compendium of mathematical knowledge. It's a world of mathematics laid out on paper, word for word, symbol for symbol.

Fermat was impressed by a particular problem in Book II of the *Arithmetica* (Problem II.8)—it reads simply, "To divide a square number into two squares" and asks one to find solutions to the Pythagorean equation. In contemporary language, the problem poses the following question: what are the integer numbers x, y, and z that satisfy the equation $x^2 + y^2 = z^2$? Any solution to this problem, such as the set (3, 4, 5) or (7, 24, 25), is called a Pythagorean triple.

Fermat's interest in this problem had nothing to do with its difficulty. In its Pythagorean form, the problem must have been trivial for Fermat—it was known since Euclid that there's an infinite number of Pythagorean triples. What intrigued Fermat was the potential that the problem carried. For by simply changing the power of the equation from 2 to 3, the Pythagorean problem could be transformed into one that's orders of magnitude more difficult than the original one. Indeed, hard as one may try, one can't find three integer numbers, x, y, z, that render the equation $x^3 + y^3 = z^3$ true. The same goes if the power is changed from 2 to 4.

Fermat took one more, algebraically small but conceptually great, step. He thought about the problem in its most general form. And in the margins of his copy of the *Arithmetica*, he wrote the following remark:

> It is impossible to separate a cube into two cubes, or a fourth power into two fourth powers, or in general, any power higher than the second, into two like powers. I have discovered a truly marvelous proof of this, which this margin is too narrow to contain.

With this statement, Fermat postulated that the equation $x^n + y^n = z^n$ had no solution for any integer value of n greater than 2. This was a remarkable statement and one of immense complexity. Fermat's claim, now known as "Fermat's Last Theorem," is a statement about an infinite number of equations. No matter what the value of n is, as long as n is an integer greater than 2, there's no solution to the equation. Out of an infinite number of combinations of three integer numbers, there's no combination that makes any one of an infinite number of Pythagorean-like equations true. It's as if Fermat had glanced through infinity and found nothing that could solve the equation in its general (n greater than 2) form.

An aside: History is tantalizingly cruel to storytellers. Two centuries before Fermat's glance into infinity, someone else wrote a comment while engaging with the *Arithmetica*. This time it was John Chortasmenos, a Byzantine monk and mathematician. Chortasmenos didn't add a problem to Diophantus's list, nor did he offer a solution to one. He noted instead his exasperation with the problems. "Thy soul, Diophantus," he wrote, "be with Satan because of the difficulty of your other theorems and particularly of the present theorem."[4] Many scholars have related Chortasmenos's comment to Problem II.8 and argued that it was the expression of Chortasmenos's frustration with the same problem that gave birth to Fermat's Last Theorem. Such an interpretation of Chortasmenos's comment makes for a nice story. Through Diophantus, the ancient Pythagorean problem challenges both a Byzantine monk and the "Prince of Amateurs"[5]; the former sees only vaguely what the latter conceived of clearly, and the former sends Diophantus to the devil, whereas the latter conjures up a problem of truly devilish complexity. Alas, the truth is less intriguing than the foregoing story. Although scholars have initially attributed Chortasmenos's comment to Problem II.8, such an attribution now appears to have been unduly quick. It's unlikely that Chortasmenos would have sent Diophantus to the devil for this problem, at least in the form expressed by Diophantus.[6] It's too easy of a problem to have been the cause for such harsh action. In all likelihood, it was a different problem that caused Chortasmenos's frustration.

Back to the story: For about three hundred years after its inception, Fermat's Last Theorem looked unprovable. The theorem had been proven for specific values of n (elsewhere in his copy of the *Arithmetica*, Fermat offered a proof for $n = 4$). Yet such proofs meant little to mathematicians. The Last Theorem is about an infinite number of equations (or values of n) so to prove it, one has to prove it for every possible positive integer greater than 2. Proving it for some, even millions, of values of n still leaves an infinite number of integers for which the theorem hasn't been proven. In his book, *The Last Problem*, published in 1961 and which detailed the history of Fermat's Last Theorem, the mathematician E. T. Bell predicted that civilization would come to an end before the theorem could be proven.[7] Bell's prediction wasn't a flippant pronouncement; it was a sober assessment of the future of mathematics based on a history filled with failed attempts to prove the theorem.

Bell was wrong. Not only that but, unbeknownst to him, the publication of his book set in motion a long series of events that would eventually lead to the capitulation of Fermat's Last Theorem. Two years after its publication, *The Last Problem* fell into the hands of a ten-year-old curious boy. Andrew Wiles borrowed a copy of Bell's book from his local library, and through it he was introduced to the greatest mathematical mystery. "It looked so simple, and yet all the great mathematicians in history couldn't solve it," he recalls.[8] "Here was a problem that I as a 10-year-old could understand, and I knew from that moment that I would never let it go. I had to solve it."[9] It wasn't just Wiles that couldn't resist the allure of Fermat's Last Theorem. The theorem "was a mathematical siren, luring geniuses toward it."[10] Scores of mathematicians before him have tried to prove it. They all failed.

Wiles devoted his life to Fermat's Last Theorem. At the age of forty-two, after years of difficult, frustrating, and mostly solitary work, he proved Fermat right. He showed, beyond any doubt, that the equation $x^n + y^n = z^n$ had no solution for any integer value of n greater than 2. In doing so, he formalized Fermat's glance into infinity and expressed it in a series of mathematical equations, theorems, and statements, all contained in two articles published in May 1995.[11] The proof is a remarkable achievement akin, perhaps, to the discoveries of DNA or of the atomic structure of matter.

• • •

When telling the story of the proof, it's easy to personify success, to view it, that is, as the accomplishment of certain singular and independent individuals. It's also tempting to revert to hagiographic narratives about mathematical or otherwise heroes who've done that which once seemed inconceivable. Yet, no individual is an island, and no cognitive enterprise occurs in an emotional or intellectual vacuum.

Wiles is the hero of this story, no doubt. But he isn't the only one. Fermat deserves credit—both for having conceived of the problem and for expressing it in such a provocative manner. Scores of mathematicians who have tried but failed to prove the theorem also deserve credit: their failures paved the way for its eventual solution. And so do many other mathematicians whose work was put to use by Wiles.

But more important for our purposes, the proof of Fermat's Last Theorem is a discovery fraught in frustration and baptized in failure. Because of that we can't afford to lose track of the emotional forces that moved the various actors, including Wiles. Indeed, in the case of Fermat's Last Theorem, the psychology of frustration proves to be didactic. By appreciating frustration's force and character, we can come to understand better not only the psychology of failure, but also that of perseverance and success.

Fermat's Last Theorem frustrated Wiles. And it's that frustration that made the theorem a central part of Wiles's life. "You might ask how could I devote an unlimited amount of time to a problem that might simply not be soluble," Wiles says.[12] "The answer is that I just loved working on this problem and I was obsessed. I enjoyed pitting my wits against it."[13] Our waking life is characterized by our goals (both short- and long-term, both trivial and profound) and their pursuit. What we choose to do, and what we persist in doing depends on what we wish to accomplish. The jobs that we take, the friends that we make, the money that we spend, the responsibilities that we carry, the hardships that we endure: these are the means that lead to some goal that we value and wish to pursue. Life, however, is messy, hard, and insensitive to our own wishes. Our relentless pursuit of our goals and personal projects inevitably runs into difficulties. Frustration is the emotion that we experience when we reach one of life's many stumbling blocks.

The stumbling blocks that yield frustration aren't to be ignored. Indeed, it's because we can't acquire something that we value that we feel frustrated. In other words, what lies on the other side of frustration is important to us. And the more we insist on trying to fulfill our frustrated desires, the more value we ascribe to their objects. The only way that Wiles could overcome a challenge as great and frustrating as Fermat's Last Theorem was to give it pride of place in his life and to let it frustrate him. The frustration of Fermat's Last Theorem defined Wiles's life and kept him motivated in his pursuit for a proof. "This was my childhood passion," Wiles says of Fermat's Last Theorem.[14] "There's nothing to replace that. I've solved it. I'll try other problems, I'm sure. Some of them will be very hard and I'll have a sense of achievement again, but there's no other problem in mathematics that could hold me the way Fermat did."[15]

In 1958, the American author Arthur Porges wrote a short fictional story about Fermat's Last Theorem. In it, the mathematician Simon Flagg summons the devil and proposes a Faustian deal. Flagg would pose a question and the devil has twenty-four hours to answer it. If the devil succeeds, then Flagg's soul belongs to the devil; if the devil fails, then Flagg would receive any sum of money within reason and health and happiness for as long as he lives. The devil agrees to the deal, and Flagg asks him his question: "Is Fermat's Last Theorem correct?" The devil disappears. He travels the universe in an attempt to collect enough mathematical knowledge to answer the question.

When his time is up, the devil diligently returns. Porges describes the devil's return as follows:

> There was a hiss. Rosy clouds mushroomed sulphurously. The devil stood before them, steaming noisomely on the rug. His shoulders sagged; his eyes were bloodshot; and a taloned paw, still clutching a sheaf of papers, shook violently from fatigue or nerves.
>
> Silently, with a kind of seething dignity, he flung the papers to the floor, where he trampled them viciously with his cloven hoofs. Gradually then, his tense figure relaxed, and a wry smile twisted his mouth.

"You win, Simon," he said, almost in a whisper, eyeing him with ungrudging respect. "Not even I can learn enough mathematics in such a short time for so difficult a problem. The more I got into it, the worse it became. . . . Do you know," he confided, "not even the best mathematicians on other planets—all far ahead of yours—have solved it? Why, there's a chap on Saturn—he looks something like a mushroom on stilts—who solves partial differential equations mentally; and even he's given up." The devil sighed. "Farewell." He dislimned with a kind of weary precision.[16]

What's wonderfully telling about this story isn't the devil's defeat—as Porges elsewhere reveals, the devil was never a fan of mathematics—but what occurs after the devil admits defeat. Shortly after he bids farewell to Flagg, the devil returns.

"I forgot," he mumbled. "I need to-ah!" He stooped for the scattered papers, gathering and smoothing them tenderly. "It certainly gets you," he said, avoiding Simon's gaze. "Impossible to stop just now. Why, if I could only prove one simple little lemma."[17]

The devil, turns out, can't give up on Fermat's Last Theorem, for not even the devil is immune to frustration's hold.

Wiles couldn't have done it without frustration. If he weren't frustrated by the theorem, he wouldn't have been captivated by it. And if he weren't captivated by the theorem, he wouldn't have tried so hard to prove it. Wiles, however, didn't passively surround to frustration. He instead found a way to utilize it. In a press conference at the Heidelberg Laureate Forum in September 2016, Wiles spoke about the experience of being stuck and how to deal with it.

Now what you have to handle when you start doing mathematics as an older child or as an adult is accepting this state of being stuck. People don't get used to that. Some people find this very stressful. Even people who are very good at mathematics sometimes find this hard to get used to and they feel that's where they're failing. But it isn't: it's part of the process and you have to accept [and] learn to enjoy that process. Yes, you don't understand [something at the moment] but you have faith that over time you will understand—you have to go through this.[18]

The aversive but motivating character of frustration helps us to continue our struggle, to overcome even our hardest difficulties.

• • •

There are more victories of frustration.

British author and behavioral economist Tim Harford tells the story of how frustration led to the performance of a lifetime.[19] On January 24, 1975, American pianist Keith Jarrett was preparing to play a concert at the Opera House in Cologne (Köln), Germany. This ought to have been an unremarkable concert, a performance like many others. But it wasn't. "Köln was different," Jarrett recalls, "there were just so many negative things in a row."[20]

Jarrett was exhausted—he arrived late in the afternoon after a long drive from Zurich; he hadn't slept in days and suffered from terrible back pain. In turn, the concert was organized by an inexperienced seventeen-year-old German girl named Vera Brandes and was scheduled to begin close to midnight; Jarrett would walk on stage only after the conclusion of an evening opera performance. Above all, Jarrett was presented with an unplayable piano. He had previously specified that he'd need a Bösendorfer 290 Imperial piano for the occasion—a grand concert piano with ninety-seven keys, the "Rolls-Royce of pianos."[21] Shortly before his performance, Jarrett was shown his piano. It was indeed a Bösendorfer but the wrong one. The piano that they've arranged for him was smaller than the requested one. It sounded "tinny and thin in the outer registers."[22] It was also in poor condition: as Brandes, the concert organizer, recalls, it "was completely out of tune, the black notes in the middle didn't work, the pedal stuck. It was unplayable."[23] Brandes tried to find a replacement piano but she couldn't. It was too late. Jarrett was stuck with a subpar piano. He didn't want to perform but Brandes begged him. The concert was sold out, she told him—1,400 people were eagerly waiting for his performance. Jarrett begrudgingly and reluctantly agreed.

The performance was recorded—although, according to Jarrett, "it might never have been recorded, because of everything being wrong."[24] The following year it was released as an album, *The Köln Concert*. It's the best-selling solo album in jazz history and the all-time best-selling piano album. The first reaction that it elicited from the audience isn't roaring applause but mild laughter—Jarrett began his performance by quoting the melody of the opera house's intermission bell. Laughter, however, quickly gave way to silence and awe, and what followed was a masterpiece in improvisation. Jarrett didn't give in to the limitations of the piano, nor did he try to play on an unplayable piano as if he was playing on a grand piano suitable for the occasion. He instead exploited the piano's limitations to create a piece that could only be performed on such an instrument. He focused on the middle registers. He compensated for the weak bass with the use of repetitive riffs. Instead of rolling out chord sequences, as it was customary for solo jazz performances, his performance developed around the repetition of hooks. He would improvise on one or two chords for extended periods of time. The result is a brilliantly improvised and mesmerizing performance. It's also sonically reassuring—Jarrett's reliance on the middle registers of the piano, gave the performance a tonic consistency and an organic feeling.

It's clear that such a performance was possible only because of the adversities that Jarrett faced. As Jarrett's producer and friend, Manfred Eicher later said, "[p]robably he played it the way he did because it was not a good piano. Because he could not fall in love with it he found another way to get the most out of it."[25] And Tim Harford, in his presentation of Jarrett's performance, writes: "Jarrett didn't produce a good concert in trying times. He produced the performance of a lifetime, but the shortcomings of the piano actually helped him."[26] Such a description, however, is only half of the story. The performance didn't happen the way it did just because of a subpar piano. Other musicians couldn't have done what Jarrett did. The performance was made possible because of Jarrett's tremendous skills and improvising ability. But the performance also owes its existence and character to Jarrett's emotional reaction to adversity. He didn't acquiesce to the fact that his piano was subpar. He didn't accept that he would have to perform badly. Nor did he resign from the task—he could have walked away, and no one would have blamed him. He instead persisted. Jarrett's behavior wasn't driven by apathy, sadness, resentment, or resignation. It was driven by frustration and a desire to succeed.

The creative power of Jarrett's and others' frustration hasn't gone unnoticed. In his work on the nature of creative process, psychologist D. David Sapp has developed a model of creative process that includes frustration as a necessary part. Sapp's model proceeds from the realization that most of the time creative endeavors don't flow smoothly. Just think of your last creative activity—writing a book, devising an experiment, composing a song or poem, coming up with a new algorithm or website design, or drawing a sketch. Our creative activities often come in fits and starts and are punctuated by moments of stagnation. There will be points at which we feel stuck, at which we don't know how to proceed, and at which important decisions must be made. "The scientist, artist or writer has traveled his or her familiar road of idea development up to a point where he or she meets with the limit of his or her knowledge or expressive repertoire."[27] It's at these frustrating moments that creativity unfolds, according to Sapp. "The individual confronts a conceptual/expressive boundary and is thwarted or frustrated by the boundary.... This moment in the creative process is perhaps the most significant.... It is at this moment that crucial decisions are made that will directly affect the outcome of the potential concept or product."[28]

Frustration, according to Sapp, is thus instrumental in letting us break through conceptual and expressive boundaries. It helps us to create something new and to explore previously uncharted outcomes and possibilities. Due to its motivational power, it counteracts stagnation and motivates progress. Jarrett didn't perceive his frustration at a subpar piano as the end of his night, nor as a detriment to his performance. He saw it as an opportunity to try something new. And he succeeded.

• • •

"Hurry up the machine. I have struck a big bonanza," Thomas Edison wrote to the electrical machine manufacturer William Wallace on September 13, 1878, asking for one of Wallace's electric generators.[29] Three days later, he was quoted in a *New York Sun* article boasting: "I have it now! . . . singularly enough, I have obtained it through an entirely different process than that from which scientific men have ever sought to secure it."[30] What Edison thought he had, he didn't. He will have it, eventually, more than a year later, and only after a most painful process of trial and error.

On September 8, 1878, Edison visited Wallace's workshop in Ansonia, Connecticut. Wallace had been experimenting with electricity for almost a decade and had succeeded in building a dynamo in 1874. A couple of months before Edison's visit, he had also developed an arc lighting system and produced a powerful electric motor generator. During his visit, Edison witnessed first-hand how electricity could be converted into light. The lighting system that was at display in Wallace's workshop was a modification of the carbon arc lighting that was first demonstrated in the beginning of the nineteenth century by the British chemist and inventor Humphry Davy. It consisted of an electromagnetic regulator holding two carbon plates (electrodes) at a short distance apart. When a strong current was applied to the system, the gap between the two carbon plates was bridged by the current, which would give rise to a blindingly bright light shaped in the form of an arc. Impressive as they were in converting electricity into light, arc lighting systems were plagued by many practical difficulties, chief among them was the fact that light emanating from such systems was too bright to have any kind of home application.

The shortcomings of the arc lighting system were of no importance to Edison—he had little interest in developing carbon arc lighting systems. His sights were set instead on creating an entirely different kind of lighting system—one that produces light by sending current through an incandescent material and which could be used to illuminate small spaces such as offices and homes. Edison's vision was, in fact, much more grandiose than the invention of the incandescent light bulb. He wanted to achieve the "subdivision of electric lights":[31] to manufacture a way to power numerous lights all at once; to illuminate, as he ostentatiously told the press, lower Manhattan. "I can produce a thousand—aye, ten thousand—from one machine. Indeed, the number may be said to be infinite. When the brilliancy and cheapness of the lights are made known to the public—which will be in a few weeks, or just as soon as I can thoroughly protect the process—illumination by carbureted hydrogen gas will be discarded."[32]

Edison's pronouncements turned out to be prescient. At the time of their making, however, they were baseless. Edison was no further along than scores of inventors who before him have tried but failed to create a practical incandescent light. One of the hardest challenges that inventors struggled to overcome was the discovery of the right material for the incandescent element of the lamp (the "filament"). The material needed to be such that it would neither oxidize nor melt at a temperature that would be sufficiently high to cause incandescence. Without a solution to this issue, Edison was forced to try numerous different—sometimes overly complicated and futile—approaches. As it becomes evident from the activities at his laboratory in Menlo Park, Edison worked frantically in a desperate search for a solution for over a year.

His struggles would come to an end in October 1879, when he, along with his colleagues, would finally devise a working incandescent light. Edison found that electric energy could be converted into usable light if the lamp was of high resistance, electricity was sent through carbonized material (such as sewing thread or paper), and the material was enclosed in a near-vacuum bulb. What's remarkable about the story of Edison's success isn't the fact that he was the first to dream up the idea of an incandescent light—Arthur A. Bright in *The Electric Lamp Industry* mentions over twenty other inventors who were trying to develop a practical incandescent electric light.[33] Nor is it the fact that he was the first to think of enclosing the incandescent material in a vacuum—earlier attempts to create incandescent lights tried to prevent the oxidization of the glowing element by enclosing it in vacuum. Nor is it even the fact that he was a pioneer in using carbon as the material for the filament—many had tried doing so before, and Moses G. Farmer, in a letter to Edison dated October, 1878, wrote that carbon "is the most promising" candidate.[34] What set Edison apart from other inventors also working on materializing such a lighting system were his perseverance and determination to succeed.

In their book, *Edison's Electric Light*, which details Edison's discovery, historians Robert Friedel, Paul Israel, and Bernard S. Finn ask the question: "Did Edison invent the incandescent electric lamp?" They answer: "He undoubtedly learned something from others, but he stood alone in his appreciation of the essential requirements, set his goals accordingly, overcame many obstacles that stalled his rivals, and developed not only a practical lamp but the associated components, such as improved generators and other hardware, that made a large-scale lighting system possible."[35] For Edison each failure was a small success. Each discarded method, material, or technique was the opening up of a potentially successful way forward. "The electric light has caused me the greatest amount of study and has required the most elaborate experiments. I was never myself discouraged, or inclined to be hopeless of success."[36] Edison's attitude is a model for how to utilize frustration's raw force.

●●●

Health and happiness, meaningful and sometimes passionate relationships, successful and fulfilling careers, education, a good reputation, moral distinction, recognition, fame, power, material possessions—not everyone wants everything on this list. Not everyone wants what's on this list to the same extent. All the same, the pursuit of such goods demands our unwavering dedication and their attainment, if and when it happens, is the result of a stupendous and continuous amount of effort. However one comes to conceive of one's goals and values, it's almost certain that the things that we value the most in life are either difficult to achieve or difficult to sustain.

The things that we value the most are difficult for a simple reason: they're excellent. And excellence, experience teaches us, doesn't come cheaply or easily. But are some things perceived as excellent or valuable just because they're difficult? Does effort invest value in our pursuits and goals? If it does, then emotional states that signify effort such as frustration will be instrumental in affording meaning to our lives.

It's a stubborn marketing legend that when they were first introduced, instant cake mixes were unsuccessful in attracting consumers because they made baking all too easy. The ease by which one could make a cake using the mix had the unintended consequence of excluding the consumer, primarily housewives, from the creative process. Baking the cake required neither skill nor effort, and as a result, consumers stopped buying the mix. If effortlessness was the problem, the solution was easy. And, indeed, manufactures found it. The mixes stopped including dried eggs and so consumers would have to add fresh eggs. Lo and behold, cake mixes (in their slightly more complex version) were a hit. Or so the legend goes.

The legend, as just told, is widespread—I read about it in magazines, blog posts, books, even in academic papers—but it isn't entirely true. The part about effort is true; the rest, not so much. It's false that the initial sales of instant cake mixes were disappointing—yes, the sales of instant cake mixes did flatten for a time, but that was years after their introduction to the market. It's false that manufactures only started considering requiring the addition of fresh eggs once they realized that the sales of the mixes didn't meet their expectations. And it's false that the decision (that only some companies took) to switch from a complete mix to one that required the addition of fresh eggs saved the industry. As culinary historian Laura Shapiro argues in her book *Something from the Oven: Reinventing Dinner in 1950s America,* the innovation that revitalized the market wasn't the no-dried-eggs mix but a profound reconceptualization of the very idea of cake.[37] According to this reconceptualization, the creation of a plain layer cake wasn't the end product but merely the first step in the creation of a cake. Starting in the 1950s, cakes were seen as culinary creations that were incomplete in the absence of icing and elaborate, in some cases, decorations. Cakes became more effortful because they became more than an eatable base. As a result, convenience was sacrificed but creativity was regained. American housewives could feel good about making cakes again because although they were using instant cake mixes, they were still required to expend energy in creating their culinary creation. It was effort, and partly the frustration involved in decorating a cake, that saved the instant cake mix. But does this finding generalize? Can effort, along with the negative emotions and sensations associated with it, really influence our preferences?

It's one of the few undeniable facts of life that assembling IKEA furniture is frustrating. Unlike putting together a LEGO creation, IKEA assembly isn't an activity of leisure. It's done out of necessity, and there are stakes involved—if we don't get it right, we might not have a bed to sleep in. We depend on a wordless instruction manual filled with enigmatic pictograms that feature an infuriating genderless cartoon figure who, unlike most of us, can seemingly build anything—a MALM (a bed frame), a SEKTION (a cabinet unit), even the famous and ubiquitous BILLY (bookshelf). We use tools that just don't seem to be up to the job. The screws lose their grip and come undone. The wood, or better the particleboard, breaks and chips easily. A 2006 article in *The Economist* begins with the line: "Few tasks are more exasperating than trying to assemble at-pack furniture from IKEA."[38] The title of a *Buzzfeed* article reads: "Why Building Ikea Furniture Is Probably Satan's Favorite Hobby."[39] Clinical psychologists and family therapists have studied the mostly adverse effects that assembling IKEA furniture has on relationships.[40] Putting together IKEA furniture is hard, stressful, and frustrating. Even IKEA itself can't deny that. In an attempt to ameliorate frustration, they recently partnered up with TaskRabbit, and you can now pay someone else to put together your furniture.

Researchers at the Nanyang Technological University in Singapore have taken a step further: they have created a robot that can read IKEA instructions and build a STEFAN chair.[41] The comedian Amy Poehler joked that "IKEA" is Swedish for "argument."[42] The joke works for "frustration" too.

The presence of frustration while dealing with IKEA furniture assembly is no mystery. We become frustrated because our goal (to create a finished product) is blocked, either temporally or permanently, by the materials at hand, poor instructions, inappropriate tools, or lack of skills. Frustration, as I argued in the previous chapter, can keep us motivated and can provide us with the vitality needed to finish the job. But there's more to frustration than motivation. It makes our labor and its fruits appear to be more valuable.

Harvard Business School professor Michael I. Norton, Tulane University professor of marketing Daniel Mochon, and Duke University psychologist and behavioral economist Dan Ariely devised an experiment in which fifty-two participants were randomly divided into two conditions.[43] In the first condition, participants were asked to assemble a plain black IKEA storage box. In the second condition, participants were given the box fully assembled and they were allowed to inspect it for some time. After the initial phase of the experiment (either building or inspecting the box), the researchers asked participants to make a bid on the box, that is, to say how much they would be willing to pay to take home the box. The participants were informed that at the end of the experiment the researchers would draw a random price and if their bid was equal or above that price, then they would have to pay the researchers the amount of their bid and they'd take the box home. If their bid was lower than the drawn price, they wouldn't purchase the box. What the researchers found was that participants who built the box themselves bid significantly higher for their box than nonbuilders. "[T]hose who assembled their own box were willing to pay a 63% premium compared to those who were given the chance to buy an identical preassembled box."[44]

Suppose that your employer is offering you a choice. For the same position that you're occupying right now, you can choose between two different work schedules. You can work full time (9 AM–5 PM) and make $50,000 per year or work part time (12 PM–5 PM) and make $40,000 per year. In trying to figure out which schedule to take, you will weigh various considerations. Whatever those may be, ultimately, you will have to decide whether the additional effort and frustration involved in working full time makes up for the pay difference. Full time is better in terms of monetary compensation, but it's worse in terms of effort. What such a calculation shows is that when we typically make decisions about costs and benefits, we consider effort as a cost. The effort that the IKEA builders put into assembling the box should detract from the final value of the box.

Effort also carries a biological cost.[45] Tasks that demand effort typically lead to an increase in blood pressure, ventilation, and sweating. When we exert effort the corrugator supercilii contracts. This is a small muscle close to the eye that draws the eyebrow down and leads to the appearance of frowning. The contraction of the corrugator is a reliable indication and expression of negative feelings. Additionally, when asked about their experiences, individuals performing effortful tasks routinely report feelings of anxiety, stress, fatigue, and frustration. There's even neurological evidence that suggests that the brain perceives effort as an aversive condition.

The aforementioned considerations suggest that the builders in the IKEA experiment have committed a mistake. Given that they already exerted effort in assembling the box, their effort should have been counted as a cost. Consequently, they should have bid lower, not higher, than nonbuilders—both groups of individuals, after all, were bidding for an identical piece of furniture. But what appears to be both an economic fallacy and a move that ignores biology turns out to be a commonplace phenomenon. We often take effort as a sign of value and not as a cost. Reports of experiments that demonstrate this phenomenon abound in the literature. A person who works hard to gain entry into a social group will like the group more than a different person who didn't experience any hardship to acquire membership.[46] Individuals are more willing to contribute to a charitable cause when the fundraising process is thought to be effortful than easy and enjoyable.[47] Indeed, researchers found that a charitable organization whose fundraising process involves a five-mile run would be more successful in soliciting donations than one whose fundraising process involves attending a pleasant picnic.[48] In a different study, participants listened to a selection from four records and were asked to rank them in terms of their preferences. They were told that the next day they would receive a complimentary record, either one that was randomly chosen for them or one selected by them. When they returned to pick up their complimentary record, half of them were told that their third-ranked record wasn't available and were asked to rate again the records. The researchers found that the attractiveness of the third record increased when it was no longer a possibility. The frustration of not being able to have it made the record more attractive.[49] Finally, in a series of studies in which access to food was made more difficult by the addition of a barrier, it was found that items that required more effort were selected more frequently than those which were easier to reach.[50] What such findings show is that we readily associate effort with value.

There's a breaking point, of course. We're willing to exert effort up to a point. After that, the positive correlation between effort and value no longer holds. Indeed, too much frustration might cause us to give up on the pursuit of a goal.[51] For cases, however, that the required effort isn't out of question, working hard to achieve a goal doesn't discount the goal; it makes it all the more valuable. Such a conclusion might seem obvious. We know that people value effortful activities. If they didn't, then what would explain the popularity of marathons, crossword puzzles, and Sudoku? But as the IKEA experiment shows, the relationship between effort and value isn't found only in cases where the exerted effort is seen as enjoyable—after all, there's such a thing called "runners' high" and people like the challenge of a difficult crossword puzzle or Sudoku. There's nothing pleasurable, however, in putting together an IKEA box. The product isn't unique, nor does it bear our mark. All the same, our effort and frustration add value to it. The DIY mentality of IKEA doesn't only help to keep costs down for the company, it also contributes to one's attachment to the furniture.

• • •

A structure of a truly nonhuman scale rises out of the Baltoro Glacier in the heart of the majestic Karakoram Range in northern Pakistan. K2 is a pyramid-shaped mountain of black rock, snow gullies, and hanging glaciers. It's sublime and symmetric—"the most beautiful of all the high peaks," according to Italian mountaineer Reinhold Messner, who climbed it in 1979.[52] It scrapes the sky at 8,611 meters (28,251 feet) and, in terms of height, yields only to Everest. But it's deadlier. The weather is worse, colder, and notoriously mercurial, and the ascent is much more technically demanding. As a result, around three hundred people have summited K2 as opposed to more than eight thousand who have reached the top of Everest.[53] No one has yet successfully reached its summit in the winter. For every one hundred safe returns, the mountain claims twenty-nine lives.[54]

Perhaps to shield us from the dangers that it holds, nature hid it from us. Because of its location in the heart of the Karakoram Range, K2 is guarded on all sides by other mountains. It was the Great Trigonometrical Survey, the massive undertaking by the British to measure the entire Indian subcontinent, that put K2 on Western maps. In 1856, Lieutenant T. G. Montgomerie dragged his equipment to an altitude of sixteen thousand feet on Mount Haramukh (or Harmukh) in the Ganderbal district of Jammu and Kashmir. From there, he was able to peak at Karakoram Range and labeled the two most prominent mountaintops "K1" and "K2."[55] Short, mysterious, and bleak, the name "K2"proved to be remarkably apposite. As Italian photographer, writer, mountaineer and academic Fosco Maraini writes, it's "sibylline, magical with a slight touch of fantasy . . . just the bare bones of a name, all rock and ice and storm and abyss. It makes no attempt to sound human. It is atoms and stars."[56]

Why then do people attempt to climb mountains such as K2? This is the question that George Loewenstein, professor of economics and psychology at Carnegie Mellon University, asks in an essay aimed to understand the motives of mountaineers. "This question," Loewenstein writes, "preoccupies many climbers, particularly in times of hardship. The answer to the why question constitutes a—perhaps *the*—central theme in the climbing literature."[57] Loewenstein is right, and the "why" question has been asked before, many times indeed. In 1923, it received its most famous and enigmatic answer. When famed British mountaineer George Mallory was asked, "Why did you want to climb Mount Everest?" he retorted with only four words: "Because it is there." [58]

Mallory's answer is more informative than it initially appears. But before we can get closer to understanding the motives of mountaineers, we must exclude what obviously are the wrong answers to the why question. Serious mountaineers, those who attempt to climb K2, Everest, Annapurna, and other alluring and dangerous summits don't do it for the money—trying to climb one of these mountains takes thousands of dollars and years in preparation and yields no monetary return. They don't do it for fame or recognition—at least not any more. Who among us knows the three hundredth climber of K2? And who would recognize them on the street? They clearly don't do it because it's fun or easy. "Serious mountaineering," Loewenstein notes, "tends to be one unrelenting misery from beginning to end."[59] There's terror and fear, exhaustion, physical pain, and sleeplessness. There's relentless cold, which may lead either to frostbite and the loss of extremities (fingers, toes, ears, and noses) or, worse, to death by hypothermia. There's extreme hunger and thirst. And there's acute altitude sickness that occurs at over eight thousand meters that can cause the lethal swelling of the brain or the filling of the lungs with fluid.

The answer to the why question can't be found in some tangible, universally agreed-upon good. When Mallory said that he wanted to climb Everest "because it is there," the "it" did refer to Everest but not just to that. "Everest is the highest mountain in the world and no man has reached its summit," he added.[60] Everest is the objective manifestation of a subjective challenge, and Mallory wanted to climb Everest because of the challenge that it posed. As political theorist Paul Sagar writes in his discussion of mountaineering, "[f]or most climbers, if there's something to be conquered, it's not so much the summit as some aspect of themselves. Fear and physical pain are the things to be overcome; routes and ascents are proxies for challenging oneself, not the terrain."[61] The conquering of a summit is a double win. It's the overcoming of both a physical and psychological challenge. But it's the psychological challenge that gives the physical challenge a value. If climbing the Everest or K2 was something easy, it wouldn't become the dream of so many. It's the profound difficulty of such assents that gives them value. Indeed, the more challenging the better. In an interview in the *New York Times*, the Polish mountaineer Janusz Golab was asked why he and his team wanted to attempt to climb K2 in the winter. "It's more challenging," he said, adding, "It's obvious. It's the best."[62] And Andrew W. Lock, the first Australian and the eighteenth person in the world to have climbed all fourteen of the world's eight thousand-meter mountaintops, repeats the sentiment: "For me the adventures in the outdoors have always been about taking on challenges where the outcome is uncertain. Because if it's guaranteed then for me there's no point in doing it."[63]

Difficult challenges carry with them, in addition to all sorts of physical and bodily harms and risks, a vast array of predominantly negative emotions and sensations. They're painful, exhausting, frustrating, miserable, and terrifying. But it's because of the negative psychological reactions that they elicit in us that they render our activities meaningful. It's out of these challenging emotions and sensations that value is often born. Not only do such emotions signal importance; they often create it. Take the challenge away, and the value would be removed. Bring it back and the value returns.

• • •

Frustration, it was shown in the previous chapter, is a great motivator. It energizes us. It pushes us to complete what frustrates us, to overcome the obstacles of life. Through the stories of this chapter, an additional characteristic of frustration surfaced. We found an important and double relationship between frustration and value. Because what frustrates us is something that matters to us, our frustrations are indications of values. They emerge only when goals that are important to us are blocked. At the same time, the experience of frustration itself can lead to the generation of value. What's frustrating, difficult, and effortful, can become valuable precisely because it's frustrating, difficult, and effortful.

If these features of frustration weren't enough to make it important, there's more to it. Frustration is necessary for pleasure and satisfaction. We need frustration, for without it we'd take no pleasure and satisfaction in our accomplishments. Indeed, frustration safeguards us from dullness and insipid satiation. A world in which all of our wishes are instantly and completely gratified would be a world without much meaning or value. In some ways, it would render our existence inhuman. To have everything, immediately and completely, would be unbearably easy and banal. If everything isn't just possible but doable without effort, then we deserve no praise for our accomplishments. To call such lives "ours" will be to bestow on them a title that's only honorific. "What an effort to keep alive! Erecting a monument does not require the expenditure of so much strength,"[64] writes Franz Kafka in a diary entry. Life is hard and frustrating. Because of that, it's one that's worth having.

Frustration also keeps our desires going and paves our future. To have a desire is to be cognizant of a need or a lack. A life devoid of frustrations will then be a life filled with expired desires, ones that fail to move us, and we would find ourselves without dreams and future plans. What's there to look forward to when you already have it all? In his essay on frustration, psychoanalyst Adam Phillips touches briefly upon this point. "[T]he quest for satisfaction begins and ends with a frustration," he writes, "it is prompted by frustration, by the dawning of need, and it ends with the frustration of never getting exactly what one wanted. How could we ever be anything other than permanently enraged?"[65]

• • •

It's time to take stock. Frustration is a sign of personal value—it indicates when important goals are blocked. Frustration is the creator of value—without it, our accomplishments run the risk of becoming insignificant. And frustration is a prompt for success—it animates us and permits us to persist in our efforts. The experience of frustration is the unavoidable consequence of living a life worth living—a life filled with projects and goals, suffused with desires and self-defining dreams; a difficult one, but a life of one's own. It should be clear that frustration isn't a sign of a failure. Rather, it's the experience of a setback: the realization that the road ahead is blocked. Importantly, however, frustration isn't just an indication of being stuck; it's also a call for action.

8

"Our possible existence is always greater than our destiny"

"Do you believe in the life to come?" asks Clov. "Mine was always that," Hamm replies.[1]

Twenty-seven years before the celebrated Irish novelist, playwright, and poet Samuel Beckett included those lines in his one-act play, *Endgame*, he'd already sketched a view of our relationship to time. In a short study on Marcel Proust—a text more informative of his views than Proust's—he declares, with the help of mythology, our inescapable attachment to time. "We are rather in the position of Tantalus, with this difference, that we allow ourselves to be tantalised."[2] Like Tantalus, human beings are constantly and forever tormented by time, "that double-headed monster of damnation and salvation."[3] Unlike Tantalus, the tantalizing itself bears our responsibility—we allow ourselves, somehow, to be taunted by time.

In Book XI of *The Odyssey*, Odysseus finds Tantalus in Tartarus—an abyss in the deepest part of the Underworld, located "as far below Hades as heaven lies above the earth"[4]; a place reserved for the punishment and suffering of the wicked. Standing in a pool of water, Tantalus is thirsty: the water recedes every time he attempts to drink from it. Standing underneath trees heavy with pears, pomegranates, apples, and figs, he is famished: the wind moves the fruits out of his reach whenever he attempts to clutch them. Homer doesn't mention Tantalus's transgressions, just his punishment. Other sources, however, do. And according to some, his punishment doesn't seem all that improper. He cut up, boiled, and offered his son Pelops as a meal to the gods.

If Tantalus's torment is grounded in his grave wrongdoing, then why are we being tantalized by time? Beckett offers no explicit reason. For him, life is a constant pendulum oscillating between the dullness of a protective and hygienic habit and a reality-revealing but unbearable suffering. Worse: life, as this is portrayed in many of Beckett's plays is a mixture of both—a tedious suffering that takes the form of waiting. Beckett's characters wait for hope, change, Godot (in *Waiting for Godot*); for medicine, the night, and the end

Propelled. Andreas Elpidorou, Oxford University Press (2020). © Andreas Elpidorou.
DOI: 10.1093/oso/9780190912963.001.0001

(in *Endgame*); for a train to come (*All That Fall*); for the bell to ring or for death to come (in *Happy Days*). In such a protracted state of waiting, time becomes suspended, impersonal, and ultimately meaningless. "What time is it?" Hamm asks in *Endgame*. "The same as usual," Clov responds.

Beckett's characters often have nothing but their waiting—their lives are devoid of any other purpose. In *Waiting for Godot*, Vladimir and Estragon play games, exercise, engage in meaningless conversation, try on boots and hats, tell stories, contradict each other, and even contemplate suicide—all to pass time, all because they have to wait. They wait, but Godot never arrives. In *Endgame,* the night or end never comes. In *Happy Days*, Winnie asymptotically approaches, but never reaches, her ending. If that's not enough, Beckett's characters have, somehow, lost their past. Vladimir and Estragon can't even establish what they did yesterday. Their memory fails them. They're incapable of reconstructing their past and of claiming a sense of identity. Hamm is disconnected from his past so much so that his parents are confined in bins. Winnie's lost past is portrayed by her continuous immersion into the ground. And Krapp, in *Krapp's Last Tape*, commits to audio events from every year but forgets what his own words signify. Beckett is unkind to his characters. He's given them neither a future nor a past—only the faintest glimpse of both.

Beckett's conception of life is bleak. I don't recommend its adoption. Still, there's a kernel of truth to it. Life is a waiting but not necessarily the one imagined by Beckett. We're always waiting for something to happen. Felt time, as French philosopher and poet Jean-Marie Guyau reminds us in *La genèse de l'idée de temps*, is "fundamentally nothing but the conscious interval between a need and its fulfillment."[5] We're waiting for work to finish, for the night to fall, for a paycheck to reach us, for a visit to show up, for our vacation to start, for the doctor to see us, for the winter to descend upon us, for a child to be born, for elections to be won, for the war to conclude, for death to come, for life to be over. There are painful waitings, joyful waitings, and waitings with affective colorations that span the whole gamut between ecstasy and misery. The fact that we're always anticipating and expecting isn't accidental. It's a defining characteristic of human life. To understand what human life is, we need to take seriously the fact that we're necessarily orientated toward the future.

•••

It used to be part of scientific orthodoxy that our brain is, more or less, passive. Although sensitive to and responsive to incoming stimulation, its activity was externally driven. The brain would passively receive waves of signals impinging our sensory systems and attempt to make sense of them by searching for and retrieving meaningful and recognizable patterns—an edge, a face, a house, a lion. The brain was given an arduous task. It had to find meaningful needles in haystacks of electrical noise, to reconstruct the world, on its own, from the bottom up.

Research in the past few decades has led to a revision of the brain's working. We know now that neurons are firing constantly.[6] Our brain is permanently on and endogenous activity is strong regardless of external stimulation. Indeed, during moments of wakeful rest, it has been noticed that there's activity in a network of brain regions that are involved in memory and imagination.[7] More important, our brain constantly engenders predictions (millions of them) of what we will encounter next. It's on account of these predictions that we come to experience the world. Our brain isn't reactive. It's a predictive machine—constantly anticipating the future, generating hypotheses of how things might come to be. We don't passively perceive the world; we instead create it (some say "model it") in virtue of our expectations, past experiences, and present context.[8]

The predictions are unconscious, quick, and short-term, as when the brain generates a prediction of the next sensory stimuli or forecasts the meaning of a continuous stream of sound by breaking it into phonemes, syllables, and words. They can also be conscious and sophisticated, as when one anticipates returning home to a grumpy partner and prepares to act and speak accordingly. It's not hard to find vivid illustrations of how our expectations affect our perception of the world. A well-known example is reproduced in Figure 8.1. If this is your first encounter with the image, you might find it difficult to see anything but a pattern of light and dark patches. Once you discover, however, that this is a picture of a cow, knowledge of the presence of the cow changes how you subsequently perceive the picture. An even more telling demonstration is found in the perception of sine-wave speech. Sine-wave speech is an artificially degraded form of natural speech. It's been synthetically manipulated so that energy maxima are replaced by simple sine waves.[9] The resulting speech is devoid of most normal speech attributes but still retains the temporal qualities of the original. When first exposed to sine-wave speech, individuals can't hear it as language—sine-wave speech sounds like noise, electronic beeps and bops. All the same, it's easy to get our brain to hear the sound as speech again. If one listens to the original audio clip and then revisits the sine-wave clip, the sine-wave speech no longer sounds like noise. Our brain is expecting to find meaning in what was previously heard as noise and it does. The change in perception is remarkable.*

* Try it for yourself: http://www.lifesci.sussex.ac.uk/home/Chris_Darwin/SWS/ or http://www.mrc-cbu.cam.ac.uk/people/matt.davis/sine-wave-speech/

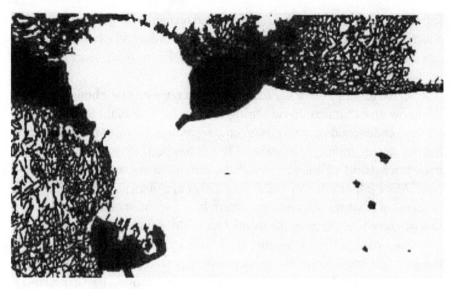

Figure 8.1 Cow illusion.
© John McCrone / Wikimedia Commons / CC-BY-SA-3.0.

Prediction is necessary. Without anticipating what's to come, our actions would always be delayed because of the noninstantaneous nature of neural processing. When it comes to vision, for example, it takes about 200 milliseconds for information to travel from our eyes to the visual cortex.[10] Without generating predictions, we'd be incapable of meeting the demands of a changing and fast-moving world. As philosopher and cognitive scientist Andy Clark writes in his meticulous synthesis of scientific findings in support of the predictive brain, "[t]o deal rapidly and fluently with an uncertain and noisy world, brains like ours have become masters of prediction."[11] Indeed, sports wouldn't exist, at least not as we know them, if we were endowed with a purely reactive brain. Our brain wouldn't be fast enough to decipher what's going on around us and at the same time guide us successfully to catch a fast moving baseball or football.

The idea that the brain is a predictive machine isn't new. Its origin can be traced back to an insight first articulated by the German physician and physicist Hermann von Helmholtz in the 1860s. Helmholtz proposed that our perceptual systems are able to estimate environmental conditions by utilizing "unconscious inferences."[12] Helmholtz's insight, however, has only recently been developed into a full-fledged model of the brain.[13] The brain, it's now thought, is built to anticipate instead of passively responding to incoming stimuli. It constantly generates hypotheses about the sources and meaning of incoming sensory data and compares them to the stimuli that it receives. The best hypothesis—that is, the one that minimizes the difference between prediction and stimulus—becomes a perception. Our neural lives are characterized by an ongoing struggle to confirm the reality of our expectations.

• • •

It's not just perception that's born out of prediction; important aspects of what we call "understanding" and "intelligence" also depend on it. Take understanding. We understand by drawing connections and recognizing patterns. But many patterns are temporal in nature. We drop a vase and it shatters; we strike a match and it lights up; we take a pill and we fall asleep; we turn on our cellphone and we get reception. To be in a position to claim understanding we must be able to predict accurately how things are going to unfold. If we can't, then our understanding is lacking. Of course, some events will occur unexpectedly. My car doesn't start when I need it the most, even though it always started before. Yet to claim that we've understood the workings of my car, we need to be able to predict its malfunctions. By constantly refining our predictions, accommodating not only for observed regularities but also for exceptions, we arrive at a nuanced understanding of the workings of the world. The point isn't that we always need to be 100% accurate in our predictions. The point rather is that if we're in the dark when it comes to predicting the workings of a phenomenon, then our understanding of that phenomenon is tenuous at best.

What holds for understanding also holds for intelligence. As Jeff Hawkins and Sandra Blakeslee note in their book, *On Intelligence*, "our intelligence tests are in essence prediction tests."[14] An IQ test is basically a test on how one makes predictions. Of course, there're other kinds of intelligence, ones that elude IQ tests. Those too seem to require prediction. Proficiency in a language requires the ability to remember and generate patterns of words. Mathematical knowledge depends on one's capacity to predict relationships between mathematical objects. Social intelligence requires one's ability to predict how others are going to behave in response to one's actions and comments. Even perspicacity and acumen in engineering, architecture, design, and technology require one's ability to generate successful predictions: predictions about the market, the desires of consumers, and the uses and abuses of one's creation.

Anticipation finds its way in other aspects of human existence. Cooperation and trust are rooted in anticipation. We make and hold our promises, plot future courses of action, and come up with fair rewards, all because we can anticipate not only others' responses in a variety of situations but also our own. Competition also is anticipatory. Successful competitors—business rivals, romantic foes, or athletic opponents—benefit from the gifts of anticipation. Being in a position to form reliable expectations of others' actions and decisions grants one an advantage. The reach of anticipation even extends into the realms of religion and modern economics. Life after death, reincarnation, final judgment, and eternal damnation are all prospective notions and are predicated upon humans' ability to think about and be concerned with the future. The same is true for our faith in currency, pension plans (when they exist), investments, credit card transactions, loans, and mortgages rates.

· · ·

Footfalls echo in the memory
Down the passage which we did not take
Towards the door we never opened

—T.S. Eliot[†]

On October 4, 1992, a Boeing 747 cargo aircraft owned by Israeli airline EL AL was on a flight from John F. Kennedy Airport, New York to Ben Gurion airport in Tel Aviv. The aircraft made a stopover at Amsterdam Schiphol Airport for a crew change and cargo processing. At 6:20 PM, local time, it departed from runway O1L. Shortly after take-off, engine no. 3 and its pylon separated from the aircraft and damaged the right wing. It also struck engine no. 4, which due to the impact separated from the wing. Without two engines and with a damaged wing, the crew was forced to make an emergency landing. Unfortunately, the severity of the damage left the crew with an aircraft that couldn't be controlled. At 6:36 PM, the aircraft crashed into an eleven-floor apartment building in Bijlmermeer, a suburb of Amsterdam. It exploded in flames. Forty-three people died.[15]

Ten months after the accident, a group of Dutch researchers distributed a questionnaire about the crash to one hundred and ninety-three people.[16] One of the questions read: "Did you see the television film of the moment the plane hit the apartment building?" One hundred seven of the respondents (55%) answered affirmatively. The researchers also sent out a modified questionnaire to a different group of individuals. The second questionnaire, in addition to asking whether the respondents had seen the television film of

† Excerpt from "Burnt Norton" from FOUR QUARTERS by T.S. Eliot. Copyright © 1936 by Houghton Mifflin Harcourt Publishing Company, renewed 1964 by T.S. Eliot. Reprinted by permission of Houghton Mifflin Harcourt Publishing Company. All rights reserved.

the crash, included questions concerning specific details of the accident as captured by the film—for example, What was the angle of the plane when it crashed? Was the plane already burning when it crashed? Sixty-six percent of the respondents said that they had seen the television film of the crashing plane. Many, in fact, remembered details of the crash.

They were wrong, all of them. There was never a TV film—no TV crew captured the crash; no amateur recorded the incident. The respondents falsely claimed to have remembered seeing the film. Simply by being asked a suggestive question by the researchers, they were manipulated into believing in an event that never happened.

In a different experiment, psychologists Gary Wells and Mary Bradfield showed participants footage of a security camera from a Target store in which a man enters the store.[17] (Figure 8.2 is a still reproduction of the man in question.) The participants were told to pay particular attention to the man because moments after the scene that they will witness, the man murders a security guard. After the participants watched the footage, they were asked to identify the man from a set of photos that, however, didn't include him. Following the

Figure 8.2 Still image from footage used in the Wells and Bradfield (1998) study.
Wells, G. L., & Bradfield, A. L., "Good, you identified the suspect": Feedback to eyewitnesses distorts their reports of the witnessing experience, *Journal of Applied Psychology, 83*(3), 360–376 (1998), APA. Image reprinted with permission from the publisher.

identification task, some participants received confirming feedback ("Good, you identified the actual suspect"), some disconfirming feedback ("Actually, the suspect is number ___"), and some no feedback. Lastly, participants were assessed on how well they had been able to see the suspect and whether they were certain of their identification.

Every participant made a false identification. That isn't all that surprising. After all, the participants were given a set of photos that didn't include the suspect. They could have easily assumed that the researchers *must* have included a picture of him in the set of pictures. What was more surprising was the effect of the researchers' feedback on participants' attitudes. Participants who received confirming feedback claimed higher confidence in their judgment, more trust in their memories, and a clearer view of the suspect than individuals who either received disconfirming feedback or no feedback at all. Such confidence and faith in their judgment and memory was, of course, baseless: they were in no better position than the other participants. Still, they thought they knew more and that they've remembered better simply because the researchers offered them some confirming remarks.

Along with many other findings, the aforementioned make it clear that our memories are susceptible to manipulation by suggestion: a question or remark can make us remember events that we couldn't have remembered.[18] Doctored photographs do the trick too. When individuals were presented with a doctored photograph showing them on a hot air balloon ride (an event that never happened to them), 50% of them created complete or partial false memories. When one of the participants was told that the photograph was fake, the participant was shocked that the hot air balloon ride didn't take place. "That's amazing, 'cause I honestly started to talk myself into believing it! . . . I still feel in my head that I actually was there; I can sort of see images of it, but not distinctly, but yeah. Gosh, that's amazing!"[19]

Imagination also affects memory. Researchers, for instance, have found that individuals who have been asked to imagine a personal event that never took place (e.g., having a nurse removing a skin sample from their little finger) were four times more likely to remember it as happening to them than individuals who have not previously imagined it.[20] In another study, students at Wesleyan University went for a walk around the campus with a researcher who asked them either to perform or to imagine performing a series of usual and unusual actions at different locations (e.g., "Check the Pepsi machine for change;" "Get down on one knee and propose marriage to the machine;" "Look up a word in the dictionary;" "Pat the dictionary and ask it how it's doing").[21] When the participants were tested two weeks later, researchers found that for both usual and unusual actions the act of imagining those actions being performed led, in many cases, to the false recollection of having actually performed them.

What do such findings show? They show that false memories are neither rare occurrences nor the products of a pathological brain. Most healthy (neurotypical) adults misremember. Most of us, in fact, can't stop it from happening. Yet that's no cause for alarm. Cases of misremembering are ordinary and frequent precisely because they're the natural and proper outcome of the operation of our brain. Strange as it may initially sound, cases of misremembering aren't signs of a malfunction. They're indications of the healthy operation of human memory and, as such, a window into memory's true character.

• • •

What is memory's main function? It can't be that its primary aim is to accurately and in detail record past events. "In a world of constantly changing environment," British psychologist Frederic Bartlett wrote in 1932, "literal recall is extraordinarily unimportant."[22] Information about the past is useful only if it can help us to face the future. But the future is rarely a repetition of the past. A memory system that simply recorded and replayed events of the past would be of little use to us in our everyday lives.

Indeed, we now know that our memory system isn't a high-fidelity, high-capacity recording system. Memories aren't mental "DVDs stored away in some library of the mind."[23] Our brain doesn't set out to record every event in perfect detail. It doesn't need to, for it's given us a better way of connecting ourselves to our past. When presented with a list of words that belong to the same theme—for example, tired, bed, rest, dream, night, pillow, blanket—individuals will later claimed to have seen words that weren't on the list but which are semantically related to them (e.g., slumber). This happens because our brain constantly seeks for patterns, meaning, and significance. It ignores details and forgets noise. We need to remember only what we need to use in the future. The rest is an unnecessary burden that takes up valuable cognitive resources. "The truth is," Argentine author Jorges Luis Borges writes in a short story about a man who is unable to forget, "that we all live by leaving behind."[24]

In the introduction to his book *Pieces of Light*, psychologist Charles Fernyhough articulates the currently accepted view of memory in the following way: "Autobiographical memories are not possessions that you either have or do not have. They are mental constructions. . . . [W]hen you have a memory, you don't retrieve something that already exists, fully formed—you create something new."[25] And Harvard University professor of psychology, Daniel Schacter, who is one of the leading memory researchers, explains how memories (specifically, autobiographical semantic memories) get constructed (or reconstructed)[‡]:

> We now know that we do not record our experiences the way a camera records them. Our memories work differently. We extract key elements from our experiences and store them. We then re-create them or reconstruct our experiences rather than retrieve copies of them. Sometimes, in the process of reconstructing we add on feelings, beliefs, or even knowledge we obtained after the experience.[26]

Autobiographical memory, decades of research shows, is essentially reconstructive. As a reconstructive capacity, it will, at times, deliver results that don't perfectly track our past. Yet this is a small price to pay given what this capacity can offer us: it can prepare us for the future by allowing us to simulate events to come. Memory is thus both past- and forward-looking. Using past knowledge, it generates mental simulations of events that may or may not have happened in the past and which may or may not occur in the future. "Memory did not evolve to allow us to reminisce about the past," UCLA neurobiologist Dean Buonomano writes in his book *Your Brain Is a Time Machine: The Neuroscience and Physics of Time*. He adds, "The sole evolutionary function of memory is to allow animals to predict what will happen, when it will happen, and how to best respond when it does happen."[27]

The constructive view of autobiographical memory is well supported. There's a wealth of imaging data that shows substantial—although not complete—overlap between the neural areas activated when individuals recall the past and when they imagine the future. When we create visions of our future we activate roughly the same areas of the brain that we activate when we think of our past, and vice versa.[28] Furthermore, it's been shown that amnesic patients with damage to the hippocampus bilaterally (one of the brain structures thought to be crucial for the formation and storage of memory)

[‡] A quick taxonomy of memory, in case anyone is interested. Psychologists typically distinguish between long-term memory and short-term memory. Long-term memory is the capacity to store and recall information for an extended period of time. Short-term memory, sometimes also called "working memory," is the ability to make available for processing some relevant information for a brief period of time. Long-term memory is divided between declarative (or explicit) memory and nondeclarative (or implicit) memory. Declarative memory is the type of memory that is accessible to consciousness—we can declare what that memory is about—and its recall often requires effort. Nondeclarative memory is the type of memory that's acquired unconsciously and can be employed without thinking and effortlessly. Declarative memory is further divided into semantic memory and episodic memory: the former is knowledge of facts, whereas the latter is memory of experienced events. Autobiographical memory is memory of events that happened to us. As such, it involves both episodic memory of our past happenings and semantic memory about facts of our lives.

experience difficulty in imagining new experiences—when asked to come up with new versions of everyday experiences, they produced imaginary scenarios of less detail and which were lacking in spatial coherence.[29] But it's not just individuals with brain injuries who experience difficulties in thinking about their personal futures. Anyone with a poor autobiographical memory is in the same situation. When asked to generate past and future events, older adults come up with descriptions of events that were less detailed than younger adults.[30] The same finding is reported in people with Alzheimer's disease, schizophrenia, and even severe depression.[31] A failing memory is correlated with an impaired ability to imagine oneself in the future.

Putting all these findings together, it's clear that our capacity to remember is intimately connected to our capacity to engage in hypothetical thinking and mental time-travel. The brain, recall, is fundamentally prospective: it constantly uses information from the past and the present to engender predictions about the future. Memory is just one of its many tools. When considering our past, we anticipate.

• • •

Emotions influence our behavior. This view of emotions seems to be as much a part of commonsense as is a part of our best science of emotions. We often speak of the causes of anger, the effects of depression, or the irresistible force of jealousy. We mention our emotional states when we want to explain our behavior to others ("I'm sorry, but I was frustrated"). We cite their presence when we want to defend ourselves in a court of law ("I did it because I loved him."). Evolutionary biologists also accept this view. In fact, they demand it. If emotions were merely epiphenomenal, they'd be powerless in granting us any adaptive or evolutionary advantage. Some psychologists take the view as an established fact—"Everyone knows," American psychologist James A. Russell writes, "that fear brings flight and anger brings fight."[32] Others conceptualize emotions to include their effects in the very idea of emotions.[33] And others find support for the view in published studies. In reading a 2001 literature review, one comes across the following sentence: "The idea that emotions exert a direct and powerful influence on behavior receives ample support in the psychological literature on emotions."[34]

It's one thing to assert that emotions affect our behavior; it's another thing entirely to articulate how they do that. Consider sadness. It can promote helping.[35] But how? Does sadness cause us to help, insofar as it directly drives behavior? Or do we help to escape sadness and to make ourselves feel better? The difference between the two possible accounts might seem inconsequential. It's not. According to the first account, sadness is the *direct* cause of our behavior. According to the second, sadness affects our behavior but in a much more complex and indirect way. We first find ourselves in a sad state. We don't like it and are motivated to get out of it. We thus decide to help only because by helping, we can alleviate our feelings of sadness. The first account makes sadness look good: because of its nature, sadness promotes prosocial behavior. The second account doesn't. The goodness of sadness is merely accidental—sadness promotes helping only because it makes us feel better. Despite their differences, both accounts of the workings of sadness accommodate findings that show that sad individuals help others more than nonsad individuals. But how then do we adjudicate between them?

Psychologists Gloria K. Manucia, Donald J. Baumann, and Robert B. Cialdini came up with a truly ingenious solution to this question.[36] They invented a mood-freezing drug called "Mnemoxine" and used it in an experiment designed to test the drug's effects on the behavior of subjects who were placed in a sad mood. All of the subjects who participated in the experiment were given Mnemoxine, but only half of them were told that Mnemoxine was designed specifically to prolong whatever emotional state the subject happens to be in when they take the drug. The experimenter explained to these subjects that "[i]f . . .you are feeling sad when it [Mnemoxine] takes effect, you will continue to be sad for the next 30 minutes or so, no matter what."[37] The other half of the participants heard nothing about Mnemoxine's remarkable mood-freezing effects. They were simply told that Mnemoxine might cause temporary dryness of the mouth.

Here's the rub. Mnemoxine was a placebo—a mere 15 cc of flat tonic water given to participants in a small medication cup. All the same, it worked. There was a significant difference between the behavior of sad individuals who thought that Mnemoxine had a mood-freezing effect and those who didn't. Those who did were less likely to help. This finding undermines the claim that sadness directly causes helping—if it were true, both groups of individuals would help. Instead, for sad individuals to help, they must think that helping will change their mood. In the absence of such a belief, helping loses both its purpose and its appeal.

In a different study, it was shown that sad people will consume more sweets than happy people but only if they believe that their moods can change.[38] In another, it was reported that anger fails to give rise to aggression when one's mood is believed to be frozen.[39] What all these findings show is that there are cases in which emotions influence our behavior not directly, but indirectly. In those cases, emotions are important determinants of our behavior only if we expect that changing our behavior will change our moods or emotions.

Without that expectation, emotions don't affect our behavior. We're moved, in other words, not by our current emotions but by our anticipated emotions—the ones that we expect to have on account of a change in our behavior.

In a 2016 study, psychologist C. Nathan DeWall and colleagues went through hundreds of published psychology articles that looked at the effects of emotions on behavior.[40] (This type of study is known as a meta-analysis and it compiles empirical evidence from numerous studies. The results of a meta-analysis are trusted more than those of individual studies because they average out the oddities intrinsic to those studies.) What they found was that most of these articles weren't able to establish a direct causal relationship between our current emotions and consequent behavior. In fact, only 22% of those studies reported a causal relationship between emotions and behavior that was statistically significant. (A result is statistically significant if there's less than 5% probability that the result could be due to chance or random variation). Although there are instances in which emotions directly cause behavioral changes, they are not as many as commonsense and received wisdom in psychology would have us believe.

The meta-analysis also investigated whether anticipated emotions affect behavior. The researchers only found a handful of studies that explored the relationship between anticipated emotions and behavior. However, and in stark contrast to the hundreds of studies exploring the relationship between current emotions and behavior, studies that considered the effects of anticipated emotions were much more successful. About 90% of these studies came up with statistically significant findings that anticipated emotions affect behavior. As one of the authors of the meta-analysis writes, "the evidence available at present suggests that behavior is much more reliably based on how people expect to feel in the future than how they feel at present."[41]

Emotions move us. But if we accept the findings of the 2016 study, most of the time we're moved not by the emotions that we have, but rather by the emotions that we wish to have. Such a realization doesn't undermine the force and importance of emotions—after all, the emotions that we want to have depend on the emotions that we have. Still, it highlights that emotions' motivational power rests, to a large extent, on anticipation.

• • •

We can distinguish between two kinds of future-orientated emotions: *anticipated* emotions and *anticipatory* emotions.[42] The former are the emotions that we predict that we will have when something occurs ("I will feel good when I make millions from this book. Thanks for buying it, btw."). The latter are the emotions that we're having *right now* because we're thinking about something in the future—these can be consciously felt ("I'm having an anxiety attack because I will someday die") or subtly processed by our brain and body (there's an increase in my skin conductance response, a measure of how well our skin conducts electricity, right before I'm about to sign papers for buying a house). The previous discussion illustrated how *anticipated* emotions affect our behavior. *Anticipatory* emotions, especially ones that are subtly processed, can do the same.

The somatic marker hypothesis, originally formulated by neuroscientist Antonio Damasio, is a neurologically grounded model that articulates how, in certain situations, our emotions can influence decision-making and behavior.[43] Although complex, the main idea behind the model is easy to summarize. Over time, and through experience, we've learned to associate certain emotional and bodily changes (what can jointly be called "somatic markers") with specific decisions and their outcomes. Because of this association, when we're faced with certain situations such as when we're asked to make a decision, the somatic markers may be reactivated. In this way, choices regarding what actions to take can be influenced emotionally by our past experiences. Importantly, this process doesn't depend on reasoning. The guidance that our (anticipatory) emotions offer is automatic and, according to some researchers, inaccessible to conscious awareness.

Evidence for the somatic marker hypothesis comes from a series of experiments that utilize the Iowa Gambling Task, a task thought to mimic real-life decision-making and which was devised by neuroscientists Antoine Bechara, Antonio Damasio, Hanna Damasio, and Steven W. Anderson when they were all at the University of Iowa.[44] In this task, a player is presented with four decks of cards (A, B, C, D) and is required to maximize profit on a loan of play money by making one hundred card selections. Players can select one card at a time from whichever deck they like and are allowed to switch decks as frequently or as infrequently as they please. Decks A and B provide higher gains than decks C and D—every time the player selects a card from either deck A or B, the subject receives $100, whereas cards from decks C and D only yield a profit of $50. However, in each of the four decks, subjects will encounter unexpected punishment cards (i.e., cards that result in money losses). The punishment is much more severe for decks A and B than it is for decks C and D. Given how the game is set up, decks A and B prove to be *disadvantageous* in the long run, and one is better off choosing cards from decks C and D.

It turns out that neurotypical participants who aren't gamblers quickly learn to move away from the "bad" decks (A and B) and instead select from decks C and D.§ Crucially, it appears that this change of behavior occurs nonconsciously. In a study conducted by Bechara and colleagues, which was published in 1997 in the journal *Science,* they recorded skin conductance responses of participants while playing the game.[45] It was revealed that participants developed different skin conductance responses depending on which deck they choose to draw from. In particular, the recorded skin conductance responses were larger preceding their choice to draw from the disadvantageous decks than the advantageous ones. Researchers also investigated when participants became cognizant of the "rules" of the game. They interrupted participants at regular intervals and asked them to describe their knowledge of what was going on in the game. What they found was that participants adopted the preferred strategy—that is, choosing from decks C and D—before they were able to report why they chose those decks over A and B. In other words, their anticipatory affective reactions biased their behavior in an advantageous manner before they were able to figure it out using reason.

Bechara and colleagues also demonstrated that patients with damage to their ventromedial prefrontal cortex—a relatively large and heterogeneous part of the brain that plays an important role in emotion regulation, decision-making, and the assessment of risk and fear—performed poorly on the task. They failed to switch from the disadvantageous decks to the advantageous ones. Unlike neurotypical subjects, the patients didn't develop anticipatory responses that would have helped them to stay away from decks A and B. Notably, even when they eventually figured out the nature of the game and thus understood that drawing from decks C and D was a better strategy, they continued to choose cards from decks A and B. Our anticipatory emotional responses—even if they're subtle or hidden from conscious awareness—are of great value to us. They're our guides into an uncertain future.

• • •

On Monday, October 29, 1945, at the Salle de Centraux in Paris, French philosopher Jean-Paul Sartre delivered a lecture that launched his reputation to towering heights. Sartre didn't become a philosopher overnight. He did, however, on account of this lecture, become, more or less, a household name. The lecture was a resounding success—in fact, it was later described as "the cultural event of the year."[46] It was widely publicized and as a result, demand for places far outstripped supply. There was yelling and arguing, pulling and

---

§ Like moths to the flame, gamblers were attracted to the high rewards promised by decks A and B, while ignoring the associated severe punishment.

shoving, broken chairs, and a destroyed box office. The hall was overflowing with a crowd that, at times, resembled a mob. The lucky ones who made it in could only stand, and people were fainting because of the heat. "Too Many Attend Sartre Lecture. Heat, Fainting Spells, Police. Lawrence of Arabia an Existentialist," read the title of a newspaper article about the event.[47]

One hour behind schedule, Sartre spoke.[48] Without notes, he delivered a captivating lecture.[49] It was a summary and defense of existentialism, a philosophical movement concerned with the nature of human existence, which found appeal outside the insular world of academia and which influenced authors, artists, political activists, and the common people alike. Sartre, a thinker whose philosophical works couldn't be readily understood by the masses, on this night made himself heard to anyone who would listen.

At the heart of existentialism, as developed and articulated by Sartre and Simone de Beauvoir, lies a paradoxical claim: human beings are characterized by a *lack*. This claim, in one form or another, is ubiquitous in the early works of Sartre. It's found, for instance, in his monumental *Being and Nothingness*, when he asserts that the foundation of human existence is "a lack of being."[50] It's also found, in various guises, in Beauvoir's influential writings. It's a guiding idea for many existentialists and a model by which one can understand human existence. What does it mean?

Within the context of existentialism, the claim receives a clear explication. To say that we're characterized by a lack is to say that our being, as human beings, is always in question. What and who we are can never be defined in advance. We have to discover and make it up as we go on living. A human being is "a being whose existence comes before its essence, a being who exists before he can be defined by any concept of it," Sartre told the audience that night, before elaborating on his position.[51] "Man"—and by that term Sartre meant any human being or person—"is not only that which he conceives of himself to be, but that which he wills himself to be, and since he conceives of himself only after he exists, just as he wills himself to be after being thrown into existence, man is nothing other than what he makes of himself. This is the first principle of existentialism."[52] Life, according to existentialism, is a perpetual project of reinventing oneself. "An existent *is* nothing other than what he *does*," Beauvoir writes in *The Second Sex*.[53]

Existence precedes essence. The "first principle of existentialism" finds its origin in the work of German philosopher Martin Heidegger. In one of the most influential, difficult, and at times abstruse philosophical works of the twentieth century, *Being and Time*, Heidegger anticipated this first principle when he wrote: "*The essence of Dasein* [Heidegger's term for human beings or persons] *lies in its existence.*"[54] In this work, Heidegger set out to answer the philosophical question, "What is the meaning of being?" Heidegger's approach was unique. Instead of approaching this question from either an abstract or scientific point of view, he proposed to understand it through an investigation of the nature of the only being for whom this question even arises—human being. For Heidegger, only humans ask the question of being. Because of that, any attempt to grasp the meaning of being must first proceed through an investigation of the meaning of human existence. What one finds when one reads *Being and Time* and follows Heidegger's tangled threads of reasoning is a radical reconceptualization of human existence, one which was instrumental for existentialists like Sartre and Beauvoir.**

• • •

What is distinctive about human beings, both Heidegger and the existentialists thought, is the fact that our existence matters to us. In existing and living our lives, we care *how* we exist. We care *what* we do and *who* we are. In the hands of Heidegger and the existentialists, this innocuous observation is quickly transformed into one of great import for it's revealing of fundamental aspects of human existence.

We care about life by constantly confronting and attempting to respond to the question "Who am I?" A response to this question, however, is neither theoretical nor optional. It isn't theoretical because the caring that characterizes our existence isn't a mere cognitive stance that we take on life. We care about life by living life—by choosing what to do and by acting, by navigating and

---

** Obligatory aside: When Heidegger used to introduce Aristotle in his lectures he had little interest in offering details about Aristotle's personality or life. "Regarding the personality of a philosopher," Heidegger used to say, "our only interest is that he was born at a certain time, that he worked, and that he died" (Heidegger 2002, p. 5). If we were to use this formula of introduction for Heidegger, it would need to be amended. When it comes to Heidegger, we should say: regarding his personality, our only interest is that he was born at a certain time, that he worked (wrote and lectured), that he was a Nazi and anti-Semite, and that he died. Heidegger's involvement with the National Socialist party is undeniable—he became a member in 1933 and while serving as a Rector of the University of Freiburg, he enthusiastically expressed his support to the party. His acceptance of National Socialist's ideas and anti-Semitic sentiments and reprehensible stereotypes is also beyond question. Scholars interested in Heidegger's writings are forced to confront difficult questions. Is Heidegger's anti-Semitism somehow rooted in his philosophical ideas, making it an unavoidable consequence of some of his theses? Or do his philosophical ideas stand independently of his involvement with National Socialism? And what does one now do with Heidegger? Do we keep reading him, or should we demand that his works be removed from "the philosophy section of libraries" and instead be put "in the historical archives of Nazism and Hitlerism," as one commentator put it (Faye 2009, p. 319)? I don't have definitive answers to these difficult questions, which incidentally don't apply just to Heidegger's corpus, but to the work of any author, artist, musician, director, etc., whose behavior is morally reprehensible. For what's worth, my current and by no means final view is that we should still read Heidegger but our engagement with his work should always be inflected by his failings. By doing so, we can perhaps decide which ideas and philosophical methods are morally dangerous and which aren't. It's not the first time that philosophers have expressed and indeed defended morally reprehensible positions. Both Aristotle and Immanuel Kant, the paradigms of rationality and the high priests of reason, held racist views.

overcoming obstacles, by forming likes and dislikes, and by risking it or playing it safe. At the same time, we have no other choice but to care about our life. Like the passage of time, life unfolds relentlessly, whether we want it to or not. Any stance on life that we might assume through our actions and decisions is already an answer to the question "Who am I?" Even lack of care, despondence, or apathy about life is still a way of responding to this question. For existentialists, our existence is an on-going, personal project of self-discovery for which we have no choice but to participate. To paraphrase Sartre, only slightly: we're condemned to care about our life by enacting who we want to become.

The significance of this conception of life is that there's always more to life than what it's given to us at any moment. Every answer to the question "Who am I?" is one that involves our future. Our existence might be lumbered by our past and anchored in our present but it's always extending into our future. Every decision we make is already informed by our future. In fact, without a view of the future, we would be stuck in a meaningfully ambiguous present. We wouldn't know precisely what to do with our present situation. We wouldn't know how to use the objects around us and how to interact with the people that surround us. How does one determine, for example, whether something or someone is a help or a hindrance without having some goal in mind?

Furthermore, in taking up any role in life, we have already (at least in part) chosen and determined our future. We've decided both who we wish to be and what goals we need to pursue to become the one we wish to be. The future is as much a part of who we are as our present and past—what options are open for us and which are closed are an integral part of who we are. Having said that, any role that we might adopt for ourselves and decide to pursue can't exhaust who we are. One is a parent, an artist, a writer, a politician, or a baseball player but one is never *just* that. One needs to keep affirming a commitment to the projects that determine one's identity. What we are fundamentally then is possibility: a possibility to become some person or another. In the words of Spanish philosopher José Ortega y Gasset, "our possible existence is always greater than our destiny or actual existence."[55] Precisely because we are, most fundamentally, a possibility, we are never complete.

Here lies the lack that existentialists find at the heart of our being. The lack isn't a sign of a human inadequacy or shortcoming. It's rather the defining mark of human existence. To live as a human being is to continually run-ahead of ourselves, to be always more than what we currently are. A human being, Heidegger writes, "is already its not-yet" and is so "constantly as long as it is."[56] We aren't just future-oriented beings; we are literally our future. Or, as Hamm says in Beckett's *Endgame*, our lives are indeed lives to come.

• • •

There isn't life without a constant view of what's to come. Our brains constantly generate predictions. Our memories are formed with a future in mind. And our lives are determined by the future that we want to come to be: the emotions that we wish to feel; the ideals that we strive for and which inspire us to become who we want to be. The ability to anticipate isn't an accouterment of human existence. Anticipation is what makes our existence recognizably human.

Yet there isn't only one type of anticipation. We anticipate wittingly or unwittingly, consciously or unconsciously, in vivid colors or in monochromatic shades, with subtle feelings or with passionate emotions. We think about our immediate or distant futures. We anticipate by ourselves or in the company of others. In anticipation, we find salvation, the apocalypse, or the trivially mundane. Anticipation can be a source of trepidation and hopelessness. It can also be a spring of optimism and a boost to move forward and to keep pursuing what really matters to us. Because of the many shades of anticipation and its varying effects, our examination of anticipation can't conclude with the realization (however important it may be) that anticipation is a necessary part of human existence. We also need to investigate what type of anticipation can promote our well-being. There's more to anticipation than its existence.

9

"And you, what do you think of optimism?"

Would you choose $100 today or $110 in a year?

If you're like most people, you'd opt for the former. A preference for a less valuable but immediate reward over one that's delayed but somewhat more valuable is common, so much so that it has its own name—"future discounting." Our choice of immediate rewards isn't baseless. Sometimes it's grounded in rationality. An immediate reward is certain, a future one need not be—who knows what can happen to us in a year. Furthermore, an immediate reward offers us opportunity in the here and the now. I can invest the $100 or use it to purchase something of pressing need; I can't do much with the mere promise of money.

Most of the time, however, future discounting is the product of our own impatience. Waiting can be unpleasant. To wait for a desired something—be it an object, a person, an experience, or a situation—is to be made painfully aware of an unfulfilled desire. Waiting signals a lack and the longer we wait, the more pronounced and entrenched the lack becomes. Hence, we tend to perceive a delay in gratification as a cost. The cost of having to wait for a year for the $110 is perceived to be, at least by many of us, greater than the benefit of the additional $10. Not only do future rewards become depreciated, immediate ones become inflated. We're willing to pay more to receive a giant inflatable swan tomorrow than in five business days. We want our rewards and we want them now. Businesses (e.g., Amazon Prime) and various financial institutions (e.g., credit card providers, pawnshops, or loan sharks) capitalize on our impatience and our tendency to discount future rewards.

The tendency to choose proximate rewards over distal ones, even if the latter are slightly higher than the former, has greatly informed (some say, misinformed) economics.[1] Indeed, for about eighty years, economists have modeled intertemporal decisions (i.e., decisions that have future consequences) precisely on the assumption that human beings discount the value of outcomes depending on how far they're in time.

Propelled. Andreas Elpidorou, Oxford University Press (2020). © Andreas Elpidorou.
DOI: 10.1093/oso/9780190912963.001.0001

Despite the impressive impact that future discounting has had on economic models and theories, it isn't hard to generate counterexamples—cases, that is, in which waiting isn't perceived as a cost but as a benefit. Here are five easy ones.

1. One doesn't rush to drink an expensive bottle of red wine, but waits for a special occasion.
2. One doesn't use up a voucher to a luxurious spa at the first opportunity—one seeks rather for the right moment, perhaps even plans the day in advance, thinks about it, and anticipates the pleasures to come.
3. The wedding industry is founded on the idea that couples take their time to plan their wedding. Couples are willing to postpone their rewards by scheduling their wedding ceremony well into the future and don't consider this as a type of discounting of their future experience.
4. Instant communication has many benefits but takes away the anticipatory delight that one experiences when one waits for a letter from a loved one.
5. Even though most companies strive to minimize the waiting period that a consumer has to experience to obtain a product or a service, waiting isn't always unwelcome or unpleasant. Dedicated music fans can wait for many hours, even days, outside of a venue to be among the first to enter a concert. El Bulli, the famous Catalan restaurant, had over three thousand customers on its waiting list, all of whom were willing to wait to experience a fleeting gustatory experience. And Apple is famous for its long lines during days on which it releases a new product. These lines aren't filled with angry or frustrated customers but with ones who are brimming with excitement, often high-fiving salespersons as they enter the store.[2]

Not all waiting is unpleasant and not all pleasures are pleasures of present things. British philosopher, social reformer, and founder of utilitarianism, Jeremy Bentham recognized this point in 1789 when he included the joys and pains of anticipation in the concept of utility.[3] The British economist William Stanley Jevons expressed his agreement with Bentham when, in his *Essays on Economics,* he wrote: "Three distinct ways are recognisable in which pleasurable or painful feelings are caused: (1) By the memory of past events; (2) By the sensation of present events; (3) By anticipation of future events."[4] Despite Bentham and Jevons's remarks, and what many ordinary experiences reveal, many economists, by overemphasizing future discounting, have missed the positive side of waiting.

In a now-classic study, behavioral economist George Loewenstein provided empirical support for the positivity of waiting.[5] Contrary to common
economic assumptions, he found that waiting can be perceived by individuals to have positive utility. Loewenstein's participants didn't seize immediate
gratification. Indeed, they were willing to incur a cost to wait. In his study,
Loewenstein asked thirty subjects to specify how much they'd be willing to
pay to obtain either $4 or a kiss from a movie star of their choice at different
points in time. He wanted to determine if the subjects' willingness to pay
would depend on whether the rewards ($4 or the kiss) are received imme-
diately, in three hours, in twenty-four hours, in three days, in one year, or in
ten years. For the monetary reward, his result was in line with the traditional
economic assumption: subjects stated that they would pay less the longer they
had to wait to receive the $4. However, the kiss exhibited a different and un-
expected pattern. Participants were willing to pay almost twice for a kiss in
three days than for an immediate one. Clearly, in the case of the kiss, individuals didn't perceive the anticipatory period as a cost. On the contrary, a
kiss for which one has to wait was valued more than a kiss that is immediate.
Loewenstein suggested that experiences such as receiving a kiss are fleeting.
They last for the shortest of times. Through anticipation, however, we can
both prolong them and bring about their pleasurable effects long before they
actually take place.

• • •

The fact that anticipation has the capacity to enhance the experience of an action doesn't mean that the action ought to be performed. Not all anticipatory
pleasures are created equally. Anticipation isn't a moral compass. A sadist, for
instance, may eagerly anticipate an upcoming torment and a political tyrant
might be delighted by the prospect of imprisoning his political opponents.

Economists Martin G. Kocher, Michal Krawczyk, and Frans van Winden
have suggested that positive anticipatory emotions can explain even some of
our addictive and unsalutary habits.[6] Specifically, the researchers looked at
the experiences of individuals who buy lottery tickets. From an economic perspective, lottery is a puzzling phenomenon. It's tremendously popular despite
the fact that it offers one of the lowest payout rates of any commercial gambling. So, why do so many individuals buy lottery tickets instead of engaging
in some other form of gambling? The answer, or at least part of the answer, lies
in anticipation. Lottery involves an anticipatory phase that individuals find
pleasant and exciting. "[L]ottery players," the researchers write, "can 'cherish
the hope' of winning a million in the time between buying a ticket and the

drawing. Hence, players are willing to accept a lower expected value than in other sorts of gambling . . . [because] they get additional utility from the waiting period."[7] Anticipation and its associated pleasures can move us in various ways, even in ways that make little rational sense.

In a series of experiments, psychologists Amit Kumar, Matthew A. Killingsworth, and Thomas Gilovich set out to determine whether people receive more utility from the anticipation of experiential purchases (e.g., paying for a vacation) than from the anticipation of material purchases (e.g., buying a computer).[8] In one of their experiments, they asked participants who were already planning either a material or experiential purchase about the nature of their anticipatory experiences. They found that although both anticipatory experiences were perceived as pleasurable, the anticipation of an upcoming experience was more pleasurable than that of an upcoming possession. The former was characterized by pleasant feelings of excitement, whereas the latter, although still positive, was tinged with impatience. In a follow-up experiment, over two thousand participants were notified at random times during waking hours by an iPhone application and were asked a variety of questions regarding their moods and plans. Participants reported thinking about a future purchase in response to about 20% of the probes. After analyzing their data, the researchers reported that individuals who were thinking about an upcoming experiential purchase were happier than individuals who weren't thinking about a future experiential purchase. Thinking about a material purchase, however, had no effect on the reported levels of happiness. The results strongly suggest that experiential purchases come with benefits, even before their consumption. As the researchers write, "the utility people derive from a purchase—or any event—is not only in the here and now, but also in anticipation."[9]

The results of the experiments by Kumar and colleagues are broadly consistent with the findings of a different study conducted by marketing professor Marsha L. Richins.[10] This study showed that before the purchase of a product that's thought to be important, materialist individuals (ones who tend to believe that material possession will make them happier) experience more anticipatory pleasure than nonmaterialist individuals. However, the overall happiness of materialist consumers was lower than that of nonmaterialist. Richins proposes that "that while materialists are getting their pleasure boosts from products, those low in materialism are getting emotional fulfillment somewhere else."[11] Given Richins' findings, such alternative sources of fulfillment appear to have a more lasting effect on one's happiness. All the same, the study, just like the one conducted by Kumar and colleagues, found that anticipation can be pleasurable, even if what we're anticipating for is a plain old material pleasure (a new computer, a pair of shoes, or that inflatable swan). The pleasures of anticipation might not be life's panacea, but they're pleasures nonetheless.

• • •

Stretched out on the grass
a boy and a girl.
Sucking their oranges, giving their kisses
like waves exchanging foam.

Stretched out on the bench
a boy and a girl.
Sucking their limes, giving their kisses
like clouds exchanging foam.

Stretched out underground
a boy and a girl.
Saying nothing, never kissing,
giving silence for silence.

—"Engaged"*

"Savoring" means to dwell on our positive experiences, to stretch them out temporally, to magnify them with our attention, and to squeeze from them every drop of joy (Figure 9.1). Within the context of psychology, savoring is understood to be a method of regulating one's emotions. In particular, it's a way of *up*regulating (i.e., improving) already positive emotions and is described as the capacity "*to attend to, appreciate, and enhance the positive experiences in one's life.*"[12] One savors a positive experience and in doing so, one intensifies or prolongs the enjoyment.

Savoring might seem like a minor thing—the icing on the cake of an already flourishing life. But it shouldn't. Our capacity to savor our experiences has clear implications for our happiness and well-being. Indeed, the fact that one might experience positive emotions doesn't guarantee that one is capable of enjoying them. One can fail to take appropriate notice of them, one might experience guilt while having them, or one can even become a killjoy for oneself. The pursuit of the good life isn't a happening but a doing. It's not an innate

* By Octavio Paz, translated by Muriel Rukeyser, from EARLY POEMS 1935–1955, copyright ©1973 by Octavio Paz and Muriel Rukeyser. Reprinted by permission of New Directions Publishing Corp.

Figure 9.1 The "Face Savoring Food" emoji. The fact that such an emoji exists suggests that savoring is an important part of everyday life, one that needs to be communicated to others efficiently via emojis.
© Vincent Le Moign / Wikimedia Commons / CC-BY-4.0.

talent but a skill that involves, centrally, the ability to react properly to our emotions. Savoring, as a way of appreciating, managing, and even enhancing our pleasurable experiences, is one of the tools that we have at our disposal for living a good life. In Octavio Paz's poem, the boy and the girl are savoring life. They do it when they're young and life is good ("sucking their oranges"). They also do it when they're old and life is hard ("sucking their limes"). They cease to savor only when they're dead ("Saying nothing, never kissing, / giving silence for silence").

It might also seem that savoring is an exclusively present-orientated activity. This too is a false impression. Granted, savoring is something that we often do while we're having an experience. I savor a dessert by eating it slowly and attentively and by describing to myself and others the joys that I'm currently experiencing. This isn't, however, the whole story. Savoring is often related to memory and, thus, to the past. I can savor a past experience as a way to relive it, even faintly, in my imagination. I can also savor a past experience as a way of savoring a present one. "Oh, how wonderful was this espresso yesterday!" I say to myself, before taking a sip with my eyes closed. More important, savoring involves anticipation for the future. In fact, one of the methods that we use to savor an experience is to anticipate it. Savoring thus isn't exhausted by a mindful presence to what we're currently experiencing. It also involves thinking ahead, mentally cataloguing what experiences are likely to come, how they'll unfold in our mind, and how pleasant, divergent, even baroque they'll be. Simone de Beauvoir expresses this point eloquently when she discusses the future dimensions of pleasure: "To enjoy a good thing is to use it, to throw oneself with it toward the future. To enjoy the sun or the shade is to feel its presence as a slow enrichment. . . . While looking at the path traveled, I look at those valleys toward which I am going; I look at my future. All enjoyment is project. It surpasses the past toward the future, toward the world that is the fixed image of the future."[13]

The importance of anticipation in savoring is attested by the manner in which psychologists measure individuals' capacity to savor their experiences. Psychologist Fred B. Bryant, a leading scholar in the psychology of savoring, has devised a questionnaire, the Savoring Beliefs Inventory, that consists of twenty-four statements and that allows researchers to assess one's capacity for savoring.[14] Individuals are instructed to indicate on a 7-point scale how true each of the twenty-four statements is for them. The final score can be used to determine one's capacity for savoring. The relevance of anticipation is obvious to anyone who reads the questionnaire. One third of the statements concern one's attitudes toward the future and anticipation. When one completes the questionnaire, one must indicate the extent to which statements such as "Get pleasure from looking forward," "Can feel the joy of anticipation," and "Can enjoy events before they occur" are true for oneself.

In a series of studies, Bryant explored the relationship between savoring and well-being. In one of them, Bryant found that older adults who score high on the Savoring Beliefs Inventory questionnaire report having experienced greater happiness in the past week than those who score lower.[15] This result was confirmed by a 2014 study conducted by Jennifer L. Smith and Linda Hollinger-Smith, researchers at the Mather LifeWays Institute of Aging in Evanston, Illinois. Smith and Hollinger-Smith reported that, for older adults, a greater ability to savor positive experiences predicted greater happiness, lower depression, and greater satisfaction with life.[16] In a joint study conducted by Smith and Bryant, older adults who were instructed to savor valuable life lessons that they had learned while growing older reported more positive perception of aging and higher life satisfaction than both older adults who were instructed to reflect on physical losses that they experienced in aging and older adults who were asked to do neither.[17] What's more, Bryant also found that higher scores in the part of the Savoring Beliefs Inventory that deals specifically with anticipation predicted greater reported enjoyment of taking a vacation. In other words, individuals who were capable of taking pleasure in anticipating a vacation were able to have a more pleasant experience in the present.[18]

An intriguing study conducted by researchers Jordi Quoidbach, Elizabeth W. Dunn, K. V. Petrides, and Moïra Mikolajczak explored the relationship between wealth and happiness. The researchers were motivated to pursue this investigation because of the known finding in the happiness literature that objective life circumstances in general, and wealth in particular, explain little of the observed variance in happiness.[†] So, why is it that money can't really buy happiness? Quoidbach and colleagues found a negative relationship between the ability to savor one's experience and financial wealth. "In a large sample of working adults, we found," the researchers report, "that wealthier individuals reported lower savoring ability."[19] It should be noted that Quoidbach and colleagues used a different measure of savoring, but their measure, just like Bryant's, considers anticipation to be an integral part of savoring. Why would wealth undermine one's ability to savor? The hypothesis offered by the researchers is both simple and intuitive. Financial wealth corrodes one's ability to savor because, after one has experienced the best things in life, other more mundane pleasures pale in comparison.

• • •

Doodlebug is mercifully short. A three-minute, low-budget, black-and-white film that director Christopher Nolan wrote, directed, and shot in 1997, when he was a student at University College London, a year before he released his critically acclaimed *Following* and almost a decade before he started the production of his blockbusters. The story of *Doodlebug* is simple. A man, in a state of disarray, wearing a worn-out white tank top, black trousers, and no shoes, jumps around his dilapidated apartment with a shoe in hand. He tries, desperately, to crush what appears to be, at least initially, a bug. After many failed attempts, he comes face to face with the bug. But it isn't a bug. It's a miniature version of his future self—in the film, the actions of the miniature version are replicated, a few seconds later, by the man. The miniature version of the man

---

[†] Sadly, this finding goes against the teachings of popular twenty-first-century philosopher, Arianna Grande, who in "7 Rings" sings "Happiness is the same price as red-bottoms." If only happiness were that easy to achieve! Note for the uninitiated: Red-bottoms are luxury shoes characterized by their shiny red-lacquered outsoles and designed by Christian Louboutin. In summer 2018, a European Union high court ruled that red-bottoms are trademarked by Louboutin and that no other company could make red-soled shoes without infringing upon Louboutin's rights. See Wood (2018).

crushes something with his shoe, presumably a miniature version of the miniature man. After a couple of seconds, the man in the apartment follows suit. He victoriously crushes his miniature version. And right before the end, as the man grins, a giant version of himself squashes him with a giant shoe.

The short film is intentionally ambiguous. Is the man driven to insanity because he's been chasing a version of himself? Is his demise a consequence of this chase? Is the film an allegory of the dangers of chasing one's dreams? Regardless of how we settle these and other interpretative questions, Nolan's short film presents us with a counterintuitive, perhaps even impossible, relationship between our future and present self. Our future self seems to cause (or somehow affect) our present self. But future events aren't meant to do that. The future isn't causally related to the present. Causation moves forward, not backwards in time.

Although Nolan might be cinematically toying with a scientifically, perhaps even logically, impossible relationship between future and present, there's a sense in which our future self affects our current self. This claim doesn't rest on some weird metaphysical principle that involves backward causation. It's rather a simple matter of appreciating anticipation's force. Mental future imaging has been shown to have an effect on behavior. When registered voters in Ohio were asked to picture themselves voting from the third-person perspective, they adopted a stronger pro-voting mindset than those imagining themselves from the first-person perspective and were consequently more likely to vote.[20] Students who envisioned the steps leading to receiving a high grade on an exam performed better on the exam than students who had simply imagined that they had received a high grade.[21] Homeowners who imagined themselves using cable TV and enjoying its benefits were more likely to subsequently sign up for such a service than those who were merely told about the benefits.[22] The way in which we portray to ourselves our future self can affect our present self.

• • •

When we think of our future we typically think of it in positive terms. In fact, our predictions about our future are characterized by a double optimism: we overestimate the likelihood of future positive events and underestimate the likelihood of future negative events. We think that we will live longer than what objective measures predict and that our chances for divorce are much lower than 50% (if we're living in the Western world).[23] We overestimate our chances of success in the job market.[24] We underestimate our chances of getting into an accident or suffering cancer.[25] Our future looks bright, even when, objectively speaking, it shouldn't.[26]

The majority of the population (of the Western industrialized world) displays a bias toward a better personal future. According to some accounts, 80% of us have a tendency to prospect with rosy glasses. Even some animals share our relentless optimism. The fact that such a tendency is so ubiquitous invites important theoretical questions. First, is our (often unrealistic) optimism a good thing?

Optimism carries some risks. It can bias our decision-making by making us either overconfident about our own abilities or about the outcomes of our projects. For instance, it's been repeatedly shown that what we think we can accomplish within a given timeframe and what we can actually get done are two different things. This is called the "planning fallacy," and most of us commit it every time we draw up a to-do list. A famous case of the fallacy involves the construction of the Sydney Opera House. Originally, it was expected that its construction would conclude in 1963, and it would cost $7 million. As it turned out, it wasn't finished until 1973 and the total cost was $102 million. There are additional dangers associated with being optimistic, but those have to do with overoptimism—that is, optimism above and beyond the typical optimistic attitude that most of us exhibit. For instance, individuals who are excessively optimistic about their future prospects might engage in potentially harmful activities such as smoking, overspending, and unhealthy eating, precisely because they severely underestimate the chances of anything bad happening to them.[27]

Notwithstanding the aforementioned risks, optimism is, on the whole, a boon. Optimists enjoy longer and healthier lives. Studies have found that optimism predicts lower mortality and lower rates of heart attack and fatal coronary heart disease.[28] Optimism reduces anxiety and stress and is correlated with better immune functioning and quick recovery from bypass surgery,[29] and optimistic HIV patients show better survival rates than those who are pessimistic.[30] Optimism has also been associated with health-promoting strategies, such as eating healthily and exercising, and in the workplace, it's been related to professional success.[31]

That's not all. Optimism comes with a motivational boost.[32] When we expect good things to happen to us, we're motivated to chase after them. In turn, optimism is related to the perception of a meaningful life. In a 2018 paper, psychologists Wijnand A. P. van Tilburg and Eric R. Igou explored the hypothesis that anticipated happiness and optimism for the future carries existential benefits.[33] They concluded that optimism is a meaning-creating strategy insofar as the tendency to anticipate a brighter future contributes to the perception that one's life is meaningful.

• • •

Why are we optimistic about the future? This isn't an easy question to answer. Indeed, the answer depends on what perspective we're choosing to adopt when addressing the question. If we're looking for the mechanisms that lead to future bias, then the answer might lie in the fact that we tend to update our beliefs more in the face of positive information about the future than in the face of negative information. This hypothesis was explored and confirmed by a study conducted by neuroscientists Tali Sharot, Christoph W. Korn, and Raymond J. Dolan.[34]

The researchers asked participants to estimate the likelihood of encountering forty negative events in their lifetime—these included, among others, Parkinson's disease and car theft. After each response, participants were shown the actual probability of the event happening to someone like them—this probability had been extracted from actuarial statistics. Once the participants went through the whole list of events and the actual probability of each event happening to them was revealed, they were asked once again to estimate the likelihood of those events happening to them. The point of this study was to examine how individuals respond to objective information about future events and how their brain processes this information.

The researchers found that participants were unlikely to update their estimate if the actual probability of an event happening to them was higher than what they initially estimated. Yet, if the actual probability was lower, they were much more likely to update their estimate to reflect the actual probability. In other words, if their initial response was too optimistic, participants ignored corrective information. If their initial response, however, was too pessimistic, then participants readily incorporated corrective information and became *less* pessimistic. Subjects thus exhibited a preferential orientation toward positive information: information that makes our future look better is duly noted; information that challenges our rosy vision of the future gets ignored.

The researchers also collected functional magnetic resonance imaging data while the subjects were providing their likelihood estimates. They observed a failure of frontal lobe regions to code errors in prediction. In particular, "when optimistic individuals are confronted with unexpected statistics about the likelihood of encountering negative events, their right inferior frontal gyrus exhibits reduced coding of information that calls for a negative update."[35] This finding concerning neural activity wasn't replicated in cases where the corrective information was better than expected. In such cases, regions of the prefrontal cortex coded for information efficiently, both for individuals high and low in optimism. As the researchers write, "optimism was related to diminished coding of undesirable information about the future, in a region of the frontal cortex (right IFG [inferior frontal gyrus]) identified as sensitive to negative estimation errors."[36] The brain of the optimist ignores bad news.

Impressive and important as this study is, the neurological explanation doesn't fully address *why* we tend to be optimists. It provides a helpful description of a mechanism that would lead to optimistic forecasts, but it still doesn't tell us why our human brains are wired to behave in such a manner. An intriguing suggestion and possible answer to the why question can be found in a short paper written by biologist Ajit Varki titled, "Human Uniqueness and the Denial of Death."[37] Drawing upon the work of geneticist Danny Brower, Varki posited that our optimism about the future is an evolutionary-programmed response to the bleak future that awaited most of our distant ancestors. The emergence of self-consciousness and prospection might have been the catalyst for most abilities and achievements that are distinctively human and that have conferred to us, as a species, a great advantage. Yet this emergence also gave rise to an unbearable dread and anxiety about the future. Self-consciousness and prospection revealed to our distant ancestors the ills of their future life and the existential nothingness of death—the latter still looms large even in our modern, relatively safe lives. A constant awareness of impending sickness, pain, misfortune, and death would have impeded daily functions and activities necessary for survival. Optimism, Varki suggests, offered our ancestors, a refuge. It diverted the mind away from future misfortunes. It filled the soul with positive feelings and attitudes about the future.

• • •

"Optimism is the opium of the people!" reads a postcard that Ludvik Jahn, prize student and gifted musician, sent as a joke to his girlfriend in Milan Kundera's novel *The Joke*.[38] The postcard was misinterpreted. Ludvik was summoned to the office of the District Party Secratariat and was interrogated by three comrades. He recalls the incident:

And you, what do you think of optimism? they asked. Optimism? I asked. What should I think of it? Do you consider yourself an optimist? they went on. I do, I said timidly. I like a good time, a good laugh, I said, trying to lighten the tone of the interrogation. Even a nihilist can like a good laugh, said one of them. He can laugh at people who suffer. A cynic also can like a good laugh, he went on. Do you think socialism can be built without optimism? asked another of them. No, I said.[39]

Ludvik, a loyalist of the Communist Party, is ultimately thrown out of the party, expelled from university, and sent to a labor camp, all because of a joke. Optimism, however, is no joke. If Varki is right, it might be an evolutionary inevitability. But even if it's not, it's still a requirement for a healthy comportment to life.

In the 1990s, psychologist Andrew MacLeod and colleagues devised a measure of future thinking called the Future-Thinking Task.[40] When administrating this measure, researchers instruct individuals to list both events that they are looking forward to and ones that they aren't looking forward to, in various future times (e.g., next week, next year, or in five to ten years). When MacLeod and colleagues used the Future-Thinking Task in a range of clinical and nonclinical participants, a number of interesting results were found. First, it was shown that there was no correlation between future positive thoughts and future negative thoughts—our ability (or inability) to produce future events that we're looking forward to isn't related to our ability (or inability) to produce future events that we aren't looking forward to, and vice versa.[41] Second, compared to nondepressed individuals, depressed patients show reduced positive anticipation (they generate fewer events that they're looking forward to) without, however, showing an increase in negative anticipation (they don't generate more events that they aren't looking forward to).[42] The findings of depression are duplicated in the case of suicidal participants. Just like depressed patients, suicidal individuals show a reduced ability to generate positive future events, even though they don't exhibit an increase in the number of negative future events that they anticipate.[43] Lastly, suicidal patients' performance on the Future-Thinking Task was shown to be related to hopelessness about the future.[44] Measurements of hopelessness rely largely on a self-report measure that was the outcome of Aaron T. Beck's pioneering work on the topic—the Beck Hopelessness Scale (BHS).[45] BHS consists of twenty statements (e.g., "My future seems dark to me," "The future seems vague and uncertain to me," "I look forward to the future with hope and enthusiasm") and individuals are asked to evaluate whether the statements are true or false for them. The scale is meant to assess one's global outlook for the future. It's not all that surprising then that high BHS scores, which indicate high hopelessness, were found to be significantly correlated with having fewer positive thoughts.[46]

These findings are significant. The fact that both depressed patients and suicidal subjects generate fewer positive future thoughts supports the widely accepted contention that depression and suicidality overlap in important ways; it also highlights the importance and relevance of anticipation when rendering a diagnosis. Moreover, although prevalent in depression, hopelessness is an important psychological construct in its own right. In numerous published studies, hopelessness has been revealed as a powerful predictor of suicidal ideation and suicide attempts, both for depressed and nondepressed populations.[47] Hopelessness was also found to be correlated with a desire for hastened death in terminally ill cancer patients.[48]

It isn't just the lack of positive anticipation that's worrisome. Some anticipatory images can foreshadow, even bring about, the most destructive of acts. Suicidal ideas are anticipatory ideas that form quickly, sometimes without one's consent, and are incredibly powerful. A recent study reported that about half of individuals who attempted suicide made their attempt within ten minutes of having a persistent suicidal idea.[49] Such ideas can come in the form of a verbal thought but also in the form of vivid mental images. Experimental research led by psychiatrists Emily Holmes and Catharine Crane has revealed that patients with a history of depression and suicidality, experience, when in crisis, intrusive and repetitive suicide-related images. They imagine themselves, at some point in the future, committing suicide. These "flash-forwards" are realistic, vivid, rich in detail, and emotionally impactful.

I hit road and concrete. I imagine my brain splitting open like a pumpkin, seeing myself doing that, seeing myself flying down, hair and clothes flying backwards, head breaking into pieces, making a sound like a watermelon, a pop sound. The traffic stops and people scream, my mother comes out screaming, mother is crying, father is in shock, face so shattered that it is unrecognizable.[50]

The image was at first "rough."[51] Yet, according to the woman who experienced it, the image "gradually got more and more detailed to the extent it was perfectly planned."[52] She felt guilty for having this image. The image, she told the researchers, made her want to end her life by doing what she imagined herself doing. Another subject, with a history of suicidal behavior, describes a different, highly elaborate, and multisensory flash-forward.

In a deep wood, little chance of being found, fully leaved, summery dense, daytime dusky, see myself climbing the tree, tying rope to a branch above, putting the noose over my head and tightening it. I take huge overdose with alcohol & sit in tree thinking about things—verbal dialogue, hear this rewinding. Smell of woods, life accepting things, end of it, justification. The sun goes down, I fall unconscious, fall & hang. I see image of being there 6 months later, like a film cut, I found nobody cared.[53]

The reported flash-forward was, according to him, "brilliant" and vivid.[54] And the force of it made him want to act on it. He thought that it was a failsafe way of taking his own life. It promised him a "sense of closure."[55] Many others experience such flash-forwards. There're images of overdosing, of slitting one's wrists, or of throwing oneself in front of a train or over a window or cliff.

Such future imaginings can make the imagined events appear more probable and can even promote action. They can also facilitate a familiarity with suicide—their vividness and realism might undo one's inhibitions regarding the act of taking one's life. All the same, the realization that such flash-forwards occur can be a tool in the hands of medical professionals insofar as it can allow them to determine whether depressed individuals are at risk of suicide. Indeed, researchers now recommend that therapists be on the lookout for such anticipatory images. It's also recommended that cognitive therapy for suicidal ideation ought to target these flash-forwards by changing the imagined outcome and by reducing their vividness and realism.[56] The manner in which we think of the future has clear implications about our lives and well-being. If optimism is the bright side of anticipation, depression and suicidal ideation are its dark crevices.

• • •

Amyotrophic lateral sclerosis (ALS) is a neurodegenerative disease characterized by progressive muscular paralysis caused by the loss and degeneration of motor neurons in the primary motor cortex, brainstem, and spinal cord, and the degeneration of the corticospinal tract.[57] It primarily affects adults and results, typically within two to five years, in the loss of all voluntary movement, including loss of the muscles necessary for speaking, swallowing, and breathing, and ultimately death, usually due to respiratory failure.[58] In the United States alone, more than five thousand people are diagnosed with ALS each year.[59] As of yet, there's no cure. It's always fatal. One might choose to eat through a feeding tube and use an artificial ventilator for breathing, but such means, unfortunately, only prolong the inevitable.[60]

One would expect that distress would be prevalent among patients with ALS. But that isn't what scientific studies show. Nor is it what personal blogs and testimonies reveal. The latter are often characterized by optimism, cheerfulness, stoicism, resilience, and a sense of purpose.[61] "There's a lot of optimism in the ALS community," a twenty-six-year old woman with ALS stated in an interview.[62] "Even though they are living with this shitty-ass disease, they are here to experience everything they can before their time ends. I feel that way too."[63] It's not that patients ignore or forget that they have ALS. They don't. How could they? They understand their condition very well. "ALS defines me . . . it differentiates me in a way that most of those other words don't," a different ALS patient said when talking about her relationship to ALS.[64] Still, they decided not to give up, to keep hope, and to keep on living. "I've learned through my journey with ALS, that there are a lot of choices," Augie Nieto states. "I can choose to celebrate what I do have or mourn the loss of something I can no longer do by myself."[65] Most ALS patients have remarkably chosen the former.

Many studies with ALS patients show a similar pattern. A study led by Evelyn R. McDonald, co-founder of the educational and charitable foundation The New Road Map Foundation, reported that many ALS patients who receive ventilator support experience psychological well-being and live high-quality lives. "Our findings suggest," the researchers conclude, "that a high quality of life *can* exist for those who cannot breathe, walk, talk or eat on their own."[66] A 2000 study by psychiatrist Judith G. Rabkin and colleagues interviewed forty-nine ALS patients and found that 87% of them had no clinical depression and only 28% exhibited significant depressive symptoms. They reported:

> Patients were less optimistic about the future compared with general population samples and, on average, experienced mild depressive symptoms; however, there was almost no major psychopathology. Virtually all remained engaged in whatever social, recreational, and intellectual activities their circumstances permitted."[67]

A 2015 follow-up study by Rabkin and colleagues revealed confirming results.[68] Only 12% of ALS patients who were interviewed for the purpose of the study had minor or major depression. According to the authors of the study, "depressive disorders are not necessarily to be expected in the context of an invariably progressive, untreatable and fatal illness."[69] Indeed, they found that "most patients are able to find enjoyment in the present and maintain some hope for the future."[70]

Other studies confirmed this trend. A longitudinal study conducted by neuropsychologist Dorotheé Lulé and colleagues found out that only 28% of patients with ALS had clinically depressive symptoms. They also found no correlation between depressive symptoms and the extent of physical impairment that follows from ALS. Furthermore, when they assessed the subjective quality of life among ALS patients, it was found to be comparable to that of normal control subjects. They write: "ALS patients can experience a satisfactory quality of life without depressive manifestations even if they are severely physically impaired, including in the terminal phase."[71] A different study, which focused on late-stage ALS, also reported that although the prevalence of depression in patients with ALS is, as expected, higher than that of the total population, it's still not a necessary consequence of ALS. Indeed, it was found to be lower than other groups of medically ill patients.[72]

What could explain such findings? What is it that allows some ALS patients to continue living and persevering, sometimes even adopting an upbeat outlook on life, despite their harsh everyday reality? When an ALS patient who lost the ability to speak, swallow, or walk without help, was asked this question, he responded by typing the following message: "When my back is to the wall, my face is to life." [73] One lives not by looking back, at what one had and lost, but by looking forward, at what one can expect and wait for. It's through anticipation that one finds meaning, a sense of purpose, and the drive to live.

• • •

Even in our darkest moments, anticipation doesn't disappear. How could it? It's part of what it means to be human. Anticipation might sometimes yield despair, but it also begets resilience, a sense of purpose, and the motivation to keep going. Anticipation is a necessary link between the now and the future. Whatever form it takes, we're always at both of its ends.

10

"Immobile paradises promise us nothing"

It's time for conclusions.

Boredom, frustration, and anticipation are related: all three constitute elements of a good life insofar as they help us to regulate and to direct our behavior. It's a recent lesson from the psychology of self-regulation that we're better adjusted, happier, and more successful in accomplishing our goals if we're able to move from state to state. Movement, it turns out, is key to the fulfillment of our desires, to personal growth, and even to flourishing. Boredom, frustration, and anticipation all move us. All three ensure that we keep pursuing what matters to us and that we don't linger too much in situations that don't meet our expectations and desires. Boredom, frustration, and anticipation might be all-too-familiar psychological states, yet they're important. Much value lies in them; more, perhaps, lies through them.

• • •

Not to become my Mum
Lose anger
To be loved
To be less negative
Travel more
Pay off debts
To relax more
To be happy
Learn how to drive
Meet someone and fall in love
To be a nicer person
Learn a new language
To have children and a family
Have a bath in a bathroom, not just a shower
Losing 2kg

Propelled. Andreas Elpidorou, Oxford University Press (2020). © Andreas Elpidorou.
DOI: 10.1093/oso/9780190912963.001.0001

The list is a verbatim reproduction of responses given by participants in a study conducted by psychologists Katherine L. Sherratt and Andrew K. MacLeod.[1] Participants were given the prompt "In the future it will be important for me to..." and were asked to list as many completions of this sentence as possible. The provided responses differed along a number of dimensions. Some were more specific than others; some expressed events far in the future; some focused on gaining something new; some concerned outcomes or events in the world; and others were about one's thoughts, feelings, or personality traits. All of them, however, were expressions of goals.

A goal is a representation of a future: an image, but not a literal picture, in one's mind about what lies ahead. As a representation, a goal allows us to compare our current state to a future desired one. It helps us to make adjustments and to deduce when we're close to our desired future and when we've missed the mark. A goal isn't a representation of just any future, though. It represents a future that we believe we can realize. Without its realism, a goal ceases to be a goal and becomes a fantasy.

There's more to a goal, however, than what it represents. A goal isn't an idle image that we entertain and leaves us unmoved. It's a representation of something personal that matters to us. We conjure it up precisely because it stands for our personal values and for a future that we want to realize. Due to that fact, a goal is an incentive to action. It has its own, special for each one of us, allure. We're constantly engaging with and attracted by our goals. We produce them, compare our present condition to them, and chase after them. Goals, in sum, are mental representations of a desired, realistic future that's of personal significance and that we're motivated to realize or at least to pursue.

The significance of having goals in our lives can hardly be overstated. A simple method of subtraction suffices to illustrate their necessity. Imagine your life as it is right now. Now imagine it without any goals. What's left? Not much. There's still an organism that acts in certain ways. But the organism has no dreams, motivations, or future desires. The organism seems to lack purpose. With goals there's fulfillment and disappointment, purpose and meaning. Without them, we're mere automata.

• • •

I have two stories to tell.

The first one is relatively well known. It's the story of Bartleby, the title character of Herman Melville's masterpiece of short fiction, "Bartleby, the Scrivener: A Story of Wall Street," that first appeared in two parts in the pages of *Putnam's Monthly Magazine* in 1853.[2] Bartleby is hired by the narrator, a lawyer, to help out with the increased workload at the latter's office. At first, Bartleby appears to be an exemplary worker: he works efficiently and tire-lessly, without complaints or disruptions. Quickly, however, things change. Bartleby stops performing his duties. He refuses to proofread his work and then refuses to copy documents. "I have given up copying," Bartleby, whose job is precisely to copy, declares.[3]

Nonetheless, Bartleby remains in the office. He never goes anywhere, not even for a walk. He only speaks when he must. He doesn't read. He just stands and stares outside his window at a brick wall. The lawyer soon discovers that Bartleby lives in the office. He tries to fire him, but Bartleby refuses; he prefers, he says, not to go anywhere. In a desperate attempt to rid himself of Bartleby, the lawyer decides to move to another office without Bartleby. The new ten-ants aren't happy with Bartleby's presence, his unwillingness to move out, and his stupendous strangeness. "He now persists in haunting the building gener-ally, sitting upon the banisters of the stairs by day, and sleeping in the entry by night," the lawyer is told by a representative of the new tenants.[4] The lawyer meets with Bartleby and tries to convince him to leave the premises. He even offers him to come and stay with him. He refuses. "At present I would prefer not to make any change at all," Bartleby tells him.[5] Bartleby is eventually arrested for vagrancy and put to jail. The lawyer visits Bartleby. Bartleby refuses to eat. He stares at a brick wall even though he's free to roam around. On his second visit, the lawyer finds Bartleby dead, "strangely huddled at the base of the wall, his knees drawn up, and lying on his side, his head touching the cold stones."[6]

The story doesn't end with Bartleby's demise. Clearly perturbed by Bartleby's life, the narrator makes one last attempt at understanding it. He mentions a rumor that he heard about Bartleby but can't substantiate. Bartleby, we're told, used to work as a clerk in the Dead Letter Office at Washington D.C., the place where letters that couldn't be delivered are gathered and burned. The lawyer considers what Bartleby must have experienced and through his thoughts, we're transposed there:

> For by the cartload they [the letters] are annually burned. Sometimes from out the folded paper the pale clerk takes a ring—the finger it was meant for, perhaps, moulders in the grave; a bank-note sent in swiftest charity—he whom it would re-lieve, nor eats nor hungers any more; pardon for those who died despairing; hope for those who died unhoping; good tidings for those who died stifled by unrelieved calamities. On errands of life, these letters speed to death.[7]

The lawyer's imagination offers him some kind of intellectual comfort. It allows him to treat Bartleby not as an unexplained singularity but as the consequence of a condition that can afflict many. Bartleby, perhaps mistreated by society and life or perhaps cognizant of some deep and dark truth about the world, had lost all hope and finds no meaning. In a state of prolonged existential despair, Bartleby chooses death. "Ah Bartleby! Ah Humanity!" the narrator cries before the story concludes.[8]

The narrator's cry suggests that Bartleby's condition is the human condition. But that isn't entirely accurate. Bartleby exists in a unique manner. He is a marginal case of human existence. He sits, as it were, on the side of human life but near, very near, to the event horizon of death. That's not because he's at risk of losing qualities that would grant him membership to the biological species *Homo sapiens*. Even when he's biologically alive and well, Bartleby still occupies the liminal space between human existence and inexistence. He does so because he's actively involved in the process of becoming inhuman. By his own choice, he's given up on his goals and projects. He's given up on life.

As every reader of the story quickly becomes aware, Bartleby expresses his intentions and handles his interpersonal affairs in a rather laconic and eccentric manner. He doesn't express desires, only preferences, most of which are negative. Bartleby prefers not to proofread, prefers not to copy, prefers not to let the lawyer into his office, prefers not to quit his job, prefers not to make any changes, and prefers not to dine. When the lawyer asks him to go to the post office, he replies with "I would prefer not to." The lawyer asks for clarification, "You *will* not?" But Bartleby still refuses to state a desire. He responds: "I *prefer* not."[9] Bartleby wills nothing; he merely prefers.

Bartleby's attitude is fundamentally at odds with how we live our lives. Living a life requires us to commit ourselves constantly to projects, and to declare, cultivate, and attempt to fulfill our wishes and goals. Life is that project that always begets more projects. And we live life by choosing our projects. Without this ability (even if illusory) to choose, we aren't living our life—life, instead, happens to us. The story of Bartleby is a story about an impersonal and nonhuman life. It's the closest one can get to a conception of human existence that although alive isn't lived.

• • •

"We are going to subjugate Greece first," he declares.[10]

Pyrrhus was the king of the ancient Greek state Epirus and one of the subjects of Plutarch's *Parallel Lives*. The celebrated general Hannibal, whose name became synonymous with peril, declared Pyrrhus to be "the foremost of all generals in experience."[11] Pyrrhus's name has survived through the millennia. Yet outside classicist circles, he's best known neither for his leadership nor for his strategic acuity, but rather as the originator of the term "pyrrhic victory": a title given to any kind of victory that's been accomplished at great cost. In 279 BC, in the battle of Asculum, Pyrrhus and his army fought the Romans. They won, but they barely survived. "If we are victorious in one more battle with the Romans, we shall be utterly ruined," he said when he was congratulated for the win.[12] Pyrrhus's victory was pyrrhic.

In Plutarch's *Parallel Lives*, Pyrrhus and Cineas, Pyrrhus's wise adviser, engage in a dialogue, the subject matter of which is, ostensibly, world domination. Simone de Beauvoir, in her brilliant *Pyrrhus and Cineas*, a philosophical text that articulates and defends important existentialist themes, gives her own account of the dialogue and turns it into a discussion about the rationality and meaning of human action.

"We are going to subjugate Greece first," Pyrrhus declares. "And after that?" Cineas asks. "We will vanquish Africa," Pyrrhus answers. Cineas isn't satisfied. "After Africa?" he asks. "We will go on to Asia, we will conquer Asia Minor, Arabia." "We will go on as far as India," Pyrrhus adds. "After India?" asks Cineas. "I will rest," Pyrrhus says. To which Cineas responds, "Why not rest right away?"[13] Cineas's serial questioning is important, and Beauvoir takes it seriously. "What's the use of leaving if it is to return home?" Beauvoir asks.[14] Cineas's questioning isn't just about Pyrrhus's plan of world domination. It's also about the motivations of human actions. Indeed, why do we do the things that we do? That's what Cineas is really asking without however explicitly asking it.

But isn't the answer to that question obvious? We pursue the projects that we pursue because of some end that they promise to deliver. Yet this obvious answer can't be right. If we take Cineas seriously, our ultimate ends are revealed, through reflection, to be arbitrary. Choose any desirable end—let's say, doing well in law school. Such an end makes sense only because we want to become a lawyer. But why become a lawyer instead of a doctor, or an artist, or a culinary specialist? Maybe it's because we want to help others or because we want to make money or because we want to have a stable job. But then why do we want those things and not some others? Just like Cineas, we can keep interrogating our actions and their motives. At some point, however, we're going to be left with no answer. All chains of reasoning, all explanations and forms of justification, must come to an end somewhere. When we can no longer offer an answer to the why question (to the question of why we've chosen one thing over another), we come to see our goals as arbitrary. They don't become meaningless in this light—they still matter a great deal to us. But if we're honest with ourselves, we must admit that there's no real reason why we're pursuing them.

Cineas's questioning gives rise to a double conclusion.[15] First, there's no *ultimate* ground for our goals—there's only the appearance of one. Second, because our goals lack such a ground, we can't rationally justify our projects on the basis of the goals and outcomes that they promise to deliver. One can explain why one wants to get into law school by stating, "I want to become a lawyer." But such an explanation only postpones the inevitable. The goal and wish to become a lawyer can also be questioned. And so can the goal that motivates the goal to become a lawyer. We have to accept that we do some things in life—those that are the motivations behind our most personal and self-defining projects—not because of some reason or another, but simply because we do. To borrow a famous remark by Austrian philosopher Ludwig Wittgenstein: "If I have exhausted the justifications I have reached bedrock, and my spade is turned. Then I am inclined to say: 'This is simply what I do.'"[16]

Beauvoir accepts Cineas's conclusion but doesn't think that it undermines human nature and activity. On the contrary, the conclusion reveals for Beauvoir the ultimate ground of human existence—and that isn't reason, but action. "In spite of everything, my heart beats, my hand reaches out, new projects are born and push me forward," she tells us.[17] To be human is to act, which means to have projects, one after another. There's no escape from committing ourselves to our projects, for that is what it means to have a life. We are, in other words, first and foremost, doers. "To live a love is to throw oneself through that love toward new goals: a home, a job, a common future. Since man is project, his happiness, like his pleasures, can only be projects. . . . Pascal said it perfectly: it is not the hare that interests the hunter, it's the hunt."[18] Or, in the words of Greek poet C. P. Cavafi, we should hope for the voyage of life to "be long, full of adventures."[19]

The point of human existence isn't an end but the motion toward that end; it isn't some specific goals or projects, but the continuous creation and pursuit of them. "Man is only by choosing himself; if he refuses to choose, he annihilates himself," Beauvoir writes and offers, unwittingly, a discerning diagnosis of Bartleby's condition.[20] Bartleby annihilated himself—starved himself to death—by not choosing. Both the dialogue between Pyrrhus and Cineas and Bartleby's story carry the same message: there's no life without choosing and doing. "Man has no other way of existing," Beauvoir tells us. "It is Pyrrhus and not Cineas, who is right. Pyrrhus leaves in order to conquer; let him conquer, then. 'After that?' After that, he'll see."[21]

• • •

How do we move through life? Our free choices are characterized by our aim to minimize the distance between our current situation and a desired one. We set our aims and we choose to realize them. The term "self-regulation" refers to the psychological processes that permit us to carry out this sort of directed movement. It's through such processes that we first become aware of the existence of a discrepancy between our goals and our current situation. And it's through them that we utilize the needed resources to pursue and accomplish our goals. Self-regulation allows us to think, feel, and act in ways that are consistent with, and conducive to the realization of, our standards and desires.

Self-regulation can be hard. Often it requires the exertion of effort—just think of how it feels to stick to a diet, to complete your homework, or to do your taxes. Such activities aren't pleasurable. We don't do them for their inherent rewards. Still, we make ourselves do them because of what they bring—they're the means toward the ends that we desire. As one can quickly surmise, our ability to regulate our behavior is greatly beneficial. Because of self-regulation we're able to focus and ignore distractions. We're able to do the things that matter to us. We're able to succeed.

There are different ways of thinking about and measuring self-regulation. According to regulatory mode theory, a specific and greatly influential model of self-regulation developed by psychologists Edward Tory Higgins and Arie W. Kruglanski and tested in numerous studies, human behavior is guided by two largely independent components: *assessment* and *locomotion*.[22] The distinction between these two components can be readily illustrated with the use of an example. Consider the decision to join a gym. Some individuals spend a great amount of time trying to come up with answers to the following questions: "What's the best gym?" "What type of exercises should I do?" "Should I do weights, or shall I register for classes?" "Do I need a trainer?" "Do I have the right outfit and gear?" "What's the best time of year (or month) to join?" Others just choose a gym, perhaps the first one that they see or the one closest to them, register, and just show up. They eschew an exhaustive survey of their options. They don't overthink it; they just do it. These two differing ways of approaching a possible course of action reflect the two components of regulatory mode theory—assessment and locomotion.

Assessment constitutes the comparative aspect of self-regulation. It involves the critical evaluation and comparison of different means and goals to determine which is most worthy of pursuit. When we're trying to decide on how to act, we first need to become aware of our options. We also need to think of the costs associated with each of these options and their benefits. Finally, we need to decide which goal to pursue. All of these processes and mechanisms are part of the assessment component of self-regulation.

Whereas assessment is the evaluator and decider of self-regulation, loco-motion is the doer: it's the aspect of self-regulation that involves the commit-ment of one's psychological resources to initiate and maintain goal-directed activity. It's important to note that locomotion isn't characterized by a specific end state but rather by movement itself, where movement is understood to be any change from one state (psychological or physical) to another. In other words, what locomotion does is to move us, not to a specific state, but to any state other than the current one. Locomotion abhors the status quo. It craves and seeks for change.

Neither locomotion nor assessment is an all-or-nothing matter: individuals can be characterized as low or high in either one of them. Whether one is high or low on either one of these components of self-regulation is measured with the use of two questionnaires. When responding to these questionnaires, individuals report the extent to which each of the statements comprising the questionnaires accurately describe themselves (see Table 10.1). The manner in which one responds to the questionnaires reveals whether one is a high or low assessor and a high or low locomotor.

A high locomotion focus is highly desirable. The list of its benefits is long.[23] Compared to low locomotion individuals, high locomotors are more likely to act on their intentions and are better able to cope with change.[24] In turn, high locomotors are better at time management, and more likely to accumulate savings for retirement, to get better grades in school, and to contribute more to their partners' well-being than low locomotors.[25] They also experience less regret, less nostalgia, less counterfactual thinking ("What if things had been otherwise"), and less negative affect than low locomotors.[26] Furthermore, high locomotors invest more time and effort into goal attainment.[27] They procrastinate less and finish tasks more quickly.[28] Multitasking agrees with them.[29] And they're more willing to forgive themselves and others.[30]

There are some dangers associated with too much locomotion, but only if coupled with low assessment.[31] For instance, high locomotors' desire for movement and change might make it hard for them to learn from the past. Because of their focus on motion and change, they might miss out on what's going on in the present, and they might neglect friendships. Moved by their desire to act quickly, they might even commit to a course of action that ulti-mately doesn't yield the best consequences. All the same, a large body of ev-idence clearly shows that high locomotion is a beneficial trait, even when it's not accompanied by high assessment.

Individuals high on locomotion tend to be future oriented:[32] when one is concerned with moving forward, one will inevitably be concerned with the future. Thus, a locomotion focus is a focus on the future. Indeed, studies have found that high locomotors show greater attentiveness to and concern for the

Table 10.1 Items That Make Up the Locomotion and Assessment Scales

Item
Locomotion Items

1. I don't mind doing things even if they involve extra effort.
2. When I finish one project, I often wait a while before getting started on a new one. (Reverse-scored)
3. I am a "workaholic."
4. I feel excited just before I am about to reach a goal.
5. I enjoy actively doing things, more than just watching and observing.
6. I am a "doer."
7. When I decide to do something, I can't wait to get started.
8. By the time I accomplish a task, I already have the next one in mind.
9. I am a "low energy" person. (Reverse-scored)
10. Most of the time my thoughts are occupied with the task I wish to accomplish.
11. When I get started on something, I usually persevere until I finish it.
12. I am a "go-getter."

Assessment Items

1. I never evaluate my social interactions with others after they occur. (Reverse-scored)
2. I spend a great deal of time taking inventory of my positive and negative characteristics.
3. I like evaluating other people's plans.
4. I often critique work done by myself or others.
5. I often compare myself with other people.
6. I often feel that I am being evaluated by others.
7. I am very self-critical and self-conscious about what I am saying.
8. I rarely analyze the conversations I have had with others after they occur. (Reverse-scored)
9. I am a critical person.
10. I don't spend much time thinking about ways others could improve themselves. (Reverse-scored)
11. I often think that other people's choices and decisions are wrong.
12. When I meet a new person I usually evaluate how well he or she is doing on various dimensions (e.g., looks, achievements, social status, clothes).

Source: Reproduced from Kruglanski et al. (2018).

future. They're also optimistic about the future, and they feel little guilt about the past.[33] These traits of locomotion are necessary for the pursuit of a good life. The tendency to focus on the future leads individuals to anticipate and plan for the future. A concern with motion and change motivates individuals to set goals and to commit to them. High locomotors experience life in motion. And that's a good thing.

• • •

Motion is what brings together boredom, frustration, and anticipation. All three are our antidotes to stagnation: they promote movement and contribute to the locomotion dimension of self-regulation which in turn allows us to live a life in which we commit ourselves to projects and set out to accomplish them. Consider first boredom. Given its affective, cognitive, volitional, and physiological aspects, boredom is a psychological state that has the capacity to help us achieve movement. I spoke at length about the motivational power of boredom. And although boredom's value isn't exhausted by its capacity to move us, that's a big part of it. Boredom doesn't just signal dissatisfaction with our current situation, it also acts as a push that motivates us to get out of uninteresting and meaningless situations. As such, the state of boredom contributes to the exercise of locomotion. To alleviate boredom, we're motivated to change our (physical or social) situation or to engage in a different mental activity. Boredom is a source of movement when we find ourselves at a halt.

Frustration plays a similar role. Because of its capacity to energize us, it allows us to overcome obstacles and to meet goals of personal significance. Frustration might not be what initiates the pursuit of a goal—we don't seek out a goal because it's frustrating to us—but once we're engaged with a goal and we become frustrated by our inability to achieve it, we continue to chase after it. In doing so, frustration saves us from giving up all too easily on goals that are important to us. But frustration can promote movement in an additional manner. Frustration, remember, has a breaking point. If something is too frustrating, we'll stop pursuing it and instead choose something else to do. In this way, frustration safeguards us from becoming stuck with an insurmountable obstacle. Frustration, hence, moves us. It does so either because it motivates us to overcome an obstacle that blocks the completion of an important goal, or because it pushes us to give up on a frustrating project that we can't complete or conquer. Either way, frustration doesn't let setbacks and failures immobilize us.

Given its emphasis on future, anticipation and locomotion are closely related. Without an ability to look into the future and plan, one wouldn't be able to move through life. And vice versa—those who are able to move are ones who anticipate and plan ahead. When we anticipate, our attention and effort are directed toward the future. What becomes important is that which lies ahead of us. The present is seen through the lens of whatever event we anticipate. In this way, the state of anticipation highlights not only future events but also the importance that such events hold in our life. Anticipation is a motivating mechanism that helps us to keep moving into the future so that we can achieve our goals and realize our dreams.

But because such states move us, they also help us achieve personal growth. Boredom promotes motion but not just any kind of motion. It doesn't move us from one uninteresting or meaningless state to another. Rather, it moves us from an uninteresting or meaningless state to one that is perceived by us to be interesting or meaningful. In this way, boredom promotes the pursuit of significant activities, and contributes to the buildup of personal meaning. Boredom helps us to find what matters to us. And it takes us there.

The experience of frustration is an indication of value and personal significance. Indeed, the objects of frustration are goals that are important for us but blocked. By permitting us to chase after them and by helping us to overcome the obstacles that block our goals, frustration, like boredom, promotes personal growth. It gets us closer to the completion of those goals. It adds meaning to our lives, for it keeps us moving not in an aimless direction but toward the fulfillment of matters of personal significance.

Anticipation too contributes to personal growth, and it does so almost by definition. Without anticipation there would be no goals to pursue, no aspirations to aspire to, and no ideals to model one's life after. We would be fully content with what's given to us in the present. But this form of contention with our current state is precisely the antithesis of growth. Being perpetually stuck in the present vitiates any possibility of growth.

• • •

In this book, I've argued for a conception of human existence that takes seriously both the ups and especially the downs of life. The aim has been to articulate a picture of the good life that isn't fixated on happy feelings and sensations but on the pursuit and accomplishment of meaningful projects and activities. Such an essentially active life will come with disappointments, bouts of boredom, hardships, feelings of frustration, waiting, and periods of anticipation. But precisely because it contains all of that, it's a life worth living. Temporary states of discontent (boredom, frustration, waiting in anticipation) are crucial and necessary for meaningful lives. If everything struck us as interesting, if the world constantly and too easily satisfied us, and if there was nothing to anticipate, then we'd ultimately occupy a world that carried none of our personal values. The way in which we discover and create values in the world—and develop and grow as human beings—is by having to decide what's interesting and what's not, by being forced to encounter and deal with frustrating situations, and by being asked to figure out what's worth pursuing.

Well-being isn't an one-dimensional ideal. It includes happiness and positive feelings. But it also includes the determination and pursuit of meaningful goals, the discovery and exercise of one's talents, personal growth, and the creation and maintenance of one's social and physical environment. Living well is a multidimensional dynamic process. It involves movement and progress.

It involves the taking up of interests. It requires the expression and exercise of a number of human capacities. The good life is an activity, not a happening. And because of that, motion is necessary to achieve it.

We have boredom, frustration, and anticipation to thank for our ability to move out of our present and into a better future.

"The beauty of the promised land," Beauvoir writes in *Pyrrhus and Cineas*, "is that it promised new promises. Immobile paradises promise us nothing but an eternal ennui."[34] The beauty of life lies in motion. It lies in those states of discontent that keep us going.

Acknowledgments

For a book on boredom and frustration, this has been a project of tremendous joy. Temporary impasses, moments of struggle, and difficult decisions were not, of course, absent. But overall, the journey was more than pleasant and immensely rewarding. A good part of this book was written outdoors on the premises of a paradisiacal cottage in Muskoka Lakes, Ontario, Canada. I thank Jeremy and Elayne Freeman for their generous hospitality and patience.

I'm deeply grateful to my wonderful agent, Laurie Abkemeier, for believing in the project and for being my guide from inception to conclusion. Laurie was instrumental in shaping the voice and tone of the book and in helping me "see" that often the best way to explain a difficult concept is by simplifying it. I am also grateful to my editor at Oxford University Press, Abby Gross, for her unwavering support, conversations about the book, and her many helpful suggestions. It's been a pleasure working with her, and the book has benefited greatly from her discerning edits and suggestions. I would like to thank the referees who have read and commented on the book. My thanks also go to my colleague John Gibson for the many lengthy, often late-night, conversations that we had on art, literature, and boredom. I thank James Danckert for discussions on boredom and emotions, and audiences at various conferences and workshops for their feedback. I would like to acknowledge the support of the Commonwealth Center for the Humanities and Society at the University of Louisville. With the permission of Taylor & Francis, a few sentences from my "The Good of Boredom," *Philosophical Psychology 31*, no. 3 (2018), 323–351, appear in chapters 5 and 10. A couple of passages from chapter 5 have previously appeared in a blog post that I authored for OUPBlog ("Boredom's Push," September 17, 2017). I thank the Andy Warhol Museum, the American Psychological Association, the New Directions Publishing Corporation, and the Houghton Mifflin Harcourt Publishing Company for permissions to use copyrighted material. I would also like to thank Bennett Foddy for allowing me to use screenshots of his video games, QWOP and Getting Over It with Bennett Foddy.

Above all, I owe a profound debt of gratitude to my partner, Lauren Freeman, for always being there. Every page in this book is better than it would have been had I not received her input.

Notes

Preface

1. Hinton (1881), p. 238.
2. This thought experiment is famously discussed in Nozick (1974).

Chapter 1

1. Peterson and colleagues (Peterson et al., 2005) distinguish between *three* different ways of achieving happiness: through pleasure, through meaning, and through engagement. According to them, a full or flourishing life is one that is simultaneously pleasurable, meaningful, and engaging.
2. Diener & Seligman (2002).
3. For a more detailed description, see Raman (2018) or consult your nearest neuroscience textbook.
4. Barbano & Cador (2007).
5. Raman (2018), p. 79.
6. Davidai & Gilovich (2016).
7. Wilson & Gilbert (2008).
8. Ibid., p. 379.
9. Wiggins et al. (1992), pp. 1404–5.
10. Ong et al. (2018).
11. Quoidbach et al. (2014).
12. Ibid., p. 2064.

Chapter 2

1. A description of this episode in S.M.'s life is found in Feinstein et al. (2011), supplementary information. The case of S.M. is also discussed in NPR's *Invisibilia*, "World With No Fear" episode, produced by A. Spiegel and L. Miller (January, 2015). Retrieved from https://www.npr.org/2015/01/16/377517810/world-with-no-fear
2. Feinstein (2013).
3. Feinstein et al. (2011), supplementary information.
4. NPR's *Invisibilia*, "World With No Fear."
5. Lerner et al. (2003).
6. Pitts et al. (2014).
7. Clore & Huntsinger (2007); Zadra & Clore (2011). For a defense of the effects of emotions on perception, see Clore & Proffit (2016).
8. Kelley & Schmeichel (2014).
9. Banerjee et al. (2012).

10. For a review, see Isen (2000).
11. Fredrickson & Branigan (2005).
12. Raghunathan & Trope (2002).
13. Fredrickson et al. (2008).
14. Dunn & Schweitzer (2005).
15. American Psychiatric Association (2013), p. 303.
16. Simeon (2004); Stein & Simeon (2009).
17. Simeon (2004); Simeon et al. (2001); van Ijzendoorn & Schuengel (1996).
18. For more on depersonalization/derealization disorder, see American Psychiatric Association (2013), pp. 302–306, and Simeon (2004).
19. Reported in Bockner (1949), p. 969.
20. American Psychiatric Association (2013), p. 303.
21. Simeon and Abugel (2006), p. 81.
22. Reported in Bockner (1949), p. 969.
23. Ibid.
24. The relationship between depersonalization/derealization disorder and anxiety is complex and not fully understood. A number of published studies have noted an association between the two and, indeed, it seems reasonable to hold that individuals who experience their existence as unreal and alien would also feel anxious. However, more recent work has complicated this picture. For instance, a 2012 study offered evidence for treating depersonalization/derealization as an independent condition that may or may not be significantly associated with anxiety (Sierra et al., 2012).
25. Simeon and Abugel (2006), p. 8.
26. Sifneos (1973); see also Nemiah & Sifneos (1970).
27. Sifneos (1973); Taylor et al. (1997).
28. Bagby & Taylor (1997).
29. See Heinzel et al. (2010).
30. Luminet et al. (2006); Sifneos (1973); Taylor et al. (1997).
31. De Gucht & Heiser (2003); Taylor (1997).
32. Love (2016).
33. FeldmanHall et al. (2013); Moriguchi et al. (2007).
34. Reported in Bagby & Taylor (1997), p. 34.
35. Frewen, Dozois et al. (2008).
36. Frewen, Lanius et al. (2008), p. 177; emphasis in original.
37. Ibid; emphasis in original.
38. Sartre (1939/2004), p. 44; page reference is to the English translation.

Chapter 3

1. The presentation of Clive Wearing's case is based on Wearing (2005), which is a description of his life and condition written by Clive's wife, Deborah Wearing. The particular dialogue occurs on page 158.
2. Wearing (2005), p. 160.
3. Gibson (1975).
4. Vonnegut (2009) p. 109; *Slaughterhouse-Five* was originally published in 1969.

5. Vonnegut (2009) p. 34.
6. Augustine (2006), p. 241; *Confessions* was written in Latin by Augustine in the last three years of the fourth century AD. The translation is by F. J. Sheed.
7. Vonnegut (2009), p. 34.
8. Siffre (1975), p. 431. Siffre's story is documented in Siffre (1975). Additional information about his underground adventures can be found in Foer (2008).
9. Siffre (1975).
10. Ibid., p. 428.
11. Ibid., p. 429.
12. Ibid., p. 426.
13. Ibid., p. 429.
14. Ibid., p. 432.
15. Ibid., p. 433.
16. Ibid., p. 435.
17. Ibid.
18. Quotation is taken from John E. Woods's English translation of the book. See Mann (1996), p. 63.
19. Reported in Baum et al. (1984), p. 60.
20. Shakespeare (2004), p. 111. *As You Like It* was entered in the Stationers' Register on August 4, 1600, and published in the First Folio collection of Shakespeare's work (1623).
21. Baumeister (1990), p. 100.
22. Twenge et al. (2003), p. 410.
23. Foer (2008).
24. Here's another illustration of the relationship between our subjective perception of time and the way we live our lives. According to socioemotional selectivity theory developed by psychologist Laura L. Carstensen, our subjective sense of future affects our attitudes, motivations, and ultimately actions. Specifically, when time is perceived by us as open-ended—that is, when we think that we have a long future ahead of us—we are more motivated to expand our knowledge and to seek out novel experiences. When time, however, is perceived as constrained—that is, when we think that we might die soon—we tend to attach less significance to goals that aim to expand our horizons. Instead, we are motivated to pursue short-term goals that can furnish our lives with meaning and emotional satisfaction. For an accessible presentation of socioemotional selectivity theory, see Carstensen (2006).
25. Noyes & Kletti (1977), p. 377.
26. Ibid., p. 378.
27. For a review, see Droit-Volet & Meck (2007).
28. Waits & Sharrock (1984).
29. Droit-Volet et al. (2004); Effron et al. (2006); Gil et al. (2007); Tipples (2011).
30. Angrilli et al. (1997).
31. Campbell & Bryant (2007); see also Sterlini & Bryant (2002).
32. Bschor et al. (2004); Gil & Droit-Volet (2009); Kuhs et al. (1991); Tysk (1984).
33. Wittmann et al. (2006).
34. Proust (2005), p. 205. *In the Shadow of Young Girls in Flower*, originally published in 1919, is the second volume of Proust's celebrated seven-volume *In Search of Lost Time*.

35. Quoted in Droit-Volet & Meck (2007).
36. Bauby (1998).
37. Ibid., p. 20.
38. Ibid.
39. Ibid., p. 101.
40. Frankl (2006), pp. 70–71; *Man's Search for Meaning* was originally published in 1946.
41. Block & Reed (1978); Flaherty et al. (2005); Fraisse (1963); Ornstein (1970); Poynter (1983).
42. For support for this claim, see Block & Zakay (1997) and Zakay & Block (2004).
43. James (1886), p. 390.
44. Twenge et al. (2003).
45. Ibid., p. 421.
46. Ibid.
47. Ibid.
48. Wittmann et al. (2006), p. 360.
49. Ibid., p. 361.
50. Ibid.
51. Baum et al. (1984).

Chapter 4

1. For discussions of *Vexations*, see Orledge (1998) and Whittington (2003).
2. Quoted in Whittington (2003).
3. Cage's performance is discussed in Ross (2007) and Sweet (2013). The *New York Times* sent eight critics to cover the performance and published a review on September 11, 1963, p. 45 of the New York edition.
4. Higgins (1981), p. 21.
5. Ibid.
6. Ibid., p.22.
7. See Watson (2003).
8. Danto (2009), p. 79.
9. Reported in Danto (2009), p. 78.
10. Mekas (1965), p. 12.
11. Battcock (1969), p. 39.
12. Ibid.
13. Bourdon (1989), p. 188.
14. Danto (2009), p. 77.
15. Myers (1967), p. 138.
16. Austen (2003), p. 244; *Emma* was originally published in 1815.
17. The National Center on Addiction and Substance Abuse, 2003. Retrieved from https://www.centeronaddiction.org/addiction-research/reports/national-survey-american-attitudes-substance-abuse-teens-parents-2003
18. GPC Research & Health Canada, 2003; cited in Eastwood et al. (2007).
19. Reported in Spacks (1995), p. 3.

20. Vessel & Russo (2015).
21. Roach (2010), p. 27.
22. R. Wright (1998).
23. Hollingham (2013).
24. Hazen (1937), p. 150.
25. Warhol & Hatchett (1980), p. 64.
26. Cage (1973), p. 93.
27. Goldsmith (2004).
28. Mauriac (2005), pp. 113–114; *Thérèse Desqueyroux* was originally published in 1927.
29. Phillips (1993), p. 78.
30. See, e.g., Sinkewicz (2003) and Cassian (2000). For a discussion of the role of boredom in religious life, see Raposa (1999).
31. Dante (1995), *Inferno*, Canto VII, 121-123; translation by Mark Musa. *The Divine Comedy* was written between 1308–1321.
32. Reported in Maltsberger et al. (2000).
33. Ibid., p. 84.
34. Ibid.
35. Ibid.
36. Ibid.
37. Heidegger (1983).
38. Bernstein (1975), p. 517.
39. Ibid.
40. The original French reads: "Des plaines de l'Ennui, profondes et désertes."
41. Kierkegaard (1987), p. 285; *Either/Or* was originally published in 1843.
42. Ibid.
43. Ibid., p. 290.
44. Ibid., p. 285.
45. See, e.g., Ahmed (1990); Fahlman et al. (2009, 2013); Farmer & Sundberg (1986); Gana & Akremi (1998); Goldberg et al. (2011); Malkovsky et al. (2012); Mercer-Lynn et al. (2013); Rupp & Vodanovich, (1997).
46. Farmer & Sundberg (1986); Goldberg et al. (2011).
47. Roe & Ronen (2003), p. 323.
48. Ibid.
49. Ibid.
50. Isacescu & Danckert (2018).
51. For reviews see Elpidorou (2017b), Vodanovich (2003), and Vodanovich & Watt (2015).
52. Fisher (1993); Loukidou et al. (2009).
53. Drory (1982).
54. Wallace et al. (2002).
55. Cheyne et al. (2006).
56. Leong & Schneller (1993); Tolor (1989); Watt & Vodanovich (1999).
57. Farmer & Sundberg (1986).
58. Fahlman et al. (2009); Weinstein et al. (1995).
59. Eastwood et al. (2012); Martin et al. (2006).
60. Dahlen et al. (2004).

61. Blaszczynski et al. (1990); Dahlen et al. (2005); Lee et al. (2007); LePera (2011); Stickney & Miltenberger (1999).
62. Britton & Shipley (2010).

Chapter 5

1. Levé (2011), p. 8.
2. Ibid., p. 25.
3. Ibid., p. 29.
4. Ibid., p. 92.
5. Ibid.
6. Nietzsche (2003), p. 57; passage is from *Gay Science: With a Prelude in German Rhymes and an Appendix of Songs,* published initially in 1882 and then in an expanded version in 1887.
7. Sontag (2012), p. 144.
8. Russell (2006), p. 39.
9. Phillips (1993), p. 69.
10. Wallace (2012), p. 440.
11. Ibid., p. 548.
12. Dialogue reported in Alex's obituary in *The Economist.* The obituary is titled "Alex the African Grey" and was published online on September 20, 2007. Retrieved from https://www.economist.com/obituary/2007/09/20/alex-the-african-grey
13. My discussion of Alex draws, primarily, from Pepperberg (2002), Pepperberg & Gordon (2005), and Pepperberg (2012).
14. Pepperberg & Gordon (2005), p. 201.
15. Alex's "None" response wasn't a singular, meaningless reaction. Throughout his trials, he would be asked, at random intervals, "What color X?" for a numerical quantity that wasn't present. His accuracy in those unexpected "None" trials was 83%.
16. Kierkegaard (1987), p. 285.
17. Wilson et al. (2014), supplementary material.
18. Ibid., p. 76.
19. Ibid., reported in the data from the study.
20. Havermans et al. (2015).
21. Nederkoorn (2016).
22. Blaszczynski et al. (1990); Dahlen et al. (2005); Lee et al. (2007); LePera (2011); Moynihan et al. (2017); Stickney & Miltenberger (1999).
23. This section of the chapter that discusses boredom's capacity to lead to harm (of ourselves or of others) was originally published in Elpidorou (2017a).
24. Carroll (2009), pp. 11–12; emphasis in original. *Alice's Adventures in Wonderland* was first published in 1865.
25. van Aart et al. (2010).
26. Details for the project can be found at http://www.alice.id.tue.nl
27. Roy (1959); Skowronski (2012).
28. Van Tilburg & Igou (2016, 2017b).
29. Harris (2000); Martin et al. (2006).
30. Killingsworth & Gilbert (2010).

31. Franklin et al. (2011); Mooneyham & Schooler (2013).
32. Killingsworth & Gilbert (2010).
33. Mooneyham & Schooler (2013).
34. Ruby et al. (2013).
35. Baird et al. (2012).
36. Ibid., p. 1120.
37. BALL, AIR, BOWL.
38. Schubert (1977), p. 236.
39. Morin (1971).
40. Mann & Cadman (2014).
41. Gasper & Middlewood (2014).
42. Haager et al. (2018).
43. See, e.g., Bench & Lench (2013); Danckert et al. (2018); Elpidorou (2014); Pekrun et al. (2010); Sansone et al. (1992); J. L. Smith et al. (2009); Van Tilburg & Igou (2012, 2017a).
44. For an elaboration and defense of this view, see Elpidorou (2018a, 2018b).
45. Quoted in Kuhn (2017), p. 332.
46. Washburn & David (2016).
47. Russell (2006), p. 38.
48. See also Bench & Lench (2013, 2019).
49. Bar-On et al. (2002); Baxter & Olszewski (1960); Nagasako et al. (2003); Swanson (1963); Thrush (1973).

Chapter 6

1. Taylor & Taylor (2003), p. 123.
2. The incident is discussed in Pepperberg (2012).
3. Ibid., p. 52.
4. See also Killeen (1994).
5. See, e.g., Amsel (1962, 1991, 1992a, 1992b); Amsel & Roussel (1952).
6. Amsel (1992a), p. 43.
7. Papini & Dudley (1997).
8. Davenport & Thompson (1965), Dubreuil et al. (2006), Jakovcevic et al. (2013), Roma et al. (2006).
9. Crossman et al. (2009).
10. Stout et al. (2003).
11. Rogers (2017).
12. Quoted in Benenson (2011).
13. Quoted in Wiltshire (2018).
14. Vlotis (2018).
15. Review by user named "epicepicman78" on App Store (January 30, 2018).
16. Review by user named "Birhd" on App Store (February 4, 2018).
17. Review by user named "LordCee" on App Store (February 1, 2018).
18. Review by user named "Chrisco80" on App Store (February 7, 2018).
19. Quoted in Vlotis (2018).
20. Review by user named "Zepi23" on App Store (February 2, 2018).

21. Reported in a Kickoff.com article, April 24, 2018. Retrieved from https://www.kickoff.com/news/articles/local/categories/nedbank-cup/nedbank-comment-moses-mabhida-mayhem-kai/588855
22. Reported in Makhaya (2018).
23. Quoted in Govender (2018).
24. Munyo & Rossi (2013), p. 140.
25. Priks (2010).
26. Card & Dahl (2011).
27. Guerra et al. (1995).
28. Catalano et al. (1993).
29. Harris (1974).
30. Dollard et al. (1939).
31. The Yale researchers understood frustration not as an internal state, but as an objective happening in the world. Frustration, accordingly, is any barrier that obstructs an agent's goal. The benefit of this particular understanding of frustration is that the presence of frustration can be easily observed: an unexpected loss is frustration, my inability to put together IKEA furniture is frustration, and so is a cancelled flight. The original frustration-aggression hypothesis also included a thesis that pertains to when aggression stops. The researchers proposed that frustration ends when one experiences catharsis, that is, a release of tension.
32. Palmer (1903), p. 185.
33. Cohen (1944), p. 379.
34. Kregarman & Worchel (1961). See also Barlett et al. (2016) and Krieglmeyer et al. (2009).
35. See studies reported in Breuer & Elson (2017).
36. Pastore (1950), p. 279.
37. Anderson (1989); Anderson et al. (1997).
38. Kenrick & MacFarlane (1986).
39. Reifman et al. (1991).
40. Gailliot et al. (2007); Gailliot & Baumeister (2018).
41. Rojas & Sanchi (1941).
42. Virkkunen (1983).
43. Fabrykant & Pacella (1948); Lustman et al. (1991); Wilson (1951).
44. Virkkunen (1984).
45. Virkkunen et al. (1989).
46. Benton & Owens (1993).
47. Miller et al. (1941), p. 339.
48. Ovid (1995), pp. 68–69; Ovid's epic poem was composed around 8 AD.
49. This characterization is given by Socrates in Plato's *Philebus* dialogue.
50. Olesha (2004), p. 185.
51. Kant (2017), p. 222; *The Metaphysics of Morals* was originally published in 1797.
52. Aristotle (1941), *Rhetoric*, Bk II, Chapter 10.
53. Davidson (1912), p. 322.
54. Melville (1998), p. 257.
55. Sayers (2004), p. 94.
56. Mandeville (1988); poem originally published in 1705.

57. Ibid.
58. Ibid.
59. van de Ven et al. (2009).
60. R. H. Smith et al. (2008), p. 294.
61. van de Ven et al. (2009), pp. 425–426.
62. Vroman et al. (2009), p. 980.
63. West et al. (2012).
64. Sturgeon & Zautra (2010).
65. Currie & Wang (2004); Hestbaek et al. (2003).
66. Baliki et al. (2008).
67. Vroman et al. (2009), p. 981.
68. Schlesinger (1996), p. 253; emphasis in original.
69. Dow et al. (2012).
70. Ibid.
71. Ibid., p. 186.
72. Vroman et al. (2009), p. 984.
73. Råheim & Håland (2006), p. 747.
74. Dow et al. (2012), p. 184.
75. Ibid.
76. Evans & de Souza (2008), p. 494.
77. Schlesinger (1996), p. 252.
78. Vroman et al. (2009), p. 982.
79. Ibid.
80. Råheim & Håland (2006), p. 748.
81. Vroman et al. (2009), p. 984.
82. Crowe et al. (2010), p. 1482.
83. West et al. (2012), p. 1287.
84. Ibid.
85. Vroman et al. (2009), p. 981.
86. Ibid.
87. Sturgeon & Zautra (2010), p.110.
88. Edward et al. (2009), p. 590.
89. Machida et al. (2013), p. 1060.
90. Eisenberger et al. (2003).
91. Etkin et al. (2011); Lieberman & Eisenberger (2015).
92. Singer et al. (2004).
93. Hariri et al. (2000); Petrovic et al. (2002).
94. Zhang et al. (1999).
95. Abler et al. (2005).
96. Ibid., p.672.
97. Klöppel et al. (2010); Zalla et al. (2000).
98. LeDoux (1998).
99. Rich et al. (2005, 2007); Deveney et al. (2013).
100. Bierzynska et al. (2016).
101. Ibid., p. 8.

102. Yu (2016), p. 234.
103. Yu et al. (2014).
104. Yu (2016), p. 234.
105. Ibid.
106. Hebb (1955), p. 249.

Chapter 7

1. Phillips (2013), p. 15.
2. Merzbach & Boyer (2011), p. 161.
3. Herrin (2013), pp. 313–316.
4. Quoted in Acerbi (2013).
5. This is how E. T. Bell calls Fermat; see Bell (1965), p. 56.
6. Acerbi (2013).
7. Bell (1961); reported in Singh (1997), p.68.
8. Reported in Singh (1997), p. 6.
9. Ibid.
10. Ibid., p. 145.
11. Wiles's struggles and eventual proof of Fermat's Last Theorem are documented in Singh's wonderful *Fermat's Enigma* (Singh, 1997). Singh also offers an overview of the history of attempts to prove Fermat's Last Theorem.
12. Singh (1997), p. 231.
13. Ibid.
14. Ibid., p.285.
15. Ibid.
16. Porges (1997), p. 68.
17. Ibid., p. 69.
18. "Andrew Wiles: what does it feel to do maths?" Interview with Andrew Wiles. Retrieved from https://plus.maths.org/content/andrew-wiles-what-does-if-feel-do-maths
19. Harford (2016).
20. Quoted in Da Fonseca-Wollheim (2008).
21. Wikipedia contributors. (2019, June 13). Imperial Bösendorfer. *Wikipedia*. Retrieved from https://en.wikipedia.org/w/index.php?title=Imperial_B%C3%B6sendorfer&oldid=901703025
22. Da Fonseca-Wollheim (2008).
23. Quoted in Harford (2016), p. 2.
24. "At 70, Keith Jarrett Is Learning How To Bottle Inspiration." Keith Jarrett being interviewed by NPR's Rachael Martin. The interview was heard on Weekend Edition Sunday (May 10, 2015). Transcript retrieved from https://www.npr.org/2015/05/10/404975326/at-70-keith-jarrett-is-learning-how-to-bottle-inspiration
25. Quoted in Da Fonseca-Wollheim (2008).
26. Harford (2016), p. 3.
27. Sapp (1992), p. 24.
28. Ibid. pp. 24–25.

29. Reported in Friedel et al. (2010), p. 8.
30. "Edison's Newest Marvel," anonymous article in the *New York Sun*, September 16, 1878. Reproduction of the article was retrieved from http://edison.rutgers.edu/yearofinno/EL/Doc1439_NYSun_9-16-78.pdf
31. "Subdivision of electric light" was a phrase that Edison used to describe his invention. It also appears in the patent application for an electric lamp that was filed November 4, 1879 and granted as U.S. Pattern 223,898 on January 27, 1880.
32. "Edison's Newest Marvel," *New York Sun*, September 16, 1878.
33. Bright (1949).
34. Reported in Friedel et al. (2010), p. 12.
35. Friedel et al. (2010), p. 93.
36. Quoted in Adair (1996), p. 71.
37. Shapiro (2004).
38. "Flat-Pack Accounting," *The Economist*. Published online on May 11, 2006. Retrieved from https://www.economist.com/business/2006/05/11/flat-pack-accounting
39. Calderon (2013).
40. Purtill (2015).
41. Reported in Bach (2018).
42. Reported in Collins (2011).
43. Norton et al. (2012).
44. Ibid., p. 455.
45. For the biological effects of effort and frustration, see Inzlicht et al. (2018) and references therein.
46. Aronson & Mills (1959).
47. Olivola & Shafir (2013). For a study showing that extremely painful rituals can promote prosociality, see Xygalatas et al. (2013).
48. Olivola & Shafir (2013).
49. Brehm et al. (1966).
50. H. F. Wright (1937).
51. Apps et al. (2015); Kool & Botvinick (2014); Kurzban et al. (2013); Westbrook (2013).
52. Quoted in Viesturs & Roberts (2009), p. 9.
53. A great source of information about mountaineering is Alan Arnette's blog (http://www.alanarnette.com/blog/). In a blog post dated December 17, 2017, he offers statistics regarding successful ascends to Mount Everest. The post is available at http://www.alanarnette.com/blog/2017/12/17/everest-by-the-numbers-2018-edition/
54. "Stairway to Heaven," *The Economist*, May 29, 2013. Retrieved from https://www.economist.com/graphic-detail/2013/05/29/stairway-to-heaven
55. Viesturs & Roberts (2009).
56. Reported in Viesturs & Roberts (2009), p. 82.
57. Loewenstein (1999), p. 321.
58. Quoted in "Climbing Mount Everest is Work for Supermen," *The New York Times*, March 18, 1923. Retrieved from http://graphics8.nytimes.com/packages/pdf/arts/mallory1923.pdf
59. Loewenstein (1999), p. 317.
60. "Climbing Mount Everest Is Work for Supermen," *The New York Times*, March 18, 1923.

61. Sagar (2017).
62. Quoted in Powel (2017).
63. "Speaking With: Mountaineer Andrew Lock." Podcast by David Bishop for *The Conversation*. Retrieved from https://theconversation.com/speaking-with-mountaineer-andrew-lock-30036
64. Taylor & Taylor (2003), p. 135.
65. Phillips (2013), p. 26.

Chapter 8

1. Beckett (2006); *Endgame* was first performed in Great Britain in French as *Fin de partie* on April 3, 1957 at the Royal Court Theater in London.
2. Beckett (1970), p. 3.
3. Ibid., p. 1.
4. Homer, *Illiad*, Book 8.
5. Quoted in Fraisse (1963), p. 202. Guyau's claim appears to oversimplify human psychology. Is waiting for a bad outcome the same as waiting for a need to be satisfied? And do all experiences of felt time require our monitoring of how our desires or needs are faring? It isn't clear. Or better, the answer will depend on how we understand the nature of needs and desires. But in Guyau's defense, even in cases in which we anticipate for something bad to happen (either to us or to others), we are still waiting for some need to be satisfied— perhaps, it is the need for closure, the need to find out what happens, or even the need to be proven wrong.
6. L. Smith (2012).
7. Damoiseaux et al. (2006); Mantini et al. (2007).
8. For helpful overviews of this view of the brain, see Clark (2013, 2016) and Hohwy (2013).
9. Blumstein & Myers (2014), p. 511.
10. Thorpe et al. (1996).
11. Clark (2016), p. xiv.
12. Helmholtz (1867).
13. See, e.g., Bastos et al. (2012); Brodski et al. (2015); Engel et al. (2001); Friston (2005, 2008).
14. Hawkins & Blakeslee (2005), p.96.
15. A detailed report of the accident can be found at https://reports.aviation-safety.net/1992/19921004-2_B742_4X-AXG.pdf
16. Crombag et al. (1996).
17. Wells & Bradfield (1998).
18. See also Loftus & Palmer (1974).
19. Wade et al. (2002), p. 599.
20. Fernyhough (2014), p. 137.
21. Seamon et al. (2006).
22. Bartlett (1932), p. 204.
23. Fernyhough (2014), p. 7.
24. Borges (1962), p. 113.
25. Fernyhough (2014), pp. 5–7.
26. Schacter (2002), p. 9.

27. Buonomano (2017), pp. 10–11.
28. Schacter & Addis (2007).
29. Hassabis et al. (2007).
30. Addis et al. (2008).
31. El Haj et al. (2015).
32. Russell (2003), p. 161.
33. Frijda (1986).
34. Loewenstein et al. (2001), p. 272.
35. See, e.g., Cialdini et al. (1973) and Cunningham et al. (1980). Sadness, however, doesn't always have a prosocial effect. Cialdini & Kenrick (1976) and Thompson & Hoffman (1980) discuss cases in which the link between sadness and helping breaks.
36. Manucia et al. (1984).
37. Ibid., p. 360.
38. Tice et al. (2001).
39. Bushman et al. (2001).
40. DeWall et al. (2016). See also Baumeister et al. (2007).
41. Baumeister (2016), p. 216.
42. Baumgartner et al. (2008).
43. Damasio (1996).
44. Bechara et al. (1994, 1997, 2005); Damasio (1996).
45. Bechara et al. (1997).
46. Weiner (2001), p. 123.
47. Ibid., p. 225.
48. Aronson (2013).
49. Although captivating and tremendously influential, the lecture did contain some seemingly paradoxical or even contradictory remarks. For instance, Sartre claimed both that existentialism is a form of atheism and that the existence of God does not matter for existentialists.
50. Sartre (1984), p. 86; reference is to the English translation.
51. Sartre (2007), p. 22; reference is to the English translation.
52. Ibid.
53. Beauvoir (2011), p. 270.
54. Heidegger (1927), p. 42; emphasis in original.
55. Ortega y Gasset (1993), p. 41.
56. Heidegger (1927), p. 245.

Chapter 9

1. Loewenstein (1992); O'Donoghue & Rabin (1999).
2. See Ryan et al. (2018).
3. Bentham (1970).
4. Jevons (1905), p. 3.
5. Loewenstein (1987).
6. Kocher et al. (2014).
7. Ibid., p. 30.

8. Kumar et al. (2014).

9. Ibid., p. 6.

10. Richins (2012).

11. Ibid., p. 14.

12. Bryant & Veroff (2007), p. 2; emphasis added.

13. Beauvoir (2004), p. 96.

14. Bryant (2003).

15. Ibid.

16. J. L. Smith & Hollinger-Smith (2015).

17. J. L. Smith & Bryant (2019).

18. Bryant (2003).

19. Quoidbach et al. (2010), p. 762.

20. Libby et al. (2007).

21. Pham & Taylor (1999).

22. Gregory et al. (1982).

23. Sharot (2011a); Baker & Emery (1993).

24. Hoch (1985).

25. Weinstein (1980).

26. For more discussion, see Sharot (2011a, 2011b). As psychologist Martin E. P. Seligman and colleagues have shown in a number of publications, optimism can be influenced by personality, upbringing, and social factors. See, e.g., Seligman (1991), Lee & Seligman (1997), and Forgeard & Seligman (2012). In fact, Seligman and colleagues developed the view that optimism should be understood as an explanatory strategy or tendency. Specifically, optimists tend to explain positive events as being due to internal, stable causes and negative events as arising from external and often transient (or temporary) causes. What such an explanatory strategy entails is that the optimist would conceive of positive events as their own doing (as the products of some stable characteristics that they possess) and consequently, as events that are likely to happen again in the future. On the contrary, because optimists understand negative events to be ones that are due to external and transient causes, they will conceive of them as events that aren't likely to be repeated.

27. The phenomenon or idea of *depressive realism* is also of relevance here. In a now classic study in psychology (Alloy & Abramson, 1979), participants were asked to judge the degree of correspondence/connectedness between their act of pressing a button and a light coming on. Although the connection between the two was not under participants' control (it was set by the researchers), Alloy and Abramson (1979) reported that depressed individuals were able to offer more accurate judgments of the connection. Specifically, participants who were low in depressive symptoms overestimated the extent to which they were in control of the outcome (the light coming on), whereas participants who scored above a threshold for depressive symptoms did not exhibit the same bias. The Alloy and Abramson study gave rise to the notion of "sadder but wiser," that is, the idea that at least sometimes depressive moods might be beneficial insofar as they can help us to judge our situation more accurately. There is a lot of discussion of depressive realism in the relevant literature. Here I wish to make the following brief remarks. First, researchers weren't able to replicate the Alloy and Abramson findings when they used participants who met the clinical criteria for depression (as opposed to individuals with mild depressive symptoms)

(see, e.g., Carson et al., 2010; Dobson & Pusch, 1995). Second, many studies that claimed to have measured a bias in likelihood judgments of future events haven't utilized an objective benchmark against which such judgments could be compared (for discussion, see MacLeod, 2017, pp. 57–62). Third, there are findings that oppose the idea of depressive realism. For instance, Strunk and colleagues (Strunk et al., 2006) reported that individuals who scored high in depression were *less* accurate than nondepressed individuals. Fourth, and final point, even if there are cases in which a depressive mood could lead to more accurate judgments, it's hard to see optimism as anything but a good thing, given its connection to both emotional and physical well-being.

28. Giltay (2004); Segerstrom et al. (2017).
29. Diener & Chan (2011); Tindle et al. (2009).
30. Ironson & Hayward (2008).
31. Puri & Robinson (2007).
32. Nes et al. (2005); Segerstrom (2001).
33. Van Tilburg & Igou (2019).
34. Sharot et al. (2011).
35. Sharot (2011b), p. R943.
36. Ibid.
37. Varki (2009).
38. Kundera (1992), p. 34.
39. Ibid., pp. 36–37.
40. MacLeod et al. (1993).
41. MacLeod (2017).
42. Ibid.
43. MacLeod et al. (1993).
44. MacLeod et al. (2005).
45. Beck et al. (1974).
46. See MacLeod (2017), pp. 34–36.
47. Beck et al. (1985, 1993); Beevers & Miller (2004); Brezo et al. (2006); Joiner et al. (2005); Minkoff et al. (1973).
48. Abbey et al. (2006).
49. Crane et al. (2012).
50. Ibid., p. 62.
51. Ibid.
52. Ibid.
53. Ibid., p. 65.
54. Ibid.
55. Ibid.
56. Holmes et al. (2007).
57. Wang et al. (2011).
58. Vitale & Genge (2007).
59. http://www.alsa.org/about-als/facts-you-should-know.html
60. "Amyotrophic Lateral Sclerosis (ALS) Early Symptoms, Causes, and Prognosis" in MedicineNet.com. Retrieved from https://www.medicinenet.com/amyotrophic_lateral_sclerosis/article.htm#what_is_the_treatment_for_the_symtptoms_of_als_is_there_cure

61. See, e.g., the following website: http://alsworldwide.org/perspectives
62. Quoted in Rudulph (2014).
63. Ibid.
64. Coglianese (2015).
65. Quoted in Griffo (2014).
66. McDonald et al. (1996), p. 40; emphasis in original.
67. Rabkin et al. (2000), p. 277.
68. Rabkin et al. (2015).
69. Ibid., p. 265 (from the abstract).
70. Ibid., p. 272.
71. Lulé et al. (2008), p. 397 (from the abstract).
72. Rabkin et al. (2005).
73. Quoted in Rabkin et al. (2000), p. 277.

Chapter 10

1. Sheratt & MacLeod (2013).
2. Melville (1998).
3. Ibid., p.22.
4. Ibid., p.29.
5. Ibid., p.31.
6. Ibid., p.34.
7. Ibid., p.35.
8. Ibid.
9. Ibid., p. 14.
10. Beauvoir (2004), p. 90.
11. Plutarch (1920), p. 367.
12. Ibid., p. 417.
13. The dialogue appears in Beauvoir (2004), p. 90.
14. Ibid.
15. For more discussion, see Webber (2018).
16. Wittgenstein (1968), §217.
17. Beauvoir (2004), p. 91.
18. Ibid., p. 98.
19. Cavafi (2008), p. 37.
20. Beauvoir (2004), p. 113.
21. Ibid.
22. Higgins et al. (2003); Kruglanski et al. (2000, 2013).
23. Kruglanski et al. (2013, 2018).
24. Kruglanski et al. (2007); Mannetti et al. (2010).
25. Kim et al. (2013); Kruglanski et al. (2000, 2018); Kumashiro et al. (2007).
26. Hong et al. (2004); Kruglanski et al. (2000); Pierro et al. (2008); Pierro, Pica et al. (2013).
27. Kruglanski et al. (2000).
28. Pierro et al. (2011).
29. Pierro, Giacomantonio et al. (2013).

30. Pierro et al. (2014); cited in Kruglanski et al. (2018).
31. For some discussion of the drawbacks of high locomotion, see Kruglanski et al. (2016).
32. Kruglanski et al. (2016, 2018).
33. Kruglanski et al. (2018).
34. Beauvoir (2004), p. 98.

References

Abbey, J. G., Rosenfeld, B., Pessin, H., & Breitbart, W. (2006). Hopelessness at the end of life: the utility of the hopelessness scale with terminally ill cancer patients. *British Journal of Health Psychology, 11*(2), 173–183.

Abler, B., Walter, H., & Erk, S. (2005). Neural correlates of frustration. *NeuroReport, 16*(7), 669–672.

Acerbi, F. (2013). Why John Chortasmenos sent Diophantus to the devil. *Greek, Roman, and Byzantine Studies, 53*(2), 379–389.

Adair, G. (1996). *Thomas Alva Edison: Inventing the electric age.* New York, NY: Oxford University Press.

Addis, D. R., Wong, A. T., & Schacter, D. L. (2008). Age-related changes in the episodic simulation of future events. *Psychological science, 19*(1), 33–41.

Ahmed, S. M. S. (1990). Psychometric properties of the boredom proneness scale. *Perceptual and Motor Skills, 71*(3), 963–966.

Alloy, L. B., & Abramson, L. Y. (1979). Judgment of contingency in depressed and nondepressed students: Sadder but wiser? *Journal of Experimental Psychology: General, 108*(4), 441–485.

American Psychiatric Association. (2013). *Diagnostic and statistical manual of mental disorders* (5th ed.). Arlington, VA: Author.

Amsel, A. (1962). Frustrative nonreward in partial reinforcement and discrimination learning: Some recent history and a theoretical extension. *Psychological Review, 69*(4), 306–328.

Amsel, A. (1991). What I learned about frustration at Iowa. In J. H. Cantor (Ed.), *Psychology at Iowa: Centennial essays* (pp. 151–167). Hillsdale, NJ: Erlbaum.

Amsel, A. (1992a). *Frustration theory: An analysis of dispositional learning and memory.* Cambridge, UK: Cambridge University Press.

Amsel, A. (1992b). Frustration theory: Many years later. *Psychological Bulletin, 112*(3), 396–399.

Amsel, A., & Roussel, J. (1952). Motivational properties of frustration: I. Effect on a running response of the addition of frustration to the motivational complex. *Journal of Experimental Psychology, 43*(5), 363–368.

Anderson, C. A. (1989). Temperature and aggression: ubiquitous effects of heat on occurrence of human violence. *Psychological Bulletin, 106*(1), 74–96.

Anderson, C. A., Bushman, B. J., & Groom, R. W. (1997). Hot years and serious and deadly assault: empirical tests of the heat hypothesis. *Journal of Personality and Social Psychology, 73*(6), 1213–1223.

Angrilli, A., Cherubini, P., Pavese, A., & Manfredini, S. (1997). The influence of affective factors on time perception. *Perception & Psychophysics, 59*(6), 972–982.

Apps, M. A., Grima, L. L., Manohar, S., & Husain, M. (2015). The role of cognitive effort in subjective reward devaluation and risky decision-making. *Scientific Reports, 5*, 16880.

Aristotle. (1941). *The basic works of Aristotle.* Edited by R. McKeon. New York, NY: Random House.

Aronson, E., & Mills, J. (1959). The effect of severity of initiation on liking for a group. *Journal of Abnormal and Social Psychology, 59*(2), 177–181.

Aronson, R. (2013). The night Sartre became famous. *Publishers Weekly*, May 31. Retrieved from https://www.publishersweekly.com/pw/by-topic/industry-news/tip-sheet/article/57475-the-night-sartre-became-famous.html

Augustine. (2006). *Confessions* (2nd ed.). Translated by F. J. Sheed. Indianapolis, IN: Hackett. (Originally written in 397–400 AD)

Austen, J. (2003). *Emma*. Edited with an introduction by F. Stafford. London, UK: Penguin Books.

Bach, N. (2018). Watch a robot complete your most frustrating task: Assembling IKEA furniture. *Fortune*, April 19. Retrieved from http://fortune.com/2018/04/19/ikea-furniture-assembly-robot/

Bagby, R. M., & Taylor, G. J. (1997). Affect dysregulation and alexithymia. In G. J. Taylor, R. M Bagby, & J. D. A. Parker (Eds.), *Disorders of affect regulation: Alexithymia in medical and psychiatric illness* (pp. 26–45). Cambridge, UK: Cambridge University Press.

Baird, B., Smallwood, J., Mrazek, M. D., Kam, J. W., Franklin, M. S., & Schooler, J. W. (2012). Inspired by distraction: Mind wandering facilitates creative incubation. *Psychological Science, 23*(10), 1117–1122.

Baker, L. A., & Emery, R. E. (1993). When every relationship is above average. *Law and Human Behavior, 17*(4), 439–450.

Baliki, M. N., Geha, P. Y., Apkarian, A. V., & Chialvo, D. R. (2008). Beyond feeling: Chronic pain hurts the brain, disrupting the default-mode network dynamics. *Journal of Neuroscience, 28*(6), 1398–1403.

Banerjee, P., Chatterjee, P., & Sinha, J. (2012). Is it light or dark? Recalling moral behavior changes perception of brightness. *Psychological Science, 23*(4), 407–409.

Bar-On, E., Weigl, D., Parvari, R., Katz, K., Weitz, R., & Steinberg, T. (2002). Congenital insensitivity to pain: Orthopaedic manifestations. *Journal of Bone & Joint Surgery, British Volume, 84*(2), 252–257.

Barbano, M. F., & Cador, M. (2007). Opioids for hedonic experience and dopamine to get ready for it. *Psychopharmacology, 191*(3), 497–506.

Barlett, C., Witkower, Z., Mancini, C., & Saleem, M. (2016). Breaking the link between provocation and aggression: The role of mitigating information. *Aggressive Behavior, 42*(6), 555–562.

Bartlett, F. C. (1932). *Remembering: An experimental and social study*. Cambridge, UK: Cambridge University.

Bastos, A. M., Usrey, W. M., Adams, R. A., Mangun, G. R., Fries, P., & Friston, K. J. (2012). Canonical microcircuits for predictive coding. *Neuron, 76*(4), 695–711.

Battcock, G. (1969). Notes on *Empire*: A film by Andy Warhol. *Film Culture, 40*, 39–40.

Bauby, J-D. (1998). *The diving-bell and the butterfly*. Translated by J. Leggatt. New York, NY: Vintage International.

Baum, S. K., Boxley, R. L., & Sokolowski, M. (1984). Time perception and psychological well-being in the elderly. *Psychiatric Quarterly, 56*(1), 54–61.

Baumeister, R. F. (1990). Suicide as escape from self. *Psychological Review, 97*(1), 90–113.

Baumeister, R. F. (2016). Emotions: How the future feels (and could feel). In M. P. Seligman, P. Railton, R. F. Baumeister, & C. Sripada (pp. 207–224). New York, NY: Oxford University Press.

Baumeister, R. F., Vohs, K. D., Nathan DeWall, C., & Zhang, L. (2007). How emotion shapes behavior: Feedback, anticipation, and reflection, rather than direct causation. *Personality and Social Psychology Review, 11*(2), 167–203.

Baumgartner, H., Pieters, R., & Bagozzi, R. P. (2008). Future-oriented emotions: conceptualization and behavioral effects. *European Journal of Social Psychology, 38*(4), 685–696.

Baxter, D. W., & Olszewski, J. (1960). Congenital universal insensitivity to pain. *Brain, 83*, 381–393.

Beauvoir, S. de. (2004). Pyrrhus and Cineas. In M. A. Simons, M. Timmermann, & M. B. Mader (Eds.), *Philosophical writings, by Simone de Beauvoir*. Urbana, IL: University of Illinois Press. (Originally published in French in 1944)

Beauvoir, S. de. (2011). *The second sex*. Translated by C. Borde & S. Malovany-Chevallier. New York, NY: Random House, Inc. (Originally published in French in 1949)

Bechara, A., Damasio, A. R., Damasio, H., & Anderson, S. W. (1994). Insensitivity to future consequences following damage to human prefrontal cortex. *Cognition, 50*(1–3), 7–15.

Bechara, A., Damasio, H., Tranel, D., & Damasio, A. R. (1997). Deciding advantageously before knowing the advantageous strategy. *Science, 275*(5304), 1293–1295.

Bechara, A., Damasio, H., Tranel, D., & Damasio, A. R. (2005). The Iowa Gambling Task and the somatic marker hypothesis: some questions and answers. *Trends in Cognitive Sciences, 9*(4), 159–162.

Beck, A. T., Steer, R. A., Beck, J. S., & Newman, C. F. (1993). Hopelessness, depression, suicidal ideation, and clinical diagnosis of depression. *Suicide and Life-Threatening Behavior, 23*(2), 139–145.

Beck, A.T., Steer, R. A., Kovacs M., & Garrison, B. (1985). Hopelessness and eventual suicide: a 10-year prospective study of patients hospitalized with suicidal ideation. *American Journal of Psychiatry, 142*(5), 559–563.

Beck, A. T., Weissman, A., Lester, D., & Trexler, L. (1974). The measurement of pessimism: the hopelessness scale. *Journal of Consulting and Clinical Psychology, 42*(6), 861–865.

Beckett, S. (1970). *Proust*. New York, NY: Grove Press.

Beckett, S. (2006). *The complete dramatic works of Samuel Beckett*. London, UK: Faber & Faber.

Beevers, C. G., & Miller, I. W. (2004). Perfectionism, cognitive bias, and hopelessness as prospective predictors of suicidal ideation. *Suicide and Life-Threatening Behavior, 34*(2), 126–137.

Bell, E. T. (1961). *The Last problem*. New York, NY: Simon and Schuster.

Bell, E. T. (1965). *Men of mathematic*. New York, NY: Simon & Schuster.

Bench, S. W., & Lench, H. C. (2013). On the function of boredom. *Behavioral sciences, 3*(3), 459–472.

Bench, S. W., & Lench, H. C. (2019). Boredom as a seeking state: Boredom prompts the pursuit of novel (even negative) experiences. *Emotion, 19*(2), 242–254.

Benenson, F. (2011). Soul-crushing realism is a videogame hit. *Wired*, July 26. Retrieved from https://www.wired.com/2011/07/st_alpha_videogames/

Bentham, J. (1970). *Introduction to the principles of morals of legislation*. London, UK: Athlone Press. (Originally published in 1789)

Benton, D., & Owens, D. (1993). Is raised blood glucose associated with the relief of tension? *Journal of Psychosomatic Research, 37*(7), 1–13.

Bernstein, H. E. (1975). Boredom and the ready-made life. *Social Research, 42*(3), 512–537.

Bierzynska, M., Bielecki, M., Marchewka, A., Debowska, W., Duszyk, A., Zajkowski, W., . . . Kossut, M. (2016). Effect of frustration on brain activation pattern in subjects with different temperament. *Frontiers in Psychology, 6*, 1989. doi:10.3389/fpsyg.2015.01989

Blaszczynski, A., McConaghy, N., & Frankova, A. (1990). Boredom proneness in pathological gambling. *Psychological Reports, 67*(1), 35–42.

Block, R. A., & Reed, M. A. (1978). Remembered duration: Evidence for a contextual-change hypothesis. *Journal of Experimental Psychology: Human Learning and Memory, 4*(6), 656–665.

Block, R. A., & Zakay, D. (1997). Prospective and retrospective duration judgments: A meta-analytic review. *Psychonomic Bulletin & Review, 4*(2), 184–197.

Blumstein, S. E., & Myers, E. B. (2014). Neural systems underlying speech perception. In K. Oshsner & S. Kosslyn (Eds.), *Oxford handbook of cognitive neuroscience.* (Vol. 2, pp. 507–523). New York, NY: Oxford University Press.

Bockner, S. (1949). The depersonalization syndrome: Report of a case. *British Journal of Psychiatry, 95,* 968–971.

Borges, J. L. (1962). *Ficciones.* Edited by A. Kerrigan. New York, NY: Grove Press.

Bourdon, D. (1989). *Warhol.* New York, NY: Harry N. Abrahams.

Brehm, J. W., Stires, L. K., Sensenig, J., & Shaban, J. (1966). The attractiveness of an eliminated choice alternative. *Journal of Experimental Social Psychology, 2*(3), 301–313.

Breuer, J, & Elson, M. (2017). Frustration-aggression theory. In P. Sturmey (Ed.), *The Wiley handbook of violence and aggression.* Wiley Online Library. doi:10.1002/9781119057574.whbva040

Brezo, J., Paris, J., & Turecki, G. (2006). Personality traits as correlates of suicidal ideation, suicide attempts, and suicide completions: a systematic review. *Acta Psychiatrica Scandinavica, 113*(3), 180–206.

Bright, A. A. (1949). *The electric lamp industry.* New York, NY: Macmillan.

Britton, A., & Shipley, M. J. (2010). Bored to death? *International Journal of Epidemiology, 39*(2), 370–371.

Brodski, A., Paasch, G.-F., Helbling, S., & Wibral, M. (2015). The faces of predictive coding. *The Journal of Neuroscience, 35*(24), 8997–9006.

Bryant, F. (2003). Savoring Beliefs Inventory (SBI): A scale for measuring beliefs about savouring. *Journal of Mental Health, 12*(2), 175–196.

Bryant, F. B., & Veroff, J. (2007). *Savoring: A new model of positive experience.* Mahwah, NJ: Erlbaum.

Bschor, T., Ising, M., Bauer, M., Lewitzka, U., Skerstupeit, M., Müller-Oerlinghausen, B., & Baethge, C. (2004). Time experience and time judgment in major depression, mania and healthy subjects. A controlled study of 93 subjects. *Acta Psychiatrica Scandinavica, 109*(3), 222–229.

Buonomano, D. (2017). *Your brain is a time machine: The neuroscience and physics of time.* New York, NY: W. W. Norton.

Bushman, B. J., Baumeister, R. F., & Phillips, C. M. (2001). Do people aggress to improve their mood? Catharsis beliefs, affect regulation opportunity, and aggressive responding. *Journal of Personality and Social Psychology, 81*(1), 17–32.

Cage, J. (1973). *Silence: Lectures and Writings.* Middletown, CT: Wesleyan University Press.

Calderon, A. (2013). Why building Ikea furniture is probably satan's favorite hobby. *BuzzFeed,* August 29. Retrieved from https://www.buzzfeed.com/ariellecalderon/why-building-ikea-furniture-is-probably-satans-fa?utm_term=.ddA6XdV7#.tsxaxZ38

Campbell, L. A., & Bryant, R. A. (2007). How time flies: A study of novice skydivers. *Behaviour Research and Therapy, 45*(6), 1389–1392.

Card, D., & Dahl, G. B. (2011). Family violence and football: The effect of unexpected emotional cues on violent behavior. *Quarterly Journal of Economics, 126*(1), 103–143.

Carroll, L. (2009). *Alice's adventures in wonderland & Through the looking-glass.* London, UK: Pan Macmillan. (*Alice's adventures in wonderland* was first published in 1865; *Through the looking-glass* was first published in 1871.)

Carson, R. C., Hollon, S. D., & Shelton, R. C. (2010). Depressive realism and clinical depression. *Behaviour Research and Therapy, 48*(4), 257–265.

Carstensen, L. L. (2006). The influence of a sense of time on human development. *Science, 312*(5782), 1913–1915.

Cassian, J. (2000). *John Cassian, the Institutes.* Vol. 58. Translated by B. Ramsey. New York, NY: Newman Press.

Catalano, R., Dooley, D., Novaco, R. W., Hough, R., & Wilson, G. (1993). Using ECA survey data to examine the effect of job layoffs on violent behavior. *Psychiatric Services, 44*(9), 874–879.

Cavafi, C. P. (2008). *The collected poems.* Translated by E. Sachperoglou. New York, NY: Oxford University Press.

Cheyne, J. A., Carriere, J. S., & Smilek, D. (2006). Absent-mindedness: Lapses of conscious awareness and everyday cognitive failures. *Consciousness and Cognition, 15*(3), 578–592.

Cialdini, R. B., Darby, B. L., & Vincent, J. E. (1973). Transgression and altruism: A case for hedonism. *Journal of Experimental Social Psychology, 9*(6), 502–516.

Cialdini, R. B., & Kenrick, D. T. (1976). Altruism and hedonism: A social development perspective on the relationship of negative mood state and helping. *Journal of Personality and Social Psychology, 34*(5), 907–914.

Clark, A. (2013). Whatever next? Predictive brains, situated agents, and the future of cognitive science. *Behavioral and Brain Sciences, 36*(3), 181–204.

Clark, A. (2016). *Surfing uncertainty: Prediction, action, and the embodied mind.* New York, NY: Oxford University Press.

Clore, G. L., & Huntsinger, J. R. (2007). How emotions inform judgment and regulate thought. *Trends in Cognitive Sciences, 11*(9), 393–399.

Clore, G. L., & Proffitt, D. R. (2016). The myth of pure perception. *Behavioral and Brain Sciences, 39*, e235.

Coglianese, S. (2015). The 2 words I don't use when I talk about my ALS. *The Mighty,* September 28. Retrieved from https://themighty.com/2015/09/the-2-words-i-dont-use-when-i-talk-about-my-als/

Cohen, J. (1944). The consequences of frustration. *Nature, 154,* 378–380.

Collins, L. (2011, October). House perfect: Is the IKEA ethos comfy or creepy? *The New Yorker, 3,* 54–65.

Crane, C., Shah, D., Barnhofer, T., & Holmes, E. A. (2012). Suicidal imagery in a previously depressed community sample. *Clinical Psychology & Psychotherapy, 19*(1), 57–69.

Crombag, H. F., Wagenaar, W. A., & Van Koppen, P. J. (1996). Crashing memories and the problem of "source monitoring." *Applied Cognitive Psychology, 10*(2), 95–104.

Crossman, A. M., Sullivan, M. W., Hitchcock, D. M., & Lewis, M. (2009). When frustration is repeated: Behavioral and emotion responses during extinction over time. *Emotion, 9*(1), 92–100.

Crowe, M., Whitehead, L., Jo Gagan, M., Baxter, D., & Panckhurst, A. (2010). Self-management and chronic low back pain: A qualitative study. *Journal of Advanced Nursing, 66*(7), 1478–1486.

Cunningham, M. R., Steinberg, J., & Grev, R. (1980). Wanting to and having to help: Separate motivations for positive mood and guilt-induced helping. *Journal Personality Social Psychology, 38*(2), 181–192.

Currie, S. R., & Wang, J. (2004). Chronic back pain and major depression in the general Canadian population. *Pain, 107*(1-2), 54–60.

Da Fonseca-Wollheim, C. (2008). A jazz night to remember. *Wall Street Journal,* October 11. Retrieved from https://www.wsj.com/articles/SB122367103134923957

Dahlen, E. R., Martin, R. C., Ragan, K., & Kuhlman, M. M. (2004). Boredom proneness in anger and aggression: Effects of impulsiveness and sensation seeking. *Personality and Individual Differences, 37*(8), 1615–1627.

Dahlen, E. R., Martin, R. C., Ragan, K., & Kuhlman, M. M. (2005). Driving anger, sensation seeking, impulsiveness, and boredom proneness in the prediction of unsafe driving. *Accident Analysis & Prevention, 37*(2), 341–348.

Damasio, A. R. (1996). The somatic marker hypothesis and the possible functions of the prefrontal cortex. *Philosophical Transactions of the Royal Society B, 351*(1346), 1413–1420.

Damoiseaux, J. S., Rombouts, S. A. R. B., Barkhof, F., Scheltens, P., Stam, C. J., Smith, S. M., & Beckmann, C. F. (2006). Consistent resting-state networks across healthy subjects. *Proceedings of the National Academy of Sciences, 103*(37), 13848–13853.

Danckert, J., Mugon, J., Struk, A., & Eastwood, J. (2018). Boredom: What is it good for? In H. Lench (Ed.), *The function of emotions* (pp. 93–119). Cham, Switzerland: Springer.

Dante, A. (1995). *Inferno* (Indiana critical ed.). Translated and edited by M. Musa. Bloomington, IN: Indiana University Press.

Danto, C. A. (2009). *Andy Warhol*. New Haven, CT: Yale University Press.

Davenport, J. W., & Thompson, C. I. (1965). The Amsel frustration effect in monkeys. *Psychonomic Science, 3*(1–12), 481–482.

Davidai, S., & Gilovich, T. (2016). The headwinds/tailwinds asymmetry: An availability bias in assessments of barriers and blessings. *Journal of Personality and Social Psychology, 111*(6), 835–851.

Davidson, W. L. (1912). Envy and emulation. In J. Hastings, J. A. Selbie, & L. H. Gray (Eds.), *Encyclopedia of religion and ethics* (Vol. 5, pp. 322–323). New York, NY: Scribner.

de Gucht, V., & Heiser, W. (2003). Alexithymia and somatisation: quantitative review of the literature. *Journal of Psychosomatic Research, 54*(5), 425–434.

Deveney, C. M., Connolly, M. E., Haring, C. T., Bones, B. L., Reynolds, R. C., Kim, P., . . . Leibenluft, E. (2013). Neural mechanisms of frustration in chronically irritable children. *American Journal of Psychiatry, 170*(10), 1186–1194.

DeWall, C. N., Baumeister, R. F., Chester, D. S., & Bushman, B. J. (2016). How often does currently felt emotion predict social behavior and judgment? A meta-analytic test of two theories. *Emotion Review, 8*(2), 136–143.

Diener, E., & Chan, M. Y. (2011). Happy people live longer: Subjective well-being contributes to health and longevity. *Applied Psychology: Health and Well-Being, 3*(1), 1–43.

Diener, E., & Seligman, M. E. (2002). Very happy people. *Psychological Science, 13*(1), 81–84.

Dobson, K. S., & Pusch, D. (1995). A test of the depressive realism hypothesis in clinically depressed subjects. *Cognitive Therapy and Research, 19*(2), 179–194.

Dollard, J., Miller, N. E., Doob, L. W., Mowrer, O. H., & Sears, R. R. (1939). *Frustration and aggression*. New Haven, CT: Yale University Press.

Dow, C. M., Roche, P. A., & Ziebland, S. (2012). Talk of frustration in the narratives of people with chronic pain. *Chronic Illness, 8*(3), 176–191.

Droit-Volet, S., Brunot, S., & Niedenthal, P. (2004). Perception of the duration of emotional events. *Cognition and Emotion, 18*(6), 849–858.

Droit-Volet, S., & Meck, W. H. (2007). How emotions colour our perception of time. *Trends in Cognitive Sciences, 11*(12), 504–513.

Drory, A. (1982). Individual differences in boredom proneness and task effectiveness at work. *Personnel Psychology, 35*(1), 141–151.

Dubreuil, D., Gentile, M. S., & Visalberghi, E. (2006). Are capuchin monkeys (*Cebus apella*) inequity averse? *Proceedings of the Royal Society of London B: Biological Sciences, 273*(1591), 1223–1228.

Dunn, J. R., & Schweitzer, M. E. (2005). Feeling and believing: the influence of emotion on trust. *Journal of Personality and Social Psychology, 88*(5), 736–748.

Eastwood, J. D., Cavaliere, C., Fahlman, S. A., & Eastwood, A. E. (2007). A desire for desires: Boredom and its relation to alexithymia. *Personality and Individual Differences, 42*(6), 1035–1045.

Eastwood, J. D., Frischen, A., Fenske, M. J., & Smilek, D. (2012). The unengaged mind: Defining boredom in terms of attention. *Perspectives on Psychological Science, 7*(5), 482–495.

Edward, K. L., Welch, A., & Chater, K. (2009). The phenomenon of resilience as described by adults who have experienced mental illness. *Journal of Advanced Nursing, 65*(3), 587–595.

Effron, D. A., Niedenthal, P. M., Gil, S., & Droit-Volet, S. (2006). Embodied temporal perception of emotion. *Emotion, 6*(1), 1–9.

Eisenberger, N. I., Lieberman, M. D., & Williams, K. D. (2003). Does rejection hurt? An fMRI study of social exclusion. *Science, 302*(5643), 290–292.

El Haj, M., Antoine, P., & Kapogiannis, D. (2015). Flexibility decline contributes to similarity of past and future thinking in Alzheimer's disease. *Hippocampus, 25*(11), 1447–1455.

Elpidorou, A. (2014). The bright side of boredom. *Frontiers in Psychology, 5*, 1245.

Elpidorou, A. (2017a). Boredom's push. *OUPBlog*, September 16. Retrieved from https://blog. oup.com/2017/09/boredoms-push/

Elpidorou, A. (2017b). The moral dimensions of boredom: A call for research. *Review of General Psychology, 21*, 30–48.

Elpidorou, A. (2018a). The bored mind is a guiding mind: Toward a regulatory theory of boredom. *Phenomenology and the Cognitive Sciences, 17*(3), 455–484.

Elpidorou, A. (2018b). The good of boredom. *Philosophy Psychology, 31*(3), 323–351.

Engel, A. K., Fries, P., & Singer, W. (2001). Dynamic predictions: Oscillations and synchrony in top-down processing. *Nature Reviews Neuroscience, 2*(10), 704–716.

Etkin, A., Egner, T., & Kalisch, R. (2011). Emotional processing in anterior cingulate and medial prefrontal cortex. *Trends in Cognitive Sciences, 15*(2), 85–93.

Evans, S., & de Souza, L. (2008). Dealing with chronic pain: giving voice to the experiences of mothers with chronic pain and their children. *Qualitative Health Research, 18*(4), 489–500.

Fabrykant, M., & Pacella, B. (1948). Labile diabetes: Electroencephalographic status and effect of anticonvulsive therapy. *Annals of Internal Medicine, 29*(5), 860–877.

Fahlman, S. A., Mercer, K. B., Gaskovski, P., Eastwood, A. E., & Eastwood, J. D. (2009). Does a lack of life meaning cause boredom? Results from psychometric, longitudinal, and experimental analyses. *Journal of Social and Clinical Psychology, 28*(3), 307–340.

Fahlman, S. A., Mercer-Lynn, K. B., Flora, D. B., & Eastwood, J. D. (2013). Development and validation of the multidimensional state boredom scale. *Assessment, 20*(1), 68–85.

Farmer, R., & Sundberg, N. D. (1986). Boredom proneness: The development and correlates of a new scale. *Journal of Personality Assessment, 50*(1), 4–17.

Faye, E. (2009). *Heidegger: The introduction of Nazism into philosophy in light of the unpublished seminars of 1933–1935*. Translated by M. B. Smith. New Haven, CT: Yale University Press.

Feinstein, J. S. (2013). Lesion studies of human emotion and feeling. *Current Opinion in Neurobiology, 23*(3), 304–309.

Feinstein, J. S., Adolphs, R., Damasio, A., & Tranel, D. (2011). The human amygdala and the induction and experience of fear. *Current Biology, 21*(1), 34–38.

Feinstein, J. S., Buzza, C., Hurlemann, R., Follmer, R. L., Dahdaleh, N. S., Coryell, W. H., . . . Wemmie, J. A. (2013). Fear and panic in humans with bilateral amygdala damage. *Nature Neuroscience, 16*(3), 270–272.

FeldmanHall, O., Dalgleish, T., & Mobbs, D. (2013). Alexithymia decreases altruism in real social decisions. *Cortex, 49*(3), 899–904.

Fernyhough, C. (2014). *Pieces of light: The new science of memory*. New York, NY: Harper Perennial.

Fisher, C. D. (1993). Boredom at work: A neglected concept. *Human Relations, 46*(3), 395–417.

Flaherty, M. G., Freidin, B., & Sautu, R. (2005). Variation in the perceived passage of time: A cross-national study. *Social Psychology Quarterly, 68*(4), 400–410.

Foer, J. (2008). Caveman: An interview with Michel Siffre. *Cabinet Magazine, 30*, Summer. Retrieved from http://www.cabinetmagazine.org/issues/30/foer.php

Forgeard, M. J. C., & Seligman, M. E. P. (2012). Seeing the glass half full: A review of the causes and consequences of optimism. *Pratiques psychologiques, 18*(2), 107–120.

Fraisse, P. (1963). *The psychology of time.* Westport, CT: Greenwood Press.

Frankl, E. V. (2006). *Man's search for meaning.* Boston, MA: Beacon Press. (Originally published in 1946)

Franklin, M. S., Smallwood, J., & Schooler, J. W. (2011). Catching the mind in flight: Using behavioral indices to detect mindless reading in real time. *Psychonomic Bulletin & Review, 18*(5), 992–997.

Fredrickson, B. L., & Branigan, C. (2005). Positive emotions broaden the scope of attention and thought-action repertoires. *Cognition & Emotion, 19*(3), 313–332.

Fredrickson, B. L., Cohn, M. A., Coffey, K. A., Pek, J., & Finkel, S. M. (2008). Open hearts build lives: Positive emotions, induced through loving-kindness meditation, build consequential personal resources. *Journal of Personality and Social Psychology, 95*(5), 1045–1062.

Frewen, P. A., Dozois, D. J., Neufeld, R. W., & Lanius, R. A. (2008). Meta-analysis of alexithymia in posttraumatic stress disorder. *Journal of Traumatic Stress, 21*(2), 243–246.

Frewen, P. A., Lanius, R. A., Dozois, D. J., Neufeld, R. W., Pain, C., Hopper, J. W., . . . Stevens, T. K. (2008). Clinical and neural correlates of alexithymia in posttraumatic stress disorder. *Journal of Abnormal Psychology, 117*(1), 171 –181.

Friedel, R., Israel, P., & Finn, B. S. (2010). *Edison's electric light: the art of invention.* Baltimore, MD: John Hopkins University Press.

Frijda, N. H. (1986). *The emotions.* Cambridge, UK: Cambridge University Press.

Friston, K. (2005). A theory of cortical responses. *Philosophical Transactions of the Royal Society B: Biological Sciences, 360*(1456), 815–836.

Friston, K. (2008). Hierarchical models in the brain. *PLoS Computational Biology, 4*(11), e1000211.

Gailliot, M. T., & Baumeister, R. F. (2018). The physiology of willpower: Linking blood glucose to self-control. In *Self-regulation and self-control* (pp. 137–180). London, UK: Routledge.

Gailliot, M. T., Baumeister, R. F., DeWall, C. N., Maner, J. K., Plant, E. A., Tice, D. M., . . . Schmeichel, B. J. (2007). Self-control relies on glucose as a limited energy source: willpower is more than a metaphor. *Journal of Personality and Social Psychology, 92*(2), 325–336.

Gana, K., & Akremi, M. (1998). L'échelle de Disposition à l'Ennui (EDE): Adaptation française et validation du Boredom Proneness Scale (BP) [French adaptation and validation of the Boredom Proneness Scale (BP)]. *L'année Psychologique, 98,* 429–450.

Gasper, K., & Middlewood, B. L. (2014). Approaching novel thoughts: Understanding why elation and boredom promote associative thought more than distress and relaxation. *Journal of Experimental Social Psychology, 52,* 50–57.

Gibson, J. J. (1975). Events are perceivable but time is not. In J. T. Fraser, & N. Lawrence (Eds.), *The study of time II* (pp. 295–301). Hillsdale, NJ: Erlbaum.

Gil, S., & Droit-Volet, S. (2009). Time perception, depression and sadness. *Behavioural Processes, 80*(2), 169–176.

Gil, S., Niedenthal, P. M., & Droit-Volet, S. (2007). Anger and time perception in children. *Emotion, 7*(1), 219–225.

Giltay, E. J., Geleijnse, J. M., Zitman, F. G., Hoekstra, T., & Schouten, E. G. (2004). Dispositional optimism and all-cause and cardiovascular mortality in a prospective cohort of elderly Dutch men and women. *Archives of General Psychiatry, 61*(11), 1126–1135.

Goldberg, Y. K., Eastwood, J. D., LaGuardia, J., & Danckert, J. (2011). Boredom: An emotional experience distinct from apathy, anhedonia, or depression. *Journal of Social and Clinical Psychology, 30*(6), 647.

Goldsmith, K. (2004). *Being boring*. Talk presented at the First Seance for Experimental Literature. Los Angeles, CA, November. Retrieved from http://writing.upenn.edu/epc/authors/goldsmith/goldsmith_boring.html

Govender, S. (2018). Football hooligans causes R2.6m worth of damage at Moses Mabhida stadium. *BusinessDay* (businesslive.co.za/bd), April 25. Retrieved from https://www.businesslive.co.za/bd/national/2018-04-25-football-hooligans-cause-r26m-worth-of-damage-at-moses-mabhida-stadium/

Grabe, H. J., Rainermann, S., Spitzer, C., Gänsicke, M., & Freyberger, H. J. (2000). The relationship between dimensions of alexithymia and dissociation. *Psychotherapy and psychosomatics, 69*(3), 128–131.

Gregory, W. L., Cialdini, R. B., & Carpenter, K. M. (1982). Self-relevant scenarios as mediators of likelihood estimates and compliance: Does imagining make it so? *Journal of Personality and Social Psychology, 43*(1), 89–99.

Griffo, M. (2014). After a devastating diagnosis and a suicide attempt, this dad found a reason to live. *The Mighty*, September 8. Retrieved from https://themighty.com/2014/09/after-a-devastating-diagnosis-and-a-suicide-attempt-this-dad-found-a-reason-to-live/

Guerra, N. G., Huesmann, L. R., Tolan, P. H., Van Acker, R., & Eron, L. D. (1995). Stressful events and individual beliefs as correlates of economic disadvantage and aggression among urban children. *Journal of Consulting and Clinical Psychology, 63*(4), 518–528.

Haager, J. S., Kuhbandner, C., & Pekrun, R. (2018). To be bored or not to be bored—How task-related boredom influences creative performance. *Journal of Creative Behavior, 52*(4), 297–304.

Harford, T. (2016). *Messy: The power of disorder to transform*. New York, NY: Riverhead Books.

Hariri, A. R., Bookheimer, S. Y., & Mazziotta, J. C. (2000). Modulating emotional responses: effects of a neocortical network on the limbic system. *Neuroreport, 11*(1), 43–48.

Harris, M. B. (1974). Mediators between frustration and aggression in a field experiment. *Journal of Experimental Social Psychology, 10*(6), 561–571.

Harris, M. B. (2000). Correlates and characteristics of boredom proneness and boredom. *Journal of Applied Social Psychology, 30*(3), 576–598.

Hassabis, D., Kumaran, D., Vann, S. D., & Maguire, E. A. (2007). Patients with hippocampal amnesia cannot imagine new experiences. *Proceedings of the National Academy of Sciences, 104*(5), 1726–1731.

Havermans, R. C., Vancleef, L., Kalamatianos, A., & Nederkoorn, C. (2015). Eating and inflicting pain out of boredom. *Appetite, 85*, 52–57.

Hawkins, J., & Blakeslee, S. (2005). *On intelligence: How a new understanding of the brain will lead to the creation of truly intelligent machines*. New York, NY: Owl Books.

Hazen, A. T. (1937). *Samuel Johnson's prefaces and dedications*. New Haven, CT: Yale University Press.

Hebb, D. O. (1955). Drives and the CNS (conceptual nervous system). *Psychological Review, 62*(4), 243–254.

Heidegger, M. (1927). *Sein und Zeit*. Tübingen, Germany: Max Niemeyer Verlag.

Heidegger, M. (1983). *Die Grundbegriffe der metaphysik: Welt, endlichkeit, Einsamkeit*. Frankfurt, Germany: Vittorio Klostermann.

Heidegger, M. (2002). *Grundbegriffe der aristotelischen Philosophie*. Frankfurt, Germany: Vittorio Klostermann.

Heinzel, A., Schäfer, R., Müller, H. W., Schieffer, A., Ingenhag, A., Northoff, G., . . . Hautzel, H. (2010). Differential modulation of valence and arousal in high-alexithymic and low-alexithymic individuals. *NeuroReport, 21*(15), 998–1002.

Helmholtz, H. von. (1867). *Handbuch der physiologischen Optik*. Leipzig, Germany: Voss.

Herrin, J. (2013). *Margins and metropolis: Authority across the Byzantine Empire*. Princeton, NJ: Princeton University Press.

Hestbaek, L., Leboeuf-Yde, C., & Manniche, C. (2003). Is low back pain part of a general health pattern or is it a separate and distinctive entity? A critical literature review of co-morbidity with low back pain. *Journal of Manipulative and Physiological Therapeutics, 26*(4), 243–252.

Higgins, D. (1981). Boredom and danger. In G. Battcock (Ed.), *Breaking the sound barrier: A critical anthology of the new music* (pp. 20–27). New York, NY: E. P. Dutton.

Higgins, E. T., Kruglanski, A. W., & Pierro, A. (2003). Regulatory mode: Locomotion and as-sessment as distinct orientations. In M. P. Zanna (Ed.), *Advances in experimental social psy-chology* (Vol. 35, pp. 293–344). New York, NY: Academic Press.

Hinton, J. (1881). *Philosophy and religion: Selections from manuscripts of the late James Hinton*. Edited by Caroline Haddon. London, UK: Kegan Paul, Trench.

Hoch, S. J. (1985). Counterfactual reasoning and accuracy in predicting personal events. *Journal of Experimental Psychology: Learning, Memory, and Cognition, 11*(4), 719–731.

Hohwy, J. (2013). *The predictive mind*. Oxford, UK: Oxford University Press.

Hollingham, R. (2013). How to combat the loneliness of space travel. *BBC Future*, August 13. Retrieved from web.archive.org/web/20190717074631/http://www.bbc.com/future/story/20130813-how-to-combat-loneliness-in-space

Holmes, E. A., Crane, C., Fennell, M. J., & Williams, J. M. G. (2007). Imagery about suicide in depression—"Flash-forwards"? *Journal of Behavior Therapy and Experimental Psychiatry, 38*(4), 423–434.

Homer. (1998). *The Iliad*. Translated by R. Fagles, New York, NY: Penguin Books. (Originally composed around the 8th century BC)

Hong, R. Y., Tan, M. S., & Chang, W. C. (2004). Locomotion and assessment: Self-regulation and subjective well-being. *Personality and Individual Differences, 37*(2), 325–332.

Inzlicht, M., Shenhav, A., & Olivola, C. Y. (2018). The effort paradox: Effort is both costly and valued. *Trends in Cognitive Sciences, 22*(4), 337–349.

Ironson, G. H., & Hayward, H. S. (2008). Do positive psychosocial factors predict disease pro-gression in HIV-1? A review of the evidence. *Psychosomatic Medicine, 70*(5), 546–554.

Isacescu, J., & Danckert, J. (2018). Exploring the relationship between boredom proneness and self-control in traumatic brain injury (TBI). *Experimental Brain Research, 236*(9), 2493–2505.

Isen, A. M. (2000). Positive affect and decision making. In M. Lewis & J. M. Haviland-Jones (Eds.), *Handbook of emotions*. (2nd ed., pp. 417–435). New York, NY: Guilford Press.

Jakovcevic, A., Elgier, A. M., Mustaca, A. E., & Bentosela, M. (2013). Frustration behaviors in domestic dogs. *Journal of Applied Animal Welfare Science, 16*(1), 19–34.

James, W. (1886). The perception of time. *Journal of Speculative Philosophy, 20*(4), 374–407.

Jevons, W. S. (1905). *Essays on economics*. London, UK: Macmillan.

Joiner Jr., T. E., Brown, J. S., & Wingate, L. R. (2005). The psychology and neurobiology of sui-cidal behavior. *Annual Review of Psychology, 56*(1), 287–314.

Kant, I. (2017). *The Metaphysics of Morals* (Revised edition). Translated by L. Denis, edited by M. Gregor and J. Timmerman. New York, NY: Cambridge University Press. (Originally published in 1797)

Kelley, N. J., & Schmeichel, B. J. (2014). The effects of negative emotions on sensory percep-tion: Fear but not anger decreases tactile sensitivity. *Frontiers in Psychology, 5*, 942.

Kenrick, D. T., & MacFarlane, S. W. (1986). Ambient temperature and horn honking: A field study of the heat/aggression relationship. *Environment and Behavior, 18*(2), 179–191.

Kierkegaard, S. (1987). *Either/Or: Part I*. Translated by Howard V. Hong and Edna H. Hong. Princeton, NJ: Princeton University Press. (Originally published in 1843)

Killeen, P. R. (1994). Frustration: Theory and practice. *Psychonomic Bulletin & Review, 1*(3), 323–326.

Killingsworth, M. A., & Gilbert, D. T. (2010). A wandering mind is an unhappy mind. *Science, 330*(6006), 932.

Kim, H., Franks, B., & Higgins, E. T. (2013). Evidence that self-regulatory mode affects retirement savings. *Journal of Aging & Social Policy, 25*(3), 248–263.

Klöppel S., Stonnington, C. M., Petrovic, P., Mobbs, D., Tüscher, O., Craufurd, D., . . . Frackowiak, R. S. (2010). Irritability in pre-clinical Huntington's disease. *Neuropsychologia, 48*(2), 549–557.

Kocher, M. G., Krawczyk, M., & van Winden, F. (2014). "Let me dream on!" Anticipatory emotions and preference for timing in lotteries. *Journal of Economic Behavior & Organization, 98*, 29–40.

Kool, W., & Botvinick, M. (2014). A labor/leisure tradeoff in cognitive control. *Journal of Experimental Psychology: General, 143*(1), 131–141.

Kregarman, J. J., & Worchel, P. (1961). Arbitrariness of frustration and aggression. *Journal of Abnormal and Social Psychology, 63*(1), 183–187.

Krieglmeyer, R., Wittstadt, D., & Strack, F. (2009). How attribution influences aggression: Answers to an old question by using an implicit measure of anger. *Journal of Experimental Social Psychology, 45*(2), 379–385.

Kruglanski, A. W., Chernikova, M., & Jasko, K. (2018). The forward rush: On locomotors' future focus. In G. Oettingen, A. T. Sevincer, & P. M. Gollwitzer (Eds.), *The psychology of thinking about the future* (pp. 405–422). New York, NY: Guilford Press.

Kruglanski, A. W., Pierro, A., & Higgins, E. T. (2016). Experience of time by people on the go: A theory of the locomotion–temporality interface. *Personality and Social Psychology Review, 20*(2), 100–117.

Kruglanski, A. W., Pierro, A., Higgins, E. T., & Capozza, D. (2007). "On the move" or "staying put": Locomotion, need for closure and reactions to organizational change. *Journal of Applied Social Psychology, 37*(6), 1305–1340.

Kruglanski, A. W., Pierro, A., Mannetti, L., & Higgins, T. E. (2013). The distinct psychologies of "looking" and "leaping": Assessment and locomotion as the springs of action. *Social and Personality Psychology Compass, 7*(2), 79–92.

Kruglanski, A. W., Thompson, E. P., Higgins, E. T., Atash, M., Pierro, A., Shah, J. Y., & Spiegel, S. (2000). To "do the right thing" or to "just do it": Locomotion and assessment as distinct self-regulatory imperatives. *Journal of Personality and Social Psychology, 79*(5), 793–815.

Kuhn, R. (2017). *The demon of noontide: Ennui in Western literature.* Princeton, NJ: Princeton University Press. (Originally published in 1976)

Kuhs, H., Hermann, W., Kammer, K., & Tölle, R. (1991). Time estimation and the experience of time in endogenous depression (Melancholia): an experimental investigation. *Psychopathology, 24*(1), 7–11.

Kumar, A., Killingsworth, M. A., & Gilovich, T. (2014). Waiting for Merlot: Anticipatory consumption of experiential and material purchases. *Psychological Science, 25*(10), 1924–1931.

Kumashiro, M., Rusbult, C. E., Finkenauer, C., & Stocker, S. L. (2007). To think or to do: The impact of assessment and locomotion orientation on the Michelangelo phenomenon. *Journal of Social and Personal Relationships, 24*(4), 591–611.

Kundera, M. (1992). *The joke: Definitive version/fully revised by the author.* New York, NY: Harper Perennial.

Kurzban, R., Duckworth, A., Kable, J. W., & Myers, J. (2013). An opportunity cost model of subjective effort and task performance. *Behavioral and Brain Sciences, 36*(6), 661–679.

LeDoux, J. (1998). *The emotional brain: The mysterious underpinnings of emotional life.* New York, NY: Simon and Schuster.

Lee, C. M., Neighbors, C., & Woods, B. A. (2007). Marijuana motives: Young adults' reasons for using marijuana. *Addictive Behaviors, 32*(7), 1384–1394.

Lee, Y. T., & Seligman, M. E. (1997). Are Americans more optimistic than the Chinese? *Personality and Social Psychology Bulletin, 23*(1), 32–40.

Leong, F. T., & Schneller, G. R. (1993). Boredom proneness: Temperamental and cognitive components. *Personality and Individual Differences, 14*(1), 233–239.

LePera, N. (2011). Relationships between boredom proneness, mindfulness, anxiety, depression, and substance use. *New School Psychology Bulletin, 8*(2), 15–25.

Lerner, J. S., Gonzalez, R. M., Small, D. A., & Fischhoff, B. (2003). Effects of fear and anger on perceived risks of terrorism: A national field experiment. *Psychological Science, 14*(2), 144–150.

Levé, E. (2011). *Suicide.* Translated by J. Steyn. Champaign, IL: Dalkey Archive Press.

Libby, L. K., Shaeffer, E. M., Eibach, R. P., & Slemmer, J. A. (2007). Picture yourself at the polls: Visual perspective in mental imagery affects self-perception and behavior. *Psychological Science, 18 3*, 199–203.

Lieberman, M. D., & Eisenberger, N. I. (2015). The dorsal anterior cingulate cortex is selective for pain: Results from large-scale reverse inference. *Proceedings of the National Academy of Sciences, 112*(49), 15250–15255.

Loewenstein, G. (1987). Anticipation and the valuation of delayed consumption. *The Economic Journal, 97*(387), 666–684.

Loewenstein, G. (1992). The fall and rise of psychological explanations in the economics of intertemporal choice. In G. Loewenstein & J. Elster (Eds.), *Choice over time* (pp. 3–34). New York, NY: Russell Sage Foundation.

Loewenstein, G. (1999). Because it is there: The challenge of mountaineering . . . for utility theory. *Kyklos, 52*(3), 315–343.

Loewenstein, G. F., Weber, E. U., Hsee, C. K., & Welch, N. (2001). Risk as feelings. *Psychological Bulletin, 127*(2), 267–286.

Loftus, E. F., & Palmer, J. C. (1974). Reconstruction of automobile destruction: An example of the interaction between language and memory. *Journal of Verbal Learning and Verbal Behavior, 13*(5), 585–589.

Loukidou, L., Loan-Clarke, J., & Daniels, K. (2009). Boredom in the workplace: More than monotonous tasks. *International Journal of Management Reviews, 11*(4), 381–405.

Love, S. (2016). People with blunted sense of emotion may have harder time reading their body's signals. *Huffington Post,* October 20. Retrieved from https://www.huffingtonpost.com/stat/people-with-blunted-sense_b_12576950.html

Lulé, D., Häcker, S., Ludolph, A., Birbaumer, N., & Kübler, A. (2008). Depression and quality of life in patients with amyotrophic lateral sclerosis. *Deutsches Ärzteblatt International, 105*(23), 397–403.

Luminet, O., Vermeulen, N., Demaret, C., Taylor, G. J., & Bagby, R. M. (2006). Alexithymia and levels of processing: Evidence for an overall deficit in remembering emotion words. *Journal of Research in Personality, 40*(5), 713–733.

Lustman, P. J., Frank, B. L., & McGill, J. B. (1991). Relationship of personality characteristics to glucose regulation in adults with diabetes. *Psychosomatic Medicine, 53*(3), 305–312.

Machida, M., Irwin, B., & Feltz, D. (2013). Resilience in competitive athletes with spinal cord injury: The role of sport participation. *Qualitative Health Research, 23*(8), 1054–1065.

MacLeod, A. (2017). *Prospection, Well-Being, and Mental Health.* Oxford, UK: Oxford University Press.

MacLeod, A. K., Rose, G. S., & Williams, J. M. G. (1993). Components of hopelessness about the future in parasuicide. *Cognitive Therapy and Research, 17*(5), 441–455.

MacLeod, A. K., Tata, P., Tyrer, P., Schmidt, U., Davidson, K., & Thompson, S. (2005). Hopelessness and positive and negative future thinking in parasuicide. *British Journal of Clinical Psychology, 44*(4), 495–504.

Majohr, K.-L., Leenen, K., Grabe, H. J., Jenewein, J., Nuñez, D. G., & Rufer, M. (2011). Alexithymia and its relationship to dissociation in patients with panic disorder. *Journal of Nervous and Mental Disease, 199*(10), 773–777.

Makhaya, E. (2018). R2.6 million to fix damage caused by fans at Moses Mabhida Stadium. *Goal.com*, April 25. Retrieved from https://www.goal.com/en-us/news/r26-million-to-fix-damage-caused-by-fans-at-moses-mabhida/e8ryahwvforn15i3u8n4d2jna

Malkovsky, E., Merrifield, C., Goldberg, Y., & Danckert, J. (2012). Exploring the relationship between boredom and sustained attention. *Experimental Brain Research, 221*(1), 59–67.

Maltsberger, J. T., Sakinofsky, I., & Jha, A. (2000). Mansur Zaskar: A man almost bored to death. *Suicide & Life-Threatening Behavior, 30*(1), 83–90.

Mandeville, B. (1988). *The fable of the bees or private vices, Publick benefits.* 2 vols. With a commentary critical, historical, and explanatory by F. B. Kaye. Indianapolis, IN: Liberty Fund. Retrieved from http://oll.libertyfund.org/titles/846. (Poem originally published in 1705; book published in 1714)

Mann, S., & Cadman, R. (2014). Does being bored make us more creative? *Creativity Research Journal, 26*(2), 165–173.

Mann, T. (1996). *The magic mountain.* Translated by J. E. Woods. New York, NY: Alfred A. Knopf. (Originally published in German in 1924)

Mannetti, L., Giacomanatonio, M., Higgins, E. T., Pierro, A., & Kruglanski, A. W. (2010). Tailoring visual images to fit: Value orientation in persuasive messages. *European Journal of Social Psychology, 40*(2), 206–215.

Mantini, D., Perrucci, M. G., Del Gratta, C., Romani, G. L., & Corbetta, M. (2007). Electrophysiological signatures of resting state networks in the human brain. *Proceedings of the National Academy of Sciences, 104*(32), 13170–13175.

Manucia, G. K., Baumann, D. J., & Cialdini, R. B. (1984). Mood influences on helping: Direct effects or side effects? Journal of Personality and Social Psychology, 46(2), 357–364.

Martin, M., Sadlo, G., & Stew, G. (2006). The phenomenon of boredom. *Qualitative Research in Psychology, 3*(3), 193–211.

Mauriac, F. (2005). *Thérèse desqueyroux.* Translated with an introduction and noted by R. N. MacKenzie. Lanham, MD: Rowman & Littlefield.

McDonald, E. R., Hillel, A., & Wiedenfeld, S. A. (1996). Evaluation of the psychological status of ventilatory-supported patients with ALS/MND. *Palliative Medicine, 10*(1), 35–41.

Mekas, J. (1965). Movie journal. *Village Voice*, March 11. Retrieved from https://news.google.com/newspapers?nid=KEtq3P1Vf8oC&dat=19650311&printsec=frontpage&hl=en

Melville, H. (1998). *Billy Budd and other stories.* Ware, UK: Wordsworth Editions.

Mercer-Lynn, K. B., Flora, D. B., Fahlman, S. A., & Eastwood, J. D. (2013). The measurement of boredom differences between existing self-report scales. *Assessment, 20*(5), 585–596.

Merzbach, U. T., & Boyer, C. B. (2011). *A history of mathematics* (3rd ed.). Hoboken, NJ: Wiley.

Miller, N. E., Sears, R. R., Mowrer, O. H., Doob, L. W., & Dollard, J. (1941). I. The frustration aggression hypothesis. *Psychological Review, 48*(4), 337–342.

Minkoff, K., Bergman, E., Beck, A. T., & Beck, R. (1973). Hopelessness, depression, and attempted suicide. *American Journal of Psychiatry, 130*(4), 455–459.

Mooneyham, B. W., & Schooler, J. W. (2013). The costs and benefits of mind-wandering: a review. *Canadian Journal of Experimental Psychology/Revue canadienne de psychologie expérimentale, 67*(1), 11–18.

Moriguchi, Y., Decety, J., Ohnishi, T., Maeda, M., Mori, T., Nemoto, K., . . . Komaki, G. (2007). Empathy and judging other's pain: an fMRI study of alexithymia. *Cerebral Cortex, 17*(9), 2223–2234.

Morin, S. F. (1971). *Massed and Distributed work sessions in the generation of original responses.* Dissertation. Columbus, OH: Ohio State University.

Moynihan, A. B., Igou, E. R., & van Tilburg, W. A. P. (2017). Boredom increases impulsiveness: A meaning-regulation perspective. *Social Psychology, 48*(5), 293–309.

Munyo, I., & Rossi, M. A. (2013). Frustration, euphoria, and violent crime. *Journal of Economic Behavior & Organization, 89*, 136–142.

Myers, J. B. (1967). A letter to Gregory Battcock. In G. Battcock (Ed.), *New American cinema: A critical anthology* (pp. 139–140). New York, NY: EP Dutton.

Nagasako, E. M., Oaklander, A. L., & Dworkin, R. H. (2003). Congenital insensitivity to pain: An update. *Pain, 101*(3), 213–219.

Nederkoorn, C., Vancleef, L., Wilkenhöner, A., Claes, L., & Havermans, R. C. (2016). Self-inflicted pain out of boredom. *Psychiatry Research, 237*, 127–132.

Nemiah, J. C., & Sifneos, P. E. (1970). Affect and fantasy in patients with psychosomatic disorders. In O. W. Hill (Ed.), *Modern trends in psychosomatic medicine*, Vol. 2 (pp. 26–34). London, UK: Butterworths

Nes, L. S., Segerstrom, S. C., & Sephton, S. E. (2005). Engagement and arousal: Optimism's effects during a brief stressor. *Personality and Social Psychology Bulletin, 31*(1), 111–120.

Nietzsche, F. (2003). *The gay science: With a prelude in German rhymes and an appendix of songs.* Edited by B. Williams, translated by J. Nauckhoff and A. Del Caro. Cambridge, UK: Cambridge University Press. (Originally published in 1882 and then in an expanded version in 1887)

Norton, M. I., Mochon, D., & Ariely, D. (2012). The IKEA effect: When labor leads to love. *Journal of Consumer Psychology, 22*(3), 453–460.

Noyes, R., & R. Kletti. (1977). Depersonalization in response to life-threatening danger. *Comprehensive Psychiatry, 18*(4), 375–384.

Nozick, R. (1974). *Anarchy, state and utopia.* New York, NY: Basic Books.

O'Donoghue, T., & Rabin, M. (1999). Doing it now or later. *American Economic Review, 89*(1), 103–124.

Olesha, Y. (2004). *Envy.* Translated, with an introduction by T. S. Berczynski. Woodstock, NY: Ardis.

Olivola, C. Y., & Shafir, E. (2013). The martyrdom effect: When pain and effort increase prosocial contributions. *Journal of Behavioral Decision Making, 26*(1), 91–105.

Ong, A. D., Benson, L., Zautra, A. J., & Ram, N. (2018). Emodiversity and biomarkers of inflammation. *Emotion, 18*(1), 3–14.

Orledge, R. (1998). Understanding Satie's "vexations." *Music & Letters, 79*(3), 386–395.

Ornstein, R. E. (1970). *On the experience of time.* Baltimore, MD: Penguin Books.

Ortega y Gasset, J. (1993). *The revolt of the masses.* Anonymous translation. New York, NY. W. W. Norton. (Originally published in Spanish in 1930)

Ovid. *The Metamorphoses of Ovid* (1995). Translated by A. Mandelbaum. New York, NY: Harcourt, Brace. (Originally written around 8 AD)

Palmer, G. H. (1903). *The nature of goodness.* Boston, MA: Houghton Mifflin.

Papini, M. R., & Dudley, R. T. (1997). Consequences of surprising reward omissions. *Review of General Psychology, 1*(2), 175–197.

Pastore, N. (1950). A neglected factor in the frustration-aggression hypothesis: A comment. *The Journal of Psychology, 29*(2), 271–279.

Pekrun, R., Goetz, T., Daniels, L. M., Stupnisky, R. H., & Perry, R. P. (2010). Boredom in achievement settings: Exploring control-value antecedents and performance outcomes of a neglected emotion. *Journal of Educational Psychology, 102*(3), 531–549.

Pepperberg I. M. (2002). *The Alex studies: Cognitive and communicative abilities of grey parrots.* Cambridge, MA: Harvard University Press.

Pepperberg I. M. (2012). Emotional birds—Or advanced cognitive processing? In S. Watanabe & S. Kuczaj (Eds.), *Emotions of animals and humans: Comparative perspectives* (pp. 49–62). Tokyo, Japan: Springer.

Pepperberg I. M., & Gordon, J. D. (2005). Number comprehension by a grey parrot (*Psittacus erithacus*), including a zero-like concept. *Journal of Comparative Psych*ology, 119(2), 197–209.

Peterson, C., Park, N., & Seligman, M. E. (2005). Orientations to happiness and life satisfaction: The full life versus the empty life. *Journal of Happiness Studies, 6*(1), 25–41.

Petrovic, P., Kalso, E., Petersson, K. M., & Ingvar, M. (2002). Placebo and opioid analgesia–imaging a shared neuronal network. *Science, 295*(5560), 1737–1740.

Pham, L. B., & Taylor, S. E. (1999). From thought to action: Effects of process-versus outcome-based mental simulations on performance. *Personality and Social Psychology Bulletin, 25*(2), 250–260.

Phillips, A. (1993). *On kissing, tickling, and being bored: Psychoanalytic essays on the unexamined life.* Cambridge, MA: Harvard University Press.

Phillips, A. (2013). *Missing out: In praise of the unloved life.* New York, NY: Farrar, Straus and Giroux.

Pierro, A., Giacomantonio, M., Pica, G., Kruglanski, A. W., & Higgins, E. T. (2011). On the psychology of time in action: Regulatory mode orientations and procrastination. *Journal of Personality and Social Psychology, 101*(6), 1317–1331.

Pierro, A., Giacomantonio, M., Pica, G., Kruglanski, A. W., & Higgins, E. T. (2013). Locomotion and the preference for multitasking: Implications for well-being. *Motivation and Emotion, 37*(2), 213–223.

Pierro, A., Leder, S., Mannetti, L., Higgins, E. T., Kruglanski, A. W., & Aiello, A. (2008). Regulatory mode effects on counterfactual thinking and regret. *Journal of Experimental Social Psychology, 44*(2), 321–329.

Pierro, A., Pica, G., Klein, K., Kruglanski, A. W., & Higgins, E. T. (2013). Looking back or moving on: How regulatory modes affect nostalgia. *Motivation and Emotion, 37*(4), 653–660.

Pierro, A., Pica, G., Kruglanski, A. W., & Higgins, T. E. (2014). Regulatory mode orientations and self-forgiveness. Unpublished manuscript, University of Rome "La Sapienza."

Pitts, S., Wilson, J. P., & Hugenberg, K. (2014). When one is ostracized, others loom: Social rejection makes other people appear closer. *Social Psychological and Personality Science, 5*(5), 550–557.

Plutarch. *Plutarch's Lives.* The Loeb Classical Library Vol. 9. Translated by B. Perrin. London, UK: W. Heinemann, 1920.

Porges, A. (1997). The devil and Simon Flagg. In C. Fadiman (Ed.), *Fantasia mathematica* (pp. 63–69). New York, NY: Copernicus.

Powel, M. (2017). Scaling the world's most lethal mountain, in the dead of winter. *The New York Times,* May 9. Retrieved from https://www.nytimes.com/2017/05/09/sports/polish-climbers-to-scale-deadly-k2-peak-in-winter.html

Poynter, W. D. (1983). Duration judgment and the segmentation of experience. *Memory & Cognition, 11*(1), 77–82.

Priks, M. (2010). Does frustration lead to violence? Evidence from the Swedish hooligan scene. *Kyklos, 63*(3), 450–460.

Proust, M. (2005). *In the shadow of young girls in flower*. Translated by C. K. Scott Moncrieff; edited and annotated by W. C. Carter. New Haven, CT: Yale University Press. (Originally published in 1919)

Puri, M., & Robinson, D. T. (2007). Optimism and economic choice. *Journal of Financial Economics, 86*(1), 71–99.

Purtill, C. (2015). Why Ikea causes so much relationship tension. *The Atlantic*, September 20. Retrieved from https://www.theatlantic.com/business/archive/2015/09/ikea-furniture-fighting-couples-trust/406267/

Quoidbach, J., Dunn, E. W., Petrides, K. V., & Mikolajczak, M. (2010). Money giveth, money taketh away: The dual effect of wealth on happiness. *Psychological Science, 21*(6), 759–763.

Quoidbach, J., Gruber, J., Mikolajczak, M., Kogan, A., Kotsou, I., & Norton, M. I. (2014). Emodiversity and the emotional ecosystem. *Journal of Experimental Psychology: General, 143*(6), 2057–2066.

Rabkin, J. G., Albert, S. M., Del Bene, M. L., O'sullivan, I., Tider, T., Rowland, L. P., & Mitsumoto, H. (2005). Prevalence of depressive disorders and change over time in late-stage ALS. *Neurology, 65*(1), 62–67.

Rabkin, J. G., Goetz, R., Factor-Litvak, P., Hupf, J., McElhiney, M., Singleton, J., . . . ALS Cosmos Study Group. (2015). Depression and wish to die in a multicenter cohort of ALS patients. *Amyotrophic Lateral Sclerosis and Frontotemporal Degeneration, 16*(3-4), 265–273.

Rabkin, J. G., Wagner, G. J., & Del Bene, M. (2000). Resilience and distress among amyotrophic lateral sclerosis patients and caregivers. *Psychosomatic Medicine, 62*(2), 271–279.

Raghunathan, R., & Trope, Y. (2002). Walking the tightrope between feeling good and being accurate: Mood as a resource in processing persuasive messages. *Journal of Personality and Social Psychology, 83*(3), 510–525.

Råheim, M., & Håland, W. (2006). Lived experience of chronic pain and fibromyalgia: Women's stories from daily life. *Qualitative Health Research, 16*(6), 741–761.

Raman, I. M. (2018). Like it or not, the brain grades on a curve. In D. J. Linden (Ed.), *Think tank: Forty neuroscientists explore the biological roots of human experience* (pp. 75–81). New Haven, CT: Yale University Press.

Raposa, M. L. (1999). *Boredom and the Religious Imagination*. Charlottesville, VA: University of Virginia Press.

Reifman, A. S., Larrick, R. P., & Fein, S. (1991). Temper and temperature on the diamond: The heat-aggression relationship in major league baseball. *Personality and Social Psychology Bulletin, 17*(5), 580–585.

Rich, B. A., Schmajuk, M., Perez-Edgar, K. E., Fox, N. A., Pine, D. S., & Leibenluft, E. (2007). Different psychophysiological and behavioral responses elicited by frustration in pediatric bipolar disorder and severe mood dysregulation. *American Journal of Psychiatry, 164*(2), 309–317.

Rich, B. A., Schmajuk, M., Perez-Edgar, K. E., Pine, D. S., Fox, N. A., & Leibenluft, E. (2005). The impact of reward, punishment, and frustration on attention in pediatric bipolar disorder. *Biological Psychiatry, 58*(7), 532–539.

Richins, M. L. (2012). When wanting is better than having: Materialism, transformation expectations, and product-evoked emotions in the purchase process. *Journal of Consumer Research, 40*(1), 1–18.

Roach, M. (2010). *Packing for Mars: The curious science of life in the void*. New York, NY: W. W. Norton.

Roe, D., & Ronen, Y. (2003). Hospitalization as experienced by the psychiatric patient: a therapeutic jurisprudence perspective. *International Journal of Law and Psychiatry, 26*(3), 317–332.

Rogers, T. (2017). Getting over it is a game about using a sledgehammer to climb a mountain. *Kotaku*, October 6. Retrieved from https://kotaku.com/getting-over-it-is-a-game-about-using-a-sledgehammer-to-1819219469

Rojas, N., & Sanchi, A. F. (1941). Hipoglucemia en delincuentes [Hypoglycemia in delinquents]. *Archivos Medicales Legal Identificacion, 11*, 29.

Roma, P. G., Silberberg, A., Ruggiero, A. M., & Suomi, S. J. (2006). Capuchin monkeys, inequity aversion, and the frustration effect. *Journal of Comparative Psychology, 120*(1), 67–73.

Ross, A. (2007). *The rest is noise: Listening to twentieth century*. New York, NY: Picador.

Roy, D. (1959). "Banana time": Job satisfaction and informal interaction. *Human Organization, 18*(4), 158–168.

Ruby, F. J., Smallwood, J., Engen, H., & Singer, T. (2013). How self-generated thought shapes mood: The relation between mind-wandering and mood depends on the socio-temporal content of thoughts. *PloS One, 8*(10), e77554.

Rudulph, H. W. (2014). The Devastating struggles of a 26-year-old woman living with ALS. *Cosmopolitan*, August 22. Retrieved from https://www.cosmopolitan.com/lifestyle/news/a30365/the-struggles-of-a-26-year-old-woman-living-with-als/

Rupp, D. E., & Vodanovich, S. J. (1997). The role of boredom proneness in self-reported anger and aggression. *Journal of Social Behavior and Personality, 12*(4), 925–936.

Russell, B. (2006). *Conquest of happiness*. Abingdon, Oxon, UK: Routledge Classics. (Originally published in 1930)

Russell, J. A. (2003). Core affect and the psychological construction of emotion. *Psychological Review, 110*(1), 145–172.

Ryan, G., Hernández-Maskivker, G. M., & Valverde, M. (2018). Challenging conventional wisdom: Positive waiting. *Tourism Management, 64*, 64–72.

Sagar, P. (2017). Rules of ascent. *Aeon*. Retrieved from https://aeon.co/essays/why-do-mountaineers-choose-the-hardest-routes-to-the-top

Sansone, C., Weir, C., Harpster, L., & Morgan, C. (1992). Once a boring task always a boring task? Interest as a self-regulatory mechanism. *Journal of Personality and Social Psychology, 63*(3), 370–390.

Sapp, D. D. (1992). The point of creative frustration and the creative process: A new look at an old model. *Journal of Creative Behavior, 26*(1), 21–28.

Sartre, J-P. (1984). *Being and nothingness: An essay in phenomenological ontology*. Translated by Hazel E. Barnes. New York, NY: Washington Square Press. (Originally published as *L'Être et le néant: Essai d'ontologie phenomenologique*. Paris, France: Gallimard, 1943).

Sartre, J-P. (2004). *Sketch for a theory of the emotions*. Translated by Philip Mairet. London, UK: Routledge Classics. (Originally published as *Esquisse d'une theorie des emotions*. Paris, France: Hermann, 1939).

Sartre, J-P. (2007). *Existentialism is a humanism*. Translated by Carol Macomber. New Haven, CT: Yale University Press. (Originally published as *L'Existentialisme est un humanisme*. Paris, France: Nagel, 1946).

Sayers, D. L. (2004). *Letters to a diminished church: Passionate arguments for the relevance of Christian doctrine*. Nashville, TN: W Publishing Group.

Schacter, D. L. (2002). *The seven sins of memory: How the mind forgets and remembers*. Boston, MA: Houghton Mifflin.

Schacter, D. L., & Addis, D. R. (2007). The cognitive neuroscience of constructive memory: remembering the past and imagining the future. *Philosophical Transactions of the Royal Society of London B: Biological Sciences, 362*(1481), 773–786.

Schlesinger, L. (1996). Chronic pain, intimacy, and sexuality: A qualitative study of women who live with pain. *Journal of Sex Research, 33*(3), 249–256.

Schubert, D. S. (1977). Boredom as an antagonist of creativity. *Journal of Creative Behavior,* *11*(4), 233–240.

Seamon, J. G., Philbin, M. M., & Harrison, L. G. (2006). Do you remember proposing marriage to the Pepsi machine? False recollections from a campus walk. *Psychonomic Bulletin & Review, 13*(5), 752–756.

Segerstrom, S. C. (2001). Optimism, goal conflict, and stressor-related immune change. *Journal of Behavioral Medicine, 24*(5), 441–467.

Segerstrom, S. C., Carver, C. S., & Scheier, M. F. (2017). Optimism. In M. D. Robinson & M. Eid (Eds.), *The happy mind: Cognitive contributions to well-being* (pp. 195–212). Cham, Switzerland: Springer.

Seligman, M. E. P. (1991). *Learned optimism.* New York, NY: Knopf.

Shakespeare, W. (2004). *As you like it.* Edited by B. A. Mowat & P. Werstine. Folger Shakespeare Library. New York, NY: Washington Square Press.

Shapiro, L. (2004). Something from the oven: Reinventing dinner in 1950s America. New York: Viking.

Sharot, T. (2011a). *The optimism bias.* New York, NY: Pantheon Books.

Sharot, T. (2011b). The optimism bias. *Current biology, 21*(23), R941–R945.

Sharot, T., Korn, C. W., & Dolan, R. J. (2011). How unrealistic optimism is maintained in the face of reality. *Nature Neuroscience, 14*(11), 1475–1479.

Sierra, M., Medford, N., Wyatt, G., & David, A. S. (2012). Depersonalization disorder and anxiety: A special relationship? *Psychiatry Research, 197*(1-2), 123–127.

Siffre, M. (1975). Six months alone in a cave. *National Geographic,* March, 426–435.

Sifneos, P. E. (1973). The prevalence of 'alexithymic' characteristics in psychosomatic patients. *Psychotherapy and Psychosomatics, 22*(2-6), 255–262.

Simeon, D. (2004). Depersonalisation disorder. *CNS Drugs, 18*(6), 343–354.

Simeon, D., & Abugel, J. (2006). *Feeling unreal: Depersonalization disorder and the loss of the self.* New York, NY: Oxford University Press.

Simeon, D., Guralnik, O., Schmeidler, J., Sirof, B., & Knutelska, M. (2001). The role of childhood interpersonal trauma in depersonalization disorder. *American Journal of Psychiatry, 158*(7), 1027–1033.

Singer, T., Seymour, B., O'doherty, J., Kaube, H., Dolan, R. J., & Frith, C. D. (2004). Empathy for pain involves the affective but not sensory components of pain. *Science, 303*(5661), 1157–1162.

Singh, S. (1997). *Fermat's enigma: The epic quest to solve the world's greatest mathematical problem.* New York, NY: Anchor Books.

Sinkewicz, R. E. (2003). *Evagrius of Pontus: The Greek ascetic corpus.* New York, NY: Oxford University Press.

Skowronski, M. (2012). When the bored behave badly (or exceptionally). *Personnel Review, 41*(2), 143–159.

Smith, J. L., & Bryant, F. B. (2018). Enhancing positive perceptions of aging by savoring life lessons. *Aging & Mental Health, 23*(6), 762–770.

Smith, J. L., & Hollinger-Smith, L. (2015). Savoring, resilience, and psychological well-being in older adults. *Aging & Mental Health, 19*(3), 192–200.

Smith, J. L., Wagaman, J., & Handley, I. M. (2009). Keeping it dull or making it fun: Task variation as a function of promotion versus prevention focus. *Motivation and Emotion, 33*(2), 150–160.

Smith, L. (2012). Neuroscience: Idle minds. *Nature,* September 19. Retrieved from https://www.nature.com/news/neuroscience-idle-minds-1.11440

Smith, R. H., Combs, D. J., & Thielke, S. M. (2008). Envy and the challenges to good health. In R. H. Smith (Ed.), *Envy: Theory and research* (pp. 290–314). New York, NY: Oxford University Press.

Sontag, S. (2012). *As consciousness is harnessed to flesh: Journals & notebooks 1964–1980*. Edited by D. Rieff. New York, NY: Farrar, Strauss, Giroux.

Spacks, P. M. (1995). *Boredom: The literary history of a state of mind*. Chicago, IL: Chicago University Press.

Stein, D. J., & Simeon, D. (2009). Cognitive-affective neuroscience of depersonalization. *CNS Spectrums, 14*(9), 467–471.

Sterlini, G. L., & Bryant, R. A. (2002). Hyperarousal and dissociation: A study of novice skydivers. *Behaviour Research and Therapy, 40*(4), 431–437.

Stickney, M. I., & Miltenberger, R. G. (1999). Evaluating direct and indirect measures for the functional assessment of binge eating. *International Journal of Eating Disorders, 26*(2), 195–204.

Stout, S. C., Boughner, R. L., & Papini, M. R. (2003). Reexamining the frustration effect in rats: Aftereffects of surprising reinforcement and nonreinforcement. *Learning and Motivation, 34*(4), 437–456.

Strunk, D. R., Lopez, H., & DeRubeis, R. J. (2006). Depressive symptoms are associated with unrealistic negative predictions of future life events. *Behaviour Research and Therapy, 44*(6), 861–882.

Sturgeon, J. A., & Zautra, A. J. (2010). Resilience: A new paradigm for adaptation to chronic pain. *Current Pain and Headache Reports, 14*(2), 105–112.

Swanson, A. G. (1963). Congenital insensitivity to pain with anhydrosis: A unique syndrome in two male siblings. *Archives of Neurology, 8*(3), 299–306.

Sweet, S. (2013). A dangerous and evil piano piece. *The New Yorker*, September 9. Retrieved from https://www.newyorker.com/culture/culture-desk/a-dangerous-and-evil-piano-piece

Taylor, G. J. (1997). Somatoform disorders. In G. J. Taylor, R. M Bagby, & J. D. A. Parker (Eds.), *Disorders of affect regulation: Alexithymia in medical and psychiatric illness* (pp. 114–137). Cambridge, UK: Cambridge University Press.

Taylor, G. J., Bagby, R. M., & Parker, J. D. A. (1997). *Disorders of affect regulation: Alexithymia in medical and psychiatric illness*. Cambridge, UK: Cambridge University Press.

Taylor, I., & Taylor, A. F. (Eds.). (2003). *The assassin's cloak: An anthology of the world's greatest diarists*. Edinburgh, UK: Canongate Books.

Thompson, R. A., & Hoffman, M. L. (1980). Empathy and the development of guilt in children. *Developmental Psychology, 16*(2), 155–156.

Thorpe, S., Fize, D., & Marlot, C. (1996). Speed of processing in the human visual system. *Nature, 381*(6582), 520–522.

Thrush, D. C. (1973). Congenital insensitivity to pain: A clinical, genetic and neurophysiological study of four children from the same family. *Brain, 96*, 369–386.

Tice, D. M., Bratslavsky, E., & Baumeister, R. F. (2001). Emotional distress regulation takes precedence over impulse control: If you feel bad, do it! *Journal of Personality and Social Psychology, 80*(1), 53–67.

Tindle, H. A., Chang, Y. F., Kuller, L. H., Manson, J. E., Robinson, J. G., Rosal, M. C., . . . Matthews, K. A. (2009). Optimism, cynical hostility, and incident coronary heart disease and mortality in the Women's Health Initiative. *Circulation, 120*(8), 656–662.

Tipples, J. (2011). When time stands still: fear-specific modulation of temporal bias due to threat. *Emotion, 11*(1), 74–80.

Tolor, A. (1989). Boredom as related to alienation, assertiveness, internal–external expectancy, and sleep patterns. *Journal of Clinical Psychology, 45*(2), 260–265.

Twenge, J. M., Catanese, K. R., & Baumeister, R. F. (2003). Social exclusion and the deconstructed state: Time perception, meaninglessness, lethargy, lack of emotion, and self-awareness. *Journal of Personality and Social Psychology, 85*(3), 409–423.

Tysk, L. (1984). Time perception and affective disorders. *Perceptual and Motor Skills, 58*(2), 455–464.

van Aart, J., Bartneck, C., Hu, J., Rauterberg, M., & Salem, B. (2010). How to behave as Alice in Wonderland: About boredom and curiosity. *Entertainment Computing, 1*(3-4), 125–137.

van de Ven, N., Zeelenberg, M., & Pieters, R. (2009). Leveling up and down: The experiences of benign and malicious envy. *Emotion, 9*(3), 419–429.

van Ijzendoorn, M. H., & Schuengel, C. (1996). The measurement of dissociation in normal and clinical populations: Meta-analytic validation of the Dissociative Experiences Scale (DES). *Clinical Psychology Review, 16*(5), 365–382.

Van Tilburg, W. A., & Igou, E. R. (2012). On boredom: Lack of challenge and meaning as distinct boredom experiences. *Motivation and Emotion, 36*(2), 181–194.

Van Tilburg, W. A., & Igou, E. R. (2016). Going to political extremes in response to boredom. *European Journal of Social Psychology, 46*(6), 687–699.

Van Tilburg, W. A., & Igou, E. R. (2017a). Boredom begs to differ: Differentiation from other negative emotions. *Emotion, 17*(2), 309–322.

Van Tilburg, W. A., & Igou, E. R. (2017b). Can boredom help? Increased prosocial intentions in response to boredom. *Self and Identity, 16*(1), 82–96.

Van Tilburg, W. A., & Igou, E. R. (2019). Dreaming of a brighter future: Anticipating happiness instills meaning in life. *Journal of Happiness Studies, 20*(2), 541–559.

Varki, A. (2009). Human uniqueness and the denial of death. *Nature, 460*(7256), 684.

Vessel, E., & Russo, S. (2015). *Effects of reduced sensory stimulation and assessment of countermeasures for sensory stimulation augmentation* (NASA TM-218576). Retrieved from http://kinetic-cna.pl/web/pageFiles/kcfinder/files/adaptacja%20synaptyczna%20ARc.pdf

Viesturs, E., & Roberts, D. (2009). *K2: Life and death on the world's most dangerous mountain.* New York, NY: Broadway Books.

Virkkunen, M. (1983). Insulin secretion during the glucose tolerance test in antisocial personality. *British Journal of Psychiatry, 142*(6), 598–604.

Virkkunen, M. (1984). Reactive hypoglycemic tendency among arsonists. *Acta Psychiatrica Scandinavica, 69*(5), 445–452.

Virkkunen, M., DeJong, J., Bartko, J., Goodwin, F. K., & Linnoila, M. (1989). Relationship of psychobiological variables to recidivism in violent offenders and impulsive fire setters: A follow-up study. *Archives of General Psychiatry, 46*(7), 600–603.

Vitale, A., & Genge, A. (2007). Codman Award 2006: The experience of hope in ALS patients. *Axon/L'axone, 28*(2), 27–35.

Vlotis, G. (2018). Why the world's most frustrating video game is designed to 'hurt' you. *Nine. come.au.* Retrieved from https://pickle.nine.com.au/2018/01/18/12/54/getting-over-it-video-game-bennett-foddy

Vodanovich, S. J. (2003). Psychometric measures of boredom: A review of the literature. *Journal of Psychology, 137*(6), 569–595.

Vodanovich, S. J., & Watt, J. D. (2015). Self-report measures of boredom: An updated review of the literature. *Journal of Psychology, 150*(2), 196–228.

Vonnegut, K. (2009). *Slaughterhouse-five.* New York, NY: Dial Press Trade Paperbacks. (Originally published in 1969)

Vroman, K., Warner, R., & Chamberlain, K. (2009). Now let me tell you in my own words: narratives of acute and chronic low back pain. *Disability and Rehabilitation, 31*(12), 976–987.

Wade, K. A., Garry, M., Read, J. D., & Lindsay, D. S. (2002). A picture is worth a thousand lies: Using false photographs to create false childhood memories. *Psychonomic Bulletin & Review, 9*(3), 597–603.

Waits, F. N., & Sharrock, R. (1984). Fear and time estimation. *Perceptual and Motor Skills, 59*(2), 597–598.

Wallace, D. F. (2012). *The pale king.* New York, NY: Back Bay Books.

Wallace, J. C., Kass, S. J., & Stanny, C. J. (2002). The cognitive failures questionnaire revisited: dimensions and correlates. *Journal of General Psychology, 129*(3), 238–256.

Wang, S., Melhem, E. R., Poptani, H., & Woo, J. H. (2011). Neuroimaging in amyotrophic lateral sclerosis. *Neurotherapeutics, 8*(1), 63–71.

Warhol, A., & Hatchett, P. (1980). *POPism: The Warhol sixties.* New York, NY: Harcourt.

Washburn, M., & David M. (2016). Arson suspect said he lit wildfires out of boredom. *Charlotte Observer,* December 01. Retrieved from https://www.charlotteobserver.com/news/local/crime/article118292693.html

Watson, S. (2003). *Factory made: Warhol and the sixties.* New York, NY: Pantheon Books.

Watt, J. D., & Vodanovich, S. J. (1999). Boredom proneness and psychosocial development. *Journal of Psychology, 133*(3), 303–314.

Wearing, D. (2005). *Forever today: A memoir of love and amnesia.* London, UK: Corgi Books.

Webber, J. (2018). Beauvoir and the meaning of life. In S. Leach & J. Tartaglia, *The meaning of life and the great philosophers* (pp. 224–231). New York, NY: Routledge.

Weiner, S. (2001). *Enfants terrible: Youth and femininity in the mass media in France, 1945–1968.* Baltimore, MD: John Hopkins University Press.

Weinstein, L., Xie, X., & Cleanthous, C. C. (1995). Purpose in life, boredom, and volunteerism in a group of retirees. *Psychological Reports, 76*(2), 482.

Weinstein, N. D. (1980). Unrealistic optimism about future life events. *Journal of Personality and Social Psychology, 39*(5), 806–820.

Wells, G. L., & Bradfield, A. L. (1998). "Good, you identified the suspect": Feedback to eyewitnesses distorts their reports of the witnessing experience. *Journal of Applied Psychology, 83*(3), 360–376.

West, C., Stewart, L., Foster, K., & Usher, K. (2012). The meaning of resilience to persons living with chronic pain: an interpretive qualitative inquiry. *Journal of Clinical Nursing, 21*(9-10), 1284–1292.

Westbrook, A., Kester, D., & Braver, T. S. (2013). What is the subjective cost of cognitive effort? Load, trait, and aging effects revealed by economic preference. *PloS One, 8*(7), e68210.

Whittington, S. (2003). Serious immobilities: On the centenary of Erik Satie's *Vexations.* Retrieved from http://vexations.ch/Serious_Immobilities_On_the_Centenary_of.pdf

Wiggins, S., Whyte, P., Huggins, M., Adam, S., Theilmann, J., Bloch, M., . . . Canadian Collaborative Study of Predictive Testing. (1992). The psychological consequences of predictive testing for Huntington's disease. *New England Journal of Medicine, 327*(20), 1401–1405.

Wilson, D. R. (1951). Electroencephalographic studies in diabetes mellitus. *Canadian Medical Association Journal, 65*(5), 462–465.

Wilson, T. D., & Gilbert, D. T. (2008). Explaining away: A model of affective adaptation. *Perspectives on Psychological Science, 3*(5), 370–386.

Wilson, T. D., Reinhard, D. A., Westgate, E. C., Gilbert, D. T., Ellerbeck, N., Hahn, C., ... Shaked, A. (2014). Just think: The challenges of the disengaged mind. *Science, 345*(6192), 75–77.

Wilson, T. D., & Schooler, J. W. (1991). Thinking too much: introspection can reduce the quality of preferences and decisions. *Journal of Personality and Social Psychology, 60*(2), 181–192.

Wiltshire, A. (2018). Designer interview: The aesthetics of frustration in *Getting over it. Gamasutra,* January 5. Retrieved from https://www.gamasutra.com/view/news/312553/Designer_Interview_The_aesthetics_of_frustration_in_Getting_Over_It.php

Wittgenstein, L. (1968). *Philosophical investigations* (3rd ed.). Translated by G. E. M. Anscombe. New York, NY: Macmillan.

Wittmann, M., Vollmer, T., Schweiger, C., & Hiddemann, W. (2006). The relation between the experience of time and psychological distress in patients with hematological malignancies. *Palliative & Supportive Care, 4*(4), 357–363.

Wood, Z. (2018). Christian Louboutin wins ECJ ruling over red-soled shoes. *The Guardian,* June 12. Retrieved from https://www.theguardian.com/business/2018/jun/12/christian-louboutin-ecj-ruling-red-soled-shoes

Wright, H. F. (1937). The influence of barriers upon strength of motivation. *Contributions to Psychological Theory, 1*(3), 143.

Wright, R. (1998). NASA Shuttle-Mir oral history project edited oral history transcript (Interview with Norman E. Thagard). Retrieved from https://historycollection.jsc.nasa.gov/JSCHistoryPortal/history/oral_histories/Shuttle-Mir/ThagardNE/ThagardNE_9-16-98.htm

Xygalatas, D., Mitkidis, P., Fischer, R., Reddish, P., Skewes, J., Geertz, A. W., . . . Bulbulia, J. (2013). Extreme rituals promote prosociality. *Psychological science, 24*(8), 1602–1605.

Yu, R. (2016). The neural basis of frustration state. In J. R Absher & J. Cloutier (Eds.), *Neuroimaging personality, social cognition, and character* (pp. 223–243). Amsterdam, The Netherlands: Elsevier.

Yu, R., Mobbs, D., Seymour, B., Rowe, J. B., & Calder, A. J. (2014). The neural signature of escalating frustration in humans. *Cortex, 54,* 165–178.

Zadra, J. R., & Clore, G. L. (2011). Emotion and perception: The role of affective information. *Wiley Interdisciplinary Reviews: Cognitive Science, 2*(6), 676–685.

Zalla, T., Koechlin, E., Pietrini, P., Basso, G., Aquino, P., Sirigu, A., & Grafman, J. (2000). Differential amygdala responses to winning and losing: a functional magnetic resonance imaging study in humans. *European Journal of Neuroscience, 12*(5), 1764–1770.

Zhang, S., Tang, J. S., Yuan, B., & Jia, H. (1999). Electrically-evoked inhibitory effects of the nucleus submedius on the jaw-opening reflex are mediated by ventrolateral orbital cortex and periaqueductal gray matter in the rat. *Neuroscience, 92*(3), 867–875.

Index

Tables, figures and notes are indicated by *t*, *f* and *n* following the page number

For the benefit of digital users, indexed terms that span two pages (e.g., 52–53) may, on occasion, appear on only one of those pages.